THE NEW ABOLITIONISTS

THE NEW ABOLITIONISTS

The Story of Nuclear Free Zones

Gordon C. Bennett

Foreword by Mark O. Hatfield

BRETHREN PRESS
Elgin, Illinois

The New Abolitionist
The Story of Nuclear Free Zones

Copyright © 1987 by Gordon Bennett

BRETHREN PRESS, 1451 Dundee Avenue, Elgin, IL 60120

Cover design by Vista III

Library of Congress Cataloging-in-Publication Data

Bennett, Gordon C.
  The new abolitionists.

  Bibliography: p.
  1. Nuclear-weapon-free zones.
  2. Antinuclear movement.
  3. Nuclear weapons—Moral and ethical aspects. I. Title.
JX1974.735.B46   1987   327.1'74   86–18884
ISBN 0–87178–603–6

Printed in the United States of America

Contents

Acknowledgements v
Foreword vii
A Fictional Prologue. 1
1. Taking Responsibility. 5
2. Towards a New World View .31
3. Americans Opt Out: Cases and Consequences 57
4. The Abolitionist Connection .85
5. Declaring Interdependence .111
6. Is a Nuclear-Free Pacific Possible? 137
7. Addressing the Bench: Legal Issues 163
8. Divestment and Conversion. 185
9. From Paralysis to Empowerment 209
Epilogue. 235
Endnotes 241
Appendices 249

Contents

Introduction ....

Prologue ....

1. Painted Shadows ....

2. Taking Responsibility ....

3. Becoming a Man Worthy Having Someone ....

4. Ambition: The Oak, Reed, and Cottonwood ....

5. The Courageous Conversation ....

6. Taking Independence ....

7. ....

8. ....

9. ....

10. ....

11. ....

Epilogue ....

Notes ....

Index ....

Acknowledgements

I am grateful for the many who have made it possible for me to create this chronicle. My gratitude includes my wife, Ruth, and my grown children, Brad and Cherry, and many good friends at Central Baptist Church (Wayne, Pa.), who have been very encouraging. I am especially indebted to the staff at Nuclear Free America who stood by while I raided their files and responded patiently to my questions, particularly Albert Donnay, who has been my severest and most helpful critic. I thank William Durland, who read my chapter on legality, and my Eastern College colleagues W. Larry Ziglar, Harold Howard, and Van Weigle, who critiqued my venture into 19th Century abolitionism, and Ian Scott, who provided information on New Zealand from a native's perspective; and at Eastern my hallmate Betsy Morgan of the English Department has been particularly supportive. Dean Jean Kim provided sabbatical time for the project and for that too I am grateful.

Many Nuclear Free Zone organizers and advocates in this country and around the world have provided information and useful opinions. I admire their intrepid work for peace and nuclear disarmament and I appreciate their willingness to correspond or to submit to interviews. Even Prime Minister David Lange of New Zealand took the time to respond personally to my query regarding his nation's role in the NFZ movement.

In addition, I want to thank Tony Campolo for his encouragement and support, and for his connection to Senator Mark Hatfield, who has written the Foreword. I respect no one in public life more than Senator Hatfield. He is one political leader who *leads*. His integration of ethical and moral values within a political career has inspired us all, and his immense devotion to the cause of peace is apparent. I am pleased and honored that the

Senator has shared some of his thinking with us here.

Also, thanks to David Eller at the Brethren Press, who possessed the wisdom to do the book and shepherded it through revisions and production. The Brethren have long been leaders for world peace, as the titles they publish demonstrate. My hope is that this book will, together with the work of so many others, promote the ultimate goal of global nuclear disarmament.

Some people act. Others write about the actors and about what yet needs to be done. Hopefully this story will inspire others to act.

Gordon Bennett
Paoli, PA

Foreword

The continued escalation of the nuclear arms race poses a grave threat to human history. The arsenals of the Soviet Union and the United States contain over 48,000 nuclear warheads and that number is growing annually. The entire globe has become a nuclear theatre involving sixty-seven countries and territories that possess nuclear weapons or facilities such as military bases which support the nuclearism of other nations, or whose commercial reactors potentially export such militarism (see Ruth Sivard, *World Military and Social Expenditures, 1985*, pp. 20–21). Endless nuclear arms reduction talks and several so-called arms control agreements have failed to slow the escalating arms buildup. These stark facts do not bode well for our future generations. However, I continue to believe that hope still exists for a safer tomorrow.

If this nation demands an end to the nuclear arms race, our government will respond accordingly. I have cited the importance of citizen involvement in the nuclear arms debate many times, and I am gratified to see that thousands of Americans have answered the call to work for a safer future. But these thousands must become millions if we are to alter our present dangerous path.

The New Abolitionists: The Story of Nuclear Free Zones examines the Nuclear Weapons Free Zone movement, an exciting and provocative way in which people are banding together to demonstrate that they have had enough of fruitless negotiations and nuclear war fighting strategies which have become increasingly hazardous and destabilizing. This book provides a good example of the importance of citizen-sponsored initiatives.

American history is full of such successful citizen movements, including those which were instrumental in establishing rights for women and minorities; ending American involvement in Vietnam; and abolishing slavery, for which *The New Abolitionists* is so aptly titled. Indeed, the birth of our nation came only after individual colonists joined forces to free themselves from British rule.

I have witnessed the importance of citizen involvement in the nuclear arms debate. When I first introduced the nuclear freeze resolution as an amendment to the SALT II treaty in 1978, my colleagues were uninterested and unimpressed. But because people across the country contacted their Senators and expressed *their* enthusiastic support for the resolution, the nuclear freeze now boasts over forty sponsors in the Senate. Though constituent phone calls and letters may seem unimportant, they *do* make a difference.

In my own state of Oregon, citizens have taken an active role on this most important issue. Oregonians have joined nuclear freeze and NWFZ movements to express their concern about the relentless nuclear arms buildup. They have also sponsored and attended education seminars on the issue and its implications. The involvement of individual Oregonians has inspired me in my fight on Capitol Hill for a more sensible definition of national security.

Increased citizen participation could not come at a more crucial time in our history. The new advances in nuclear arms technology only serve to jeopardize the present balance of power between the United States and the Soviet Union. The construction of the MX missile and the deployment of Pershing and cruise missiles have brought us perilously closer to a nuclear conflict. The present flight time of a cruise missile in Europe to its target in the Soviet Union is a scant six minutes. In case of an accidental launch, there would be no time for warnings, and a full-scale nuclear war would be upon mankind.

The destabilizing threat to our existence which attends the arms technology spiral is best evidenced in the proposal to militarize space. The effects of these costly weapons on the balance of power is totally unpredictable; far from aiding our security, these new developments create an atmosphere of fear and danger, and worse, they sustain the fallacy that increased arms means increased security.

Our present frightening course has distorted the meaning of national security. A nation is made secure by a proper balance between military and nonmilitary spending. We must have well-trained and well-equipped personnel able to defend against attack. But national security is more than soldiers and missiles. National security is health, housing, nutrition programs, education, and an infrastructure capable of sustaining a productive economy.

Many in our government believe that the U.S. is strategically inferior to the Soviet Union in nuclear weaponry. This paranoia blinds them to the fact that the U.S. and the Soviet Union are roughly equivalent in strategic nuclear power. This type of thinking has produced dramatic excuses for continued arms buildup such as the "bomber gap," the "missile gap," and most recently, the "spending gap." The U.S. and the Soviet Union have advantages in different areas, but in the final analysis, neither country, much less the world, could survive a major nuclear war. The leadership of the world's "superpowers" must awaken to the truth which the citizens of those countries already know: nuclear arms reduction would be beneficial to all sides.

United States citizens are not alone in their concern about the nuclear arms buildup. As professor Bennett has observed, the growing peace movements around the world are a direct result of the superpowers' failure to initiate meaningful arms reductions. Understandably, many citizens in our allied countries fail to see how the U.S. can claim to protect them when we proceed to deploy more and more nuclear weapons on their soil.

Other nations may soon follow the lead of New Zealand and refuse entrance to nuclear weapons cargo. After forty years of an unending increase in nuclear arms, many of our friends have become tired of our rhetoric about arms control. Our arms escalation, ironically, promotes tensions with our allies as well as our adversaries. Many longtime friends may soon choose to abandon mutually beneficial alliances with the U.S.

The U.S. has an undeniable moral commitment to lead the way to arms reduction. Because our country was founded on the principles of freedom and justice, the world looks to us for moral leadership. We are failing in this responsibility as we persist in adding to the nuclear stock piles and magnifying the "overkill" factor. The world today has enough nuclear megatonnage to kill every man, woman, and child on the earth twelve times.

A growing number of nations are following our ominous example by producing their own stockpile of nuclear weapons. Sixty-seven countries and territories have become a part of the nuclear network in some way. No greater threat to our national and world security exists than nuclear arms in the hands of volatile and unpredictable regimes.

The escalating arms race deflects attention away from monumental problems which the world faces today. The complex issues like overpopulation, famine, and scarcity of natural resources demand that we rechannel our efforts toward life-enhancing instead of life-destroying endeavors. The citizens of this country have the will and strength to change our national priorities.

To bring about a change in our country's defense policy, citizens need to keep the debate alive by writing their Senators and Representatives, organizing locally, and discussing the issue with friends and family. Our nation needs to become more knowledgeable on the many facets of the arms race, and books like *The New Abolitionists* aid tremendously in this educational process.

The top priority of every citizen and public official should be to work for an enhanced quality of life for present and future generations. Towards this end, I will continue to promote a nuclear freeze resolution. But the efforts of a few will not be sufficient to alter our presently dangerous course. Citizens from every part of the country must pledge themselves to our survival, and therefore, each individual must make a difference. Let your voices be heard, for reform in the body politic begins in the nation's cities and towns and not in the halls of congress.

Toward that end professor Bennett is to be congratulated for exploring this topic.

Senator Mark O. Hatfield
Washington, D.C.

A Fictional Prologue

The OK Corral it wasn't. Still, the incident might go down in history, if history didn't go down first.

It happened near Centerton at the village limits two miles from the Interstate, where county routes 32 and 16 intersect. Fifteen head of McGoffey's prize milkers graze in the south field behind the old grange and, across the road at the Seven-Eleven, kids after school make their noisy rendezvous.

There was the convoy: ten olive-drab trucks with no identification. There were the adversaries: two uniformed officers, Lieutenant Peters of the State Police and Chief Adair of the Centerton Police Department, backed by support police. Adair's two police cars blocked the narrow highway. The four Centerton deputies, uneasy in their nonstandard uniforms, lined the curb behind Adair while a frisky black-spotted white dog sniffed their heels. Peters was backed by a carload of impeccably dressed state troopers.

There was the issue: would this convoy pass through Centerton on its way to the nuclear submarine base on the coast? It already had been detoured or detained several times since it left Amarillo. There were those who wanted to stop it because the convoy was said to be carrying nuclear warheads for Trident sub missiles.

"Go back to the Interstate, John," Adair said.

"Two of these monsters need fuel," Peters replied, "and some of the men are hungry. You've got some decent restaurants in Centerton."

Peters was a stocky man of fifty-two, with bushy eyebrows and a chest that strained the seams of his shirt. Adair, on the other hand, was tall, spare, and laconic, with graying hair that belied his thirty-nine years.

"Are you carrying nukes?" Adair asked.

"It makes no difference," Peters said, his face reddening. "This shipment's going through Centerton and you're not going to stop it, not with your little army! Four deputies and a Dalmation? Don't you know we can ask the governor to bring in reserves, the whole National Guard if we have to?"

"Sorry, John." Adair's voice was mellow. "We can't let this convoy pass. We don't want your lousy warheads."

"For crying out loud—they're for your defense!"

"That's what you think, John."

"Let's put philosophy aside for a minute, Adair. The point is, you can't stop the United States government from moving equipment through your town. If it's not us it's the federal marshals. I don't care what this convoy's carrying!"

"*We* care what it's carrying."

"Suppose I said it was carrying cans of corn?"

"Then I'd have to inspect those trucks. Will you open them?"

"No!"

"Well, there you are." Adair grinned. "It's a standoff."

Peters glanced at his carload of troopers, the ten trucks, whose drivers drummed nervously on the fenders, and cars backed up behind the trucks in all directions. Then he looked at Adair's deputies. A scraggly bunch. Just one of his troopers could tie up all four. He heard muttered comments, laughter. A crowd began to gather in front of the Seven-Eleven. What if somebody called the press? The issue had to be resolved before the media types arrived.

"The ordinance you passed here, Adair, to make Centerton a Nuclear Free whatever—"

"Zone."

"You know it's unconstitutional."

"You gonna take us to court?"

"It's ridiculous. What's to prevent a town from declaring itself a Yogurt Free Zone or a Lint Free Zone? Some people are against all sorts of things. You might have a nut on your council who's against trapping animals and so you declare the place a Fur Free Zone and stop any vehicle that's carrying mink or sable or rabbit skins! Or somebody on the council has a kid who hates spinach so he gets them to declare the town a Spinach Free Zone. Now they even turn back Popeye! So maybe you have hundreds of these zones and pretty soon you bring interstate commerce to a standstill! Shoot—truckers'll need a directory the size of a telephone book to figure out where they can run their freight or what route to take from Lincoln to Denver so as to avoid being stopped by some ninny with a tin badge waving a two-bit local ordinance!"

"So I'm the ninny," Adair offered.

"Nothing personal."

"John, look . . ." Adair stepped closer and put a friendly hand on the state trooper's arm, and smiled. Peters glowered at him and Adair took his hand away. He shook his head, sadly. "John, what do you tell your kids?"

"Huh?"

"When the war's about to begin, what do you say? Or when it's over, and you're sitting in a cloud of radioactive dust where your house used to be and they want to know what you did to prevent this. 'Oh,' you say, 'I made sure those warheads got to their destination so decent, godfearing people could put them in their missiles and shoot them at people they had never seen but were told they should hate.'"

"You're missing the whole point, muttonhead!" Peters yelled. "Those warheads, if in fact they happen to be in this convoy, which I have not officially confirmed or denied—"

"That's fine, you've covered yourself—"

"Those warheads are necessary to keep peace in this world. I don't like them. Nobody likes them, but they're necessary. They've held back World War III ever since World War II."

"And how long can we expect to live on the brink, John? How long?"

Peters scrutinized Adair. "Well, then . . . this little Nuclear Free Zone you've created . . . that's going to get us off the brink?"

"It adds up, John. One here and one there. Pretty soon the state, several states, whole nations, regions—who knows? It's a long shot, maybe. But it's better than sitting on our bombs, ready to hatch out misery and destruction."

"You know something, Adair? You're nuts!"

The crowd was getting boisterous. A police siren could be heard in the distance. Drivers were honking their horns a hundred feet down the highway. This was the biggest traffic jam Centerton had seen since the county fair. Peters strode ten feet toward the lead truck, stopped, turned, and walked back to Adair, scratching his head.

"What are you going to do?" Adair asked him.

"Well," he said. "I guess we can make it to Byleston with the gas we've got. I'll route the convoy south on 16 to Martin's corner." He gave Adair a dark look, turning to wave to his drivers, then stopped abruptly. "What the—"

Next to the convoy's lead truck the Bonner County Sheriff was unfolding himself from his car. Three armed men got out with him. One of them opened the trunk and pulled out a shiny, new metal highway sign. He held it up for the state police to read: "BONNER COUNTY—A NUCLEAR FREE ZONE." Lieutenant Peters scowled, and turned to Adair.

"I forgot to tell you, John," Adair smiled. "Last night the commissioners voted to make the *county* nuclear-free!"

Peters took off his hat and sailed it into the field by the Seven-Eleven. One of McGoffey's prize milkers licked it cautiously.

"How about it, John?" Adair said. "Does a County Sheriff and three deputies added to me and my four and a dog beat your six?"

"Good grief," Peters groaned. "Now where do I take these lousy trucks?"

1

Taking Responsibility

". . . I have set before you life and death, blessing and curse; therefore choose life, that you and your descendants may live."
—Deuteronomy 30:19

"Forget the channels. There simply is not time enough left before the world explodes. Concentrate instead on organizing, with so many others who are of like mind, a mass movement for peace such as there has not been before."
—George Kistiakowsky, scientist

"The arms race stops here!" they say in Northampton, Massachusetts, and in Taos County, New Mexico. "Global disarmament begins at home!" rings out in Madison, Wisconsin; Boulder, Colorado; and Ashland, Oregon. Posters in St. Helena, California, proclaim: "Some Day the Whole World Will Outlaw the Nuclear Bomb. Can't We, in St. Helena, Hasten the Day?" Citizens of these communities, in league with many others across the country and around the world, have declared themselves to be Nuclear Free Zones.

There were 129 municipal Nuclear Free Zones in the United States by November 5, 1986, with another hundred campaigns in progress or contemplated. In the 1984 presidential election fourteen of sixteen communities in which NFZs were on the ballot voted to become unclear free, including five contiguous counties in Oregon totalling 23,000 square miles. The 1986 off-year election produced five new NFZs, with only one city campaign and the statewide Oregon initiative being defeated. Interestingly, in that election citizens of Eugene, Oregon, were given the chance to vote their city, county, and state nuclear-free on the same day!

But what of major cities? On November 8, 1984, the New York City Council declared that metropolis nuclear-free, although with a nonbinding resolution. On September 12, 1985, Jersy City, NJ, became the fourth community to ban city contracts with nuclear weapons-related companies, as part of its NFZ ordinance. Then on March 13, 1986, Chicago, the home of the world's first controlled nuclear chain reaction, became the nation's largest city to pass a legally-binding Nuclear Free Zone ordinance.

The ordinance "To Establish the City of Chicago as a Nuclear Weapon Free Zone" was passed unanimously by a voice vote of the usually fractious Chicago aldermen. The law bans the design, production, deployment, launching, maintenance, and storage of nuclear weapons or components within city limits. Ron Freund, executive director of Metro Chicago Clergy and Laity Concerned, which promoted the campaign, insisted that "By passing this ordinance Chicago has taken out a long-term option on a nuclear weapon-free future."[1]

The Chicago ordinance provides for a Peace Conversion Commission to be appointed by the mayor, which in two years would provide a plan for the conversion of the nuclear weapons industry and develop alternative employment for any displaced workers. According to the city's Economic Development Committee, Chicago might lose up to two million dollars in defense contracts as a result of this ordinance but no more than sixty-three jobs would be affected.

One phase of the Chicago campaign involved circulating a citywide petition in three languages, and strong support committees were formed on the north, south, and west sides of the city. Many area churches provided support—over twenty Chicago churches and synagogues have declared their premises nuclear–free, according to Clergy and Laity Concerned. At a signing ceremony arranged by CALC at Grace Place (Episcopal) on Sunday, March 23, Mayor Harold Washington wrote Chicago's name at the top of a list of five big cities in the world that are Nuclear Free Zones: London, United Kingdom; Bonn, West Germany; Wellington, New Zealand; and Kyoto, Japan.

The nation is stirring; the world is shaking, desperately trying to free itself from the bonds of nuclear madness. Clearly, this is a movement whose time has come; or, we live in a time whose movement has come: Nuclear Free Zones.

What is a Nuclear Free Zone? The exact wording of such a declaration varies from one community to another, but it generally takes this form:

(1) The territory is declared off-limits to the design, testing, manufacture, and deployment of nuclear weapons. The declaration (ordinance) may also ban the transportation of such weapons through a community; or ban radioactive materials, whether related to weapons or nuclear waste from power plants. Signs may be erected on property declaring its NFZ status.

(2) Any activity which, in a local government's view, promotes nuclear weapons or nuclear war can be condemned or prohibited. Often this means that a community decides not to invest in or do business with industries that make nuclear weapons components.

(3) The community—or school, church, office, or other organization—renounces its right to be defended with nuclear weapons held by any government, including its own.

(4) The NFZ community or entity asks the nuclear powers to take it off their target lists. Letters are sent to the proper authorities in Paris, London, and Peking as well as to Washington and Moscow; and possibly to officials in India and Israel, whose nations may also be producing nuclear weapons.

Keep in mind that the movement is primarily directed against nuclear *weapons*; overseas, in fact, such communities tend to call themselves Nuclear Weapons Free Zones (NWFZs). Some Americans have included a ban on nuclear energy as well as nuclear weapons, but this is not generally true: most NFZ ordinances do not cover nuclear energy. In our discussion, the Nuclear Free Zone has to do with action being taken against nuclear *weapons* and designed to reduce the world's arsenals and the possibility of nuclear war.

The Background

What of the mood that has produced the movement? Call it anger, frustration, and commitment to a new world-view. A grim nightmare stalks history, the horrible specter of a third and final World War. Two immense superpowers, the US and USSR, apparently locked in a global dance of death, keep pushing the world toward the brink. Together they possess over 50,000 nuclear warheads, far more than they can possibly find targets for, with a total explosive potential exceeding one million Hiroshimas. But the arms race escalates as new weapons emerge from the Pandora's Box of horrors in the Pentagon and its Kremlin twin.

Frustration comes from knowing the sad history of arms control attempts. Six thousand arms control talks since World War II have failed to produce the dismantling of a single nuclear weapon, apart from those rendered obsolete or replaced by newer ones. The heralded SALT I and SALT II treaties, the latter unratified by the US Senate, have failed to harness the arms race; instead, by posting ceilings to work towards and implicitly encouraging the development of new weapons, they have actually boosted it. The Nuclear Weapons Freeze Campaign, an excellent approach but constantly (and deliberately?) harpooned by the defense hawks as "unilateral," has stalled in Congress following passage of a House resolution. Meanwhile, it is becoming ever more dangerous to live on the planet. The equation is: for each bomb or missile added to the world's arsenals, each of us is that much *less secure*.

The result of this is a growing grassroots protest. Feeling betrayed by their elected leadership, people are going public with their rage: "If our leaders can't act or won't act, then we must!" Albert Donnay, the Director of Nuclear Free America, international clearinghouse for the NFZ movement, argues that "nobody is going to stop the arms race for us, certainly not Congress or the President. We all have to decide for ourselves what to do about it."

Nuclear Free Zones are new in America. The County of Hawaii was the first American jurisdiction to declare itself nuclear-free—and that has resulted in the first case of NFZ-related civil disobedience ever brought to trial.

That first NFZ ordinance banned the *transport* and *storage* of nuclear materials on the Big Island of Hawaii. Although it did not ban the research and development of nuclear weapons, the ordinance brought the county to conflict with the United States Navy within three years of its passage in February, 1981. The Navy wanted its ships to visit the Big Island; in particular, the USS Ouellet, a nuclear-capable frigate, would berth in Hilo Harbor during Hilo's annual "International Festival of the Pacific." The problem was that the NFZ legislation banned ships carrying radioactive materials—like nuclear weapons. The US Navy consistently refuses to "confirm or deny" whether its ships are carrying such weapons.

The Festival's organizers muscled an eleventh-hour amendment through the County Council, excluding the military from the NFZ ordinance and making it possible for American warships to enter County waters. Hundreds of Hawaiians were outraged by this apparent gutting of the ordinance, but legal attempts to counter the amendment failed. When the USS Ouellet appeared in Hilo harbor on July 18, 1984, the day after the amendment passed, a mass protest was punctuated by a symbolic blockage of the vessel. Three Hawaiian peacemakers jumped into the water, momentarily slowing the ship. Moments later the swimmers were hauled into patrolling Coast Guard vessels. The result? All three were tried and convicted, with Jim Albertini receiving the heaviest sentence, three years in prison. The federal judge, an ex-Coast Guard officer, refused to let the three explain their reasons in court; nor would he permit any discussion of the Nuclear Free ordinance or nuclear weapons. Albertini remarked at his sentencing:

> Our action was a restrained, nonviolent, symbolic effort to uphold the spirit, if not the letter, of Hawaii County's Nuclear Free

Ordinance, the first in the United States. Our nonviolent direct action followed more than three years of repeated administrative requests and judicial actions, all to no avail.

I had no illusions of using my body to create a physical counter-force to the physical force of nuclear weapons. On the contrary, the objective of the human blockade was to offer a symbolic response to nuclear weapons from the spiritual depths of our souls—soul force versus nuclear force.

Garrett Park, Maryland, became the first American community to ban the *research* and *manufacture* of nuclear weapons, in May 1982, but the movement dates from a Zone declared in Handa, Japan, in 1958. By April 1, 1986, there were over 3,000 Nuclear Free Zones worldwide in seventeen countries, but concentrated in Europe, Australia, New Zealand, and Japan. New Zealand, Austria, Spain, and fourteen other nations have policies or laws prohibiting nuclear weapons. International NFZs have been established by treaty in South America, Antarctica, outer space, the seabed, and the South Pacific; regional Nuclear Free Zones have also been proposed for Scandinavia, the Balkans, the Mediterranean, the Middle East, Africa, and Southeast Asia. A United Nations General Assembly resolution (Res. 3472B XXX) declared that "Nuclear-Weapons-Free-Zones constitute one of the most effective means for preventing the proliferation, both horizontal and vertical, of nuclear weapons." *Horizontal* proliferation means the spread of nuclear weapons from nation to nation; *vertical* refers to the growth in number and megatonnage of existing arsenals.

The Nuclear Free Zone concept, debating for years in other parts of the globe, is now taking root in America. The key to it is the phrase, *thinking globally, acting locally*. Americans, along with many millions of planetary citizens, are assuming a direct and vigorous personal responsibility for ending the arms race. Ordinary citizens are expressing opinions about political matters traditionally left to the diplomats, because nuclear war is too important to be left to diplomats. Albert Einstein, always the insightful prophet, said that our negotiators abroad are ultimately responsible to the opinions expressed and decisions made in the village square: "From there must come America's voice . . . A message to humanity from a nation of human beings."

And if our political leaders can't hear us they will at least *see us*. They will have to stop talking to themselves long enough to *observe* what is happening in Amherst and Madison, Spain and New Zealand, indeed, everywhere—action being taken to protect humanity from its most ominous threat, action taken to move the world away from the brink, from disaster, death, and destruction to a bright new nuclear-weaponless day.

Ways and Means

The precise form of an NFZ declaration depends on the nature of the community and the areas about which people are seriously concerned. Many citizens are worried about nuclear wastes or the hazards of transporting radioactive material through town: this was the focus of the Union County, NJ, NFZ campaign. Others want to reject the federal government's Crisis Relocation Plan for Civil Defense. They contend it has no chance of success in the event of a nuclear war. Some want to divest municipal funds from nuclear weapons industries, and most want to prevent the research and development of nuclear weapons within their jurisdictions.

There are various ways and means of making a Nuclear Free Zone declaration. Often the legislation is passed by county commissioners or freeholders, and often by village or township councils or boards. Usually ordinary citizens stimulate or provoke the process, gathering signatures, researching nuclear weapons facilities in the area, lobbying local authorities, taking whatever steps are necessary to put the issue up for vote; and, sometimes, there is a local referendum on the issue, permitting every citizen to voice an opinion.

The first ordinance banning the manufacture of nuclear weapons in Garrett Park, MD, was a single, simple paragraph:

> The people of this town hereby declare the town of Garrett Park to be a Nuclear Free Zone. No nuclear weapons shall be pro-

duced, transported, stored, processed, disposed of, nor used within Garrett Park. No facility, equipment, supply, or substance for the production, transportation, storage, processing, disposal, or use of nuclear weapons will be allowed in Garrett Park.

The ordinance passed a public referendum and was warmly endorsed by Senator Mathias (R-MD) in remarks recorded in the *Congressional Record*: "Mr. President, we spend a great deal of time in this Chamber talking about the threat of nuclear war, but I am proud to say that the citizens of Garrett Park . . . are doing something about it."[2]

Some legislation is as simple as Garrett Park's; others, as objections are raised and NFZ proponents find ways of tightening the legal language, are very complex. For example, the Charter Amendment that was to have taken effect in Santa Monica, California, on December 31, 1984, had it passed, consisted of eight sections and twenty-five paragraphs.

Opponents often contend that Nuclear Free Zones are "merely" symbolic. The answer is, of course, *yes,* they are symbolic, but as one campaigner said, "So was the Boston Tea Party!" So was Gandhi's use of the spinning wheel as well as the famous Salt March of 1930; but his symbolic statements combined with nonviolent direct action destroyed the British hold on India. So were the black armbands worn to protest the Vietnam War; but again, symbolism combined with direct action to force an end to American involvement, right or wrong, in Vietnam. Symbolism is powerful. Historian Gene Sharp has catalogued the various types of symbolic action in a monumental three volume work, *The Politics of Nonviolent Action.*[3] Sharp says the key to throwing off an oppressor's yoke is recognizing the power of consent. If the followers consent, injustice continues—but the people have the power *to withhold consent.*

The fact is that we can accept or reject the ominous nuclear policies of governments. Admittedly, Soviet citizens—as our more conservative friends like to point out—don't have the same freedom to affect public policy that Americans have. Let us therefore use the freedom we have to slow the world's slide towards oblivion. Each of us has a conscience. We have minds and voices. We can say, "No you don't!" to what is called leadership, "not in my name do you build and deploy these weapons!" As we reject the nuclear technocracy governing our lives and preparing our doom we become responsible *world citizens.*

When Nuclear Free Zones are adopted as ordinances, bylaws, or charter amendments, they carry legal force—they are not *merely* symbolic. They can prevent nuclear industry from moving in to a community or they can require existing weapons firms to convert to nonmilitary production. And when the legislation includes nuclear-free investment and nuclear-free purchasing provisions, the potential effect on the nuclear industry is enormous.

Some communities have followed a two-step process. First, campaigners have sought passage of a nonbinding resolution, adopted either by city council vote or referendum, and then, often with the support of some council members, they have sought legally binding legislation.

Controversy

Nuclear Free Zone campaigns are seldom unopposed. Oberlin, Ohio, is an exception. Campaigners there were surprised by the dearth of opposition during their successful 1985 NFZ campaign. But Oberlin has a long history of espousing humanitarian causes. The College, founded in 1833, was a center for the 19th Century antislavery movement in the Midwest.

In communities where there is controversy the debates often bring more heat than light to the subject. After the aldermen voted Chicago nuclear-free, Governor James R. Thompson called the law "stupid and un-American" and worried about attracting defense contracts to Illinois; and a *New York Times* editorial (3/16/86) found the Chicago action amusing.

When the city of Chico, California, planning department was considering NFZ legislation it received many letters—some of them very sarcastic—and many from outside the state. Local journalists wondered in print if Chico were being made a "laughingstock," and local businessmen worried about the town's image and what it would do to commerce. But a resolution was passed and then an ordinance, and Councilman Bill Nichols summed up the feelings of the Chico campaigners: "Since I was fifteen years old there has been no way to make any impact on nuclear arms. At least in Chico I can take charge of my life!"

When campaigners in Key West, Florida, were pushing nuclear-free legislation, opponents became frantic and illogical. A good deal of red-baiting was done and NFZ proponents had their patriotism challenged. Patricia Axelrod, founder of the local Peace Works group, was charged on local television with being a Communist. Key West Anti-Freeze made much of the fact that the Soviet Ambassador to the UN had issued a statement supporting the growth of Nuclear Free Zones worldwide. The logic of this argument, reduced to a syllogism, becomes:

1. Whatever the Russians like is wrong and we have to be against it;
2. The Russians like Nuclear Free Zones;
3. Nuclear Free Zones are wrong and we have to oppose them.

By this logic we should ban Russian caviar from our restaurants and Tschaikovsky from our symphonies!

There were some legitimate questions raised in the Key West debates, but in a community dominated by naval personnel the fear of what it might cost the community to become nuclear-free strongly affected the decision-making process. Key West has been a slave colony to the US Navy since 1823, according to Axelrod, except for a thirteen year period, and the Navy owns one-third of the town. Even sewer lids and telephone poles in Key West have "US Navy" stamped on them!

Anti-NFZ fanatics mounted a serious threat to civil liberties in Key West. A sign on one of the cars in a motorcade read, "Kill the Pacifists!" Patricia Axelrod reports that she was arrested, chained to a wall, and questioned by police after she spoke out at an anti-NFZ rally. Even though she was acting alone, Axelrod was charged with failing to obtain a permit to assemble! The

NFZ ordinance was defeated, but Patricia Axelrod claimed, "It's a victory when people realize they have power, when they say, 'I can vote for a nuclear-free world and I'm going to start in my own backyard.'"

Open, vigorous debate is a sign of a healthy democracy and welcomed by NFZ advocates. Despite opposition in most communities, the vast majority of Nuclear Free Zone campaigns have succeeded. The more intense opposition occurs where nuclear weapons facilities already exist or where the Defense Department has a strong presence or strong plans. In Key West the development of a Forward Contingency Base for possible military excursions into Central America has militarized community sentiment and intensified opposition to the Nuclear Free Zone idea.

Participatory Democracy

Social analyst John Naisbitt reported in his popular *Megatrends*[4] that Americans in the 1970s began to lose faith in representative democracy and turn towards a more participatory form of government. This often takes the form of citizen-sponsored *initiatives* to put important political and social issues on the ballot, and *referenda,* which give voters the opportunity to ratify or reject legislation already passed on the local or state level. Western states have been more generous in permitting initiatives and referenda than other states. All told, the number of initiatives doubled in the 1970s compared with the 1960s.

Naisbitt reports that by 1979 there were 300 initiatives on the ballot. Voters considered such issues as returnable bottles, limiting the height of urban structures, even the color of street lights. In the 1984 elections voters decided the fate of tax proposals, gambling, even dentures and cloud dusting! There was tremendous interest. Votes cast for certain initiatives in Missouri, North Dakota, and Michigan exceeded the number of votes for governor. California's famous Proposition 13 drew 100,000 more votes than were cast for governor!

Many of the initiatives and referenda have to do with taxes, nuclear power, and—more recently—nuclear weapons. Citizen involvement in the weapons issue is increasingly evident. The largest peace rally in American history took place in New York City on June 12, 1982, with an estimated 750,000 participants. That fall the issue of a bilateral Nuclear Freeze drew thousands to the polls. Citizens in 8 of 9 states and 28 out of 30 cities and counties where the Freeze was on the ballot voted for it (about 60 percent pro-Freeze nationwide) in what has been called the largest referendum in the history of American democracy. David Schmidt, executive director of the Initiative Resource Center in Washington, DC, has called for a broad-based anti-nuclear referendum campaign in 1988. He contends that a nationwide referendum would unite the 5,000 diverse peace groups in the nation with the possibility that it might awaken enough interest to double or triple 1982's voter participation.

Whatever the outcome—and a good many initiatives are defeated—Naisbitt and others see a trend here:

> Technical decisions, such as nuclear energy, are moving out of the hands of so-called experts and into the political arena. That is just what you would expect in a participatory democracy where the people affected by a decision must be a part of the decision-making process.[5]

The whole process worries state legislators, who fear loss of power to the electorate. But Michael Nelson argues that, in the long run, the initiative process strengthens democracy. He cites political scientist Charles Bell, who found that half of the high election-turnout states use the initiative process while only 14 percent of low-turnout states use it; and a Cadell Poll found that 74 percent of voters said they would be more likely to vote in candidate elections if they could also vote on issues. "The assault on the governing class of officials will continue," Nelson argues. "Whether it will come through the ballot box or some less pleasant route is up to them."[6]

Acting Out Faith

The battle against the bomb draws diverse people together. Nonreligious humanists acting out of a powerful concern for the world are making a profound impact, together with the hundreds of devout Jews and Christians who share the humanists' democratic values in addition to their faith-convictions. Without discounting any other philosophies and approaches to this issue, let us examine briefly what it means to bring the Judeo-Christian heritage to the task of peacemaking.

Many Christians, unfortunately—and the author is indebted for this analysis to W. Clyde Tilley, Professor of Religion at Union University, Jackson, Tennessee[7]—hold unexamined, unbiblical views of nuclear war. Professor Tilley cites the theological fallacies of "nuclear immunity," "nuclear inevitability," and "nuclear indifference." To paraphrase: (1) "God won't let it happen!" (2) "It's God will that it happens!" (3) "It doesn't matter if it happens. The sinners have had their warning. As long as I'm saved nothing else matters!"

The first view represents a naive faith in God's protective mercy, the notion that God loves us so much that he will not allow the ultimate disaster to occur. But the biblical God is not a cosmic superman getting his people out of scrapes that they have put themselves into. Rather, God lets people feel the effects of their folly: they reap the results of sin. God did not shield Adam and Eve from the consequences of eating the forbidden fruit of the tree of knowledge, and there is no evidence that God will shield *us* from the results of our eating the fruit of *nuclear* knowledge. Theologian Ronald Sider, founder of Evangelicals for Social Action, contends that, since God has given us free will, "God will allow us in our freedom to be so stupid as to destroy the Northern Hemisphere or perhaps the planet," but adds, "I don't think that needs to happen."[8]

Theologian Douglas John Hall, in an important new work on Christian Mission,[9] offers Isaiah 28:14–22 as a warning. The passage identifies the rulers of Jerusalem who "have made a covenant with death" so that "when the overwhelming scourge passes through it will not come to us; for we have made lies our refuge and in falsehood we have taken shelter." But God said no to these people; they would not escape:

> . . . I will make justice the line,
> and righteousness the plummet;
> and hail will sweep away the refuge of lies;
> and waters will overwhelm the shelter.
> Then your covenant with death will be annulled,
> and your agreement with Sheol will not stand;
> when the overwhelming scourge passes through
> you will be beaten down by it.

Does the "overwhelming scourge" equal nuclear war? Not what Isaiah meant, probably—but the parallel's so obvious that one might almost infer that Isaiah 28:14–22 is God's warning to a twentieth century entangled in a terrible covenant with death.

There is another version of the nuclear immunity theme: the idea that America has replaced Israel as God's favored people, and that if there is to be a nuclear war, God will save America. It is a short step from this position to saying that God blesses our attempt to achieve nuclear superiority so that we may "prevail" (in Secretary of Defense Weinberger's language) over the "Evil Empire" (in President Reagan's language).

Implicit in this view is a linkage between God and country. America is God's favored nation and, therefore, Christian, or Christian and therefore, favored; or materially prosperous and, therefore, Christian and favored. However you put it, this viewpoint tends to make a god of the state, so whatever the state does to physically protect itself is approved by God. Worshiping the state leads to worshiping the state's "defense" systems, including the B-1 bomber, the Trident submarine, and cruise, Pershing, and MX missiles. In a superb speech before the House during the MX debate, Congressman Lehman (D-FL) said: "In the middle ages, the best minds of the church spent time and money debating how many angels could 'dance on the point of a pin.' Now our nuclear experts similarly confuse us with quasi-religious talk about silos, basing modes, ICBM's, MIRV's and the triad."[10] (Our substitute for the Holy Trinity?)

Peacemakers see all this as idolatry. Our faith is supposed to be in God; instead it appears to be placed in missiles and bombs. Peacemakers like to cite God's warning in Leviticus 19:4 against making "gods of metal" and apply that to nuclear missiles, which are for many the object of abject obeisance. God's warning in Isaiah 31:1-3 ("Woe to those who go down to Egypt for help and rely on horses, who trust in chariots because they are many . . .") seems more relevant as a political, as well as a moral principle: people of faith are to rely on God instead of armies and armaments. God will not protect us from the consequences of an unrestrained, irresponsible arms race. "God makes no promise to preserve and protect life *over against* the human decision that it is not worth protecting and preserving."[11] As for the favored-nation argument, what reason do Americans have to assume that the US is God's new Israel? There is equally as much evidence that we are another Babylon, Hall suggests.

The second fallacy that professor Tilley describes is that of nuclear inevitability. This is a premillenial doomsday theology that suggests that God may well be planning a holocaust as the last chapter in history. The idea comes out of a world-rejecting apocalyptic view of history: if this world is evil at its core, then a nuclear purging is to be welcomed—and God's remnant will, of course, survive or surmount the holocaust. David Wilkerson and Hal Lindsay are among the conservative authors who argue that biblical prophecy predicts a nuclear Armageddon. Indeed, there are some apocalyptic passages (2 Peter 3:7-12) which sound very much like the descriptions of Hiroshima and Nagasaki or even nuclear winter. One eminent fundamentalist said over television that the bomb's invention was a part of God's intention—nuclear war may be God-ordained! "We need to be prepared," he announced, referring to America's nuclear arsenal: "Before we go, they go." (Meaning the Russians.) "I can do that in all good conscience." Incredible; we are told that we can vaporize our enemies without a guilty conscience, for it is God's will!

Fundamentalist ideas of eschatology (the doctrine of "last things") are generally based upon ambiguous passages and questionable interpretations of scripture. For example, nuclear war as a divine punishment on mankind could apparently be supported from Isaiah 13:9–13 ("Behold, the day of the Lord comes, cruel, with wrath and fierce anger, to make the earth a desolation . . .") but the remainder of the passage localizes the warning in terms of Babylon and identifies the Medes as the instruments of God's wrath. To build a doomsday theology on scattered apocalyptic passages is to build on quicksand.

Indeed, the Bible as a whole offers a very different view of God. Tom Sine, a professor at Seattle Pacific University, has written, "No biblical basis exists for picturing God as a co-conspirator in the ultimate violence of using nuclear weapons to destroy God's good creation. One thing that the Bible teaches clearly is that God loves the world and intends to recreate it, not destroy it."[12] Sine points out that the doomsday theologians with their notion of the inevitable nuclear Armageddon are promoting a grimly deterministic view of history in which

> . . . not only can't the church make a difference, neither can God. This eschatology of despair seems to lock God outside of history, characterizing God as an impotent absentee landlord who is unable to effect any real change in the present world. All God gets to do is bring down the final curtain at the end of history."[13]

The third fallacy is that of nuclear indifference: "God may or may not permit or prevent nuclear war. So what? The sinners have had their warning. As long as I'm saved nothing else matters!" This view can be dismissed quickly. It is a self-centered view totally foreign to the spirit of scripture. If I take this position, I am rejecting the core of Christ's teaching. "It suffers from lovelessness because it takes delight in my personal salvation which is accentuated all the more by the destruction of my fellow human creatures, forgetting that we are our brother's and sister's keeper."[14]

But there is a God beyond the God of nuclear immunity, inevitability, or indifference. The Bible describes that God as one who cares about *life* (not religion) in all its variety; and who cares for the world as a whole, and for *every nation,* and not only one. God may not always approve of their conduct, but the world's races are all his: "Black and yellow, red and white, they are equal in his sight."

"When God chose Israel," says John Stott in a superb essay on Christian social involvement,[15] "he did not lose interest in the nations." Amos bravely gave voice to this God:

> The Lord says, "People of Israel, I think as much of the people of Syria as I do of you. I brought the Philistines from Crete and the Syrians from Kir, just as I brought you from Egypt," (Amos 9:7, TEV)

And the psalmist wrote:

> The Lord looks down from heaven
>   and sees all mankind.
> From where he rules, he looks down
>   on all who live on earth.
> He forms all their thoughts
>   and knows everything they do. (Ps. 33:13–15, TEV)

Surely God loves the Turks and Chinese and Chileans and Russians as much as he loves Americans. And if the entire creation is good, according to Genesis 1, then we need to love it and take care of it. It would be the ultimate crime, the heinous sin, to destroy within a few minutes that which God took millenia to produce. This planet, George Kennan, former Ambassador to the Soviet Union, suggests, is the stage upon which God intended from the beginning of time to enact a grand experiment involving human beings—to determine whether men and women could become what they are meant to become, intelligent, compassionate, *fully human,* beings: "Who are we, then, the actors, to take upon ourselves the responsibility of destroying this framework, or even risking its destruction."[16] Instead, as Hall says, we are to affirm life, we the people of faith are called to steward and sustain the Kingdom of Life within the world's king-dom of mega-death!

The Judeo-Christian tradition provides a biblical base for both the goal and means of nuclear peacemaking. That wonderful Old Testament word *shalom* describes the end-state or idealized goal; Jesus' "Sermon on the Mount," the means.

Shalom conveys a number of meanings in Hebrew: well-being, health, wholeness, happiness, salvation, serenity, peace. It is seldom applied on a personal level in the Old Testament but refers to the end-state, what God desires for society, the nation, and the world. In Hosea God speaks hopefully of restoring an earlier, harmonious relationship with a young Israel:

> Then once again she will call me her husband—she will no longer call me her Baal. I will never let her speak the name of Baal again.˙
>
> At that time I will make a covenant with all the wild animals and birds, so that they will not harm my people. I will also remove all weapons of war from the land, all swords and bows, and will let my people live in peace and safety. (Hosea 2: 16–18, TEV)

Later in the passage, God indicates that he "will answer the prayers of my people Israel" (2:21) and bring them prosperity. But even "to those who were called 'Not-My-People' I will say, 'You are my people,' and they will answer, 'You are our God.' " (2:23).

We find similar passages describing the divine age of idyllic harmony in Micah 4:1–4, and in Isaiah 2:1–4, 11:1–10, and 65:17–25. In Isaiah 11 the age of *shalom* is linked to the coming of the promised Messiah. In that day when the righteous judge of earth comes, "the wolf shall dwell with the lamb, and the leop-ard shall lie down with the kid" (11:6). We are shown a vision of a day when even traditional enemies shall be kind to one another, "for the earth shall be full of the knowledge of the Lord as the waters cover the sea." (11:9) The content of God's reign is *sha-lom,* which may be the abundant life mentioned by Jesus in John 10:10.

Both in Isaiah 2 and Micah 4 we are treated to the famous

vision of swords beaten into plowshares and spears into pruning hooks. Often we overlook the point these prophets make that peace is more than the absence of conflict. Not only in that grand day will soldiers lay down their swords; *they will beat them into plowshares.* They are to convert the instruments of war into the tools of agriculture, the means of feeding themselves and their families (or, in America's case, perhaps the world). So when we speak of the *conversion* of defense industries we are referring to a spiritual change, of course, but to a very *material* conversion as well.

The Sermon on the Mount, the central core of Jesus' ethical teaching, suggests the means. Here in Matthew 5–7 we have a description of the new-age lifestyle, the behavior Jesus prescribed for those who live as disciples in his world. It is a difficult agenda. We are to eschew materialism and go the second mile in compassion—which means literally giving others the shirt off our backs. We are to offer no resistance when attacked but welcome persecution, and we are to forgive. We are even to love and bless our enemies.

And we have the Golden Rule to guide our conduct: do unto others what we would have them do unto us. The Rule of Nuclear Deterrence is different: "Do not do (read *bomb*?) unto your neighbor (read *enemy*?) because you're afraid he might do it unto you!" This is a rule of fear. Christ showed that there is more truth and power in the Rule of Love, applied unstintingly. "Love is stronger than any atomic pestilence that stalks in darkness or any atomic destruction that wastes at noonday," Leonard Sweet writes.[17]

The people of God, those working for God's kingdom, are people who care, who forgive, who even love enemies—because *God loves their enemies.* German journalist Franz Alt, whose book on nuclear peacemaking is a best seller, in 1981 was persuaded by his study of the Sermon on the Mount that modern nuclear politics are wrong. "The atom bomb," he comments, "is not even forty years old and it is taken very seriously. The Sermon on the Mount is two thousand years old, it is repeatedly quoted, and yet it plays no role in political practise." To those who ridicule Jesus' gospel as impractical idealism in the face of Trident, SS20s, and the MX, Alt answers:

> Love of enemies is not moronic, it is intelligent. Love of ene-
> mies means having the courage to take the first step. It is mental
> sovereignty instead of anxious calculation and selfish insistence on
> being right. Love of enemies is not theological small change that
> can be traded off; it is the will of the creator.[18]

The Christian church is on the spot. Our faith is being tested. We can choose to consent as usual or to withhold consent from the preparations for nuclear war. In the words of theologian Ron Sider, "We face the fundamental free choice of whether or not we'll submit to God's way, which is the way of love and justice and peace, or go our own way . . . to death and destruction."

Taking Responsibility

Years ago, Secretary of Defense McNamara answered the question of when the arms race would be stopped by saying, "When the potential victims are brought into the debate." We are *all* potential victims, and we, the victims, must begin to assume responsibility for saving the earth. Our elected officials are apparently unable or unwilling to move against nuclear weapons: they are helpless in the face of catastrophe, so *we* must act. *Thinking globally and acting locally,* thousands of American citizens are endorsing, promoting, and voting for Nuclear Free Zones.

Nuclear Free America'a Albert Donnay, answering an article arguing that NFZ advocates should work politically instead to change policies affecting Soviet-American relations, suggested that the writer didn't understand the nature of the NFZ movement: "The people who support Nuclear Free Zones *are* changing the nation's policies. They're just doing it at the local level instead of asking (and waiting) for politicians in Washington to do it for them."

It was this spirit that propelled students and faculty at Malcolm Shabazz High School in Madison, Wisconsin, into the national spotlight. Mr. Brockmeyer's social studies class in September, 1982, was discussing ways of moving the hands of the Doomsday Clock (of the *Bulletin of Atomic Scientists*) back away from midnight. (It is currently set at three minutes to midnight.) The class decided to make Malcolm Shabazz High School nuclear-free. Signatures were obtained from 117 of the school's 130 students, as well as from many faculty and staff. Signs were placed in the corridors declaring that nuclear weapons as well as nuclear research were strictly forbidden.

Students at a Berkeley, California, high school decided to "go one better" by making Berkeley High a *Space* Weapons Free Zone. The Student Senate sent a letter to President Reagan asking him to refrain from testing or deploying any space weapons in a zone beginning at ground level at Berkeley High and extending up into the heavens!

The list of educational NFZs includes not only high schools and colleges but elementary and middle schools, junior high schools, and more specialized institutions. The Nuclear Free Zone Registry of Riverside, California, reports that many people also have been declaring their homes, shops, offices and restaurants nuclear-free. The United Farm Workers of La Paz, Keane, California, declared their headquarters nuclear-free. And (then) fourteen-year old Michelle Lee, of Pfafftown, NC, cleverly put some words in the mouth of her creek:

> I; the Creek, located behind the house at 4831 River Ridge Road, hereby declare myself and the surrounding territory a Nuclear Free Zone. Included in this declaration are the snails, salamanders, minnows, and crayfish who live in me, the beasts who live in the forest around me, my activist representative at 4831 River Ridge Road, and the double rainbow of 3 August 1984, which served as my official pronouncement against nuclear weapons to the representative.
>
> —The Creek

By April 1, 1986, over 150 churches, synagogues, and religious bodies had declared their premises nuclear-free, including the headquarters of three Protestant denominations. Many churches have tied their NFZ declarations to a concrete commitment to social justice. Some utilize their facilities for ministry: a shelter for the homeless or a soup kitchen, or perhaps a counseling center for abused women or disturbed teenagers. Some provide sanctuary for political refugees. Many Christians see these ministries as a way of renouncing the "gospel" of power politics and nuclearism, and affirming the gospel of life, justice, caring, and compassionate service in the spirit of Jesus who said, "Whatever you did for the least of these . . . you did for me." (Matt. 25:40, NIV)

From Locked-Out to Acting-Out

My own awakening came about 1959, when I heard a radio presentation by Norman Cousins, then editor of the *Saturday Review.* Cousins described the world of 1959, with nuclear weapons in their infancy, as an elephant hanging over a cliff with its tail tied to a daisy. If that was the metaphor for 1959, with only a few nuclear weapons in the world, what kind of metaphor could capture the world of 1986, with over 50,000 nuclear warheads in the world? In *The Giants,* Richard Barnet suggests that the handful of men who are deciding the fate of the earth are like "chess players in the dark absorbed in a game they can hardly see. Each player depends on the other not to upset the table."[19]

Popular astronomer Carl Sagan, extending an image invented by William Ury, likes to use the grim parable of two men standing in a room up to their hips in gasoline, arguing about who holds the most matches. Dan Wasserman drew a cartoon in which a civilian refers to this in conversation with a Pentagon general, and the general agrees that the whole thing is insane. "Why," he says, "it's the size of the match head that counts!"

In the face of this "matchhead mentality" many of us can identify with the West German anti-nuclear demonstrator who was interviewed for American television. He said the arms race was a nightmare to him, a dream in which he stood with his nose pressed against a glass window. Inside were two rooms with two tables, around each table distinguished men were discussing the fate of the world. But he could not make them hear him! He yelled and screamed, he banged his fist against the glass, but no one at either table noticed him. He was shut out from the decisions these men were making about his own future, the fate of the planet, and human survival.

It is this "locked out" feeling that provokes many Nuclear Free Zone campaigners. They are demanding a voice in history. They want to be "let in." They want to influence events, not be pushed around by them. These crusaders for planetary survival have set a goal for themselves: the abolition of nuclear weapons. They want to live in a nuclear-free world. The obstacles are formidable. The poet Auden wrote: "Nothing can save us that is possible/we who are about to die demand a miracle."

But this is possible, they say. The abolition of nuclear weapons is no miracle but a conceivable dream, and whatever we can dream we can accomplish! As a New York City poet and peacemaker (Olga Cabral) has written, "This is the moment. There may never be another. And if we stand firm in our millions, the death machine may begin to die."[20]

Perhaps it won't take *millions*. Some persons in the movement contend that if the campaigners can reach a *critical mass,* perhaps only 5–15 percent of American towns and cities—or the American population—they will have produced a radical change in public thinking and policy. The phrase is borrowed from nuclear physics, where a "critical mass" means the minimum amount of fissionable material required to sustain a nuclear chain reaction.

What will it take to initiate and sustain an anti-nuclear chain reaction—a radical change of opinion, a reversal of public policy? Numbers help, but numbers alone will not do it. "Critical mass" means that a certain number of people are *taking significant action,* severing the ties that link their community to the nuclear weapons establishment. When communities around the world withdraw their economic and moral support for the arms race, the withdrawal pains will be felt deeply in Washington and

Moscow. If a relatively small percentage of communities follow the lead of Takoma Park, MD, and others, in refusing to invest in or do business with companies that deal with nuclear weapons—then change will occur.

Henry David Thoreau, the Walden Pond philosopher-activist, seems to have thought about the idea of a critical mass in his 1849 essay *On the Duty of Civil Disobedience:*

> I know this well, that if one thousand, if one hundred, if ten men whom I could name,—if ten *honest* men only,—aye, if one HONEST man, in this state of Massachusetts, *ceasing to hold slaves,* were actually to withdraw from this copartnership, and be locked up in the county jail therefore, it would be the abolition of slavery in America . . .

Thoreau's conclusion that one person becomes that critical mass would seem to be *literally* untrue. Despite his action, Thoreau alone did not stop the Mexican War, nor end slavery; nor will one individual alone stop the arms race. But one added to one added to one may do it—and as every journey begins with a single step, so any mass action begins always with one individual.

Thoreau resorted to civil disobedience. There are civil disobedience advocates today who contend that, given the nuclear peril and the obstacles to disarmament, only massive civil disobedience is likely to turn things around.

Others refuse to cross that threshold—breaking the law is something they will not or cannot do, no matter what the peril. Nuclear Free Zones offer a course between the respectable, working-through-channels method of the Nuclear Freeze Campaign, which is going slowly during the Reagan era, and the more radical approach of civil disobedience. Nuclear Free Zones are attractive to those who want to make a strong statement locally without breaking the law or risking arrest in their pursuit of peace.

There have been many attempts to curb the arms race. Various means have been used, political and nonpolitical. All have failed. Nuclear Free Zones as a strategy may prove fruitless like the others, or not. But an increasing number of people believe this movement offers the world's best hope for altering the nuclear mindset that has brought the world to the brink of oblivion.

2

Towards a New World View

"In the right hand we have penicillin and streptomycin; in the left hand the atom and the hydrogen bomb. Now is the time for the people of the world to consider more rationally this contradiction."
—Hiroshima victim (6th grade girl at the time)

"Where there is no vision, the people perish . . ."
—Proverbs 29:18a (KJV)

First, regarding experts: the author is not one. To the extent that I have done my homework on nuclear age politics and Nuclear Free Zones, one might call me a *savant* perhaps, something of a specialist: but not an expert. My definition of *expert* is someone who seems to know about all there is to know on a topic, who has decision-making power, and in whose judgment we may have complete trust.

Today experts are suspect. Remember the mechanic who guessed wrong about the carburetor, the salesman who recommended the wrong carpet, the physician who misdiagnosed the illness, the pollsters who assured us that Dewey would defeat Truman. And I was a Boston Red Sox fan in the late forties and fifties when the prognosticators annually predicted the demise of the Yankees—and were wrong!

I experimented with a "technical" issue in one of my college group dynamics classes. I gave 15 students a problem to solve that the experts—the Human Interference Task Force of the US Department of Energy—had already "solved." The "given" was that in the coming decades, tons of radioactive material from power plants will have to be stored at carefully designed dump sites, or repositories. The problem is immense: one official estimated that the nuclear waste currently being stored could fill thirty Rose Bowls, and the waste keeps building up. Some of this material is radioactive for at least 10,000 years.

Question: how do you warn succeeding generations to stay away from these repositories when you can't even be sure that 300 generations from now human beings will be able to understand English, or any of our current languages?

The DOE Task Force had produced a report in November, 1984, detailing a large number of likely solutions. These included such strategies as creating a modern Stonehenge to ring the site, erecting large cartoon narratives depicting the hazards, and developing an "atomic priesthood" to create an oral history, a legendary curse so malevolent that it would keep people away from the site. But in 15 minutes my students independently generated solutions almost identical to the expert's best—and this without the body of information available to the experts, and without nearly as much time!

So your ideas may be just as good as those of the experts; and your *judgment* may be superior. Benjamin Spock, pediatrician and peace activist, could have been addressing all of us when he advised parents of small children: "Trust yourself. You know more than you think you do . . . Don't be overawed by what the experts say. Don't be afraid to trust your own common sense."[1]

The Experts and Arms

The atom was a mystery. Splitting it called for masterful intelligence and patience, and some of the best minds of the age were put to work on it. But it was rough going, and the experts were often mystified. Einstein said in 1932: "There is not the slightest indication that (nuclear) energy will ever be attainable. It would mean that the atom would have to be shattered at will." The atom *was* split; but after the Bomb was dropped the scientists who worked on the Manhattan project were astonished at the reports from Hiroshima and Nagasaki of an epidemic of radiation sickness and death. They were woefully ignorant about the long and short-term radiation effects.

At the time, the public wasn't aware of the experts' misgivings. News of the successful atomic tests and the destruction of Hiroshima and Nagasaki impressed most Americans and left many awed by the technicians who achieved this incredible breakthrough. In a recent book on the beginnings of the nuclear era, Paul Boyer reviews the comprehensive opinion survey done by Leonard S. Cottrell, Jr., and Sylvia Eberhart in 1946 for the Social Science Research Council. Most of the sample expected an eventual atomic war but 56 percent of the people thought an effective antibomb defense would soon be developed. Scientists were revered. "I am placing my trust in these great masterminds that are working on it now," one citizen said. Another: "As long as our government is continuing atomic research so we won't be caught by new and more drastic developments, I'm not particularly worried."[2] And Edgar Guest wrote in September 1945:

> The power to blow all things to dust
> Was kept for people God could trust,
> And granted unto them alone,
> That evil might be overthrown.[3]

And so God could trust America, and Americans would trust their revered experts to use atomic power wisely and well. How naive! In the years since 1945 our confidence in these nuclear experts has been eroded.

Look at the experts' political track record since 1945. They warned us of a "bomber gap" in the fifties—a fallacy. Then they warned us of a "missile gap" in the sixties—another fallacy. The Reagan experts warned us of a "window of vulnerability" and they too were wrong. In an excellent recent study of so-called expert advice in the political realm, Gregg Herken says that no matter how many times the experts alarm us about nonexistent or exaggerated new threats from the East, they will surely appear before long with yet another dire warning![4]

And what have the experts brought us since that first Bomb

was dropped on Hiroshima in 1945? More and more hazardous weapons, an arms race ever soaring upwards, spiraling defense budgets, a bizarre vocabulary of "throw weight," "counter-force," and "acceptable losses"; and a society suffering severely from what psychologist Robert Jay Lifton calls "nuclear numb-ing," or what someone else called "planetary anguish." How do the experts answer our pain, our outrage? "Trust us," they say, "we know what's best." And they come up with the latest tech-nological fix, a new weapons system or a radical new "defense" like "Star Wars." Psychiatrist Joel Kovel writes,

> Technology is a peculiarly intellectual form of domination. The arms control, military, or even the disarmament specialist over-whelms the citizen with a double wave of expertise: only technical knowledge counts, and only he has it. Thus subdued, the citizen allows his or her sense of values to become associated with the irrational, and sinks into the apathy of nuclear terror.[5]

The result of trusting the experts is always more talk and more arms. No wonder political analyst Sidney Lens describes arms control as a "hoax" designed to "quiet public opinion,"[6] a method of mollification, a means by which the government paci-fies the peacemakers.

Many of us are fed up with the experts: the nuclear scientists, engineers, military strategists, and politicians. The Public Agenda Foundation 1984 survey, *Voter Options on Nuclear Arms Policy,* revealed that the public wants to *share* decision-making. 68 percent said that "the issue of nuclear war is too important to leave only to the President and the experts; citizens must have a say in any decisions that are made." Citizens seem to believe they can understand the problem: by 77 percent to 21 percent they rejected the statement that "the subject of nuclear weapons is too complex for people like me to think about."

The Foundation survey included a cross-section sample of 505 Americans. The views of the public sample were then compared to expert opinion; the latter was based on interviews with 40 authorities in the nuclear defense field. The study revealed that the public has an intense fear of nuclear war and a sense of immediate peril: 68 percent believe war to be inevitable if we keep on building weapons. The experts, however, tend to regard the public fear as exaggerated, and they are less likely to think nuclear war is imminent. The study revealed that the public is skeptical about various aspects of American nuclear arms policy. The authors summarized their findings:

> To the public, overkill makes little sense; limited nuclear war will not stay limited; bargaining chips don't work because the Soviets feel obliged to match us weapon for weapon; civil defense is a cruel delusion; and nuclear war is unwinnable if winning entails the death of millions of Americans. But what is "common sense" in the public view may not be sense to some experts.[7]

In *Counsels of War,* Gregg Herken contends that we have been victimized, not so much by nuclear technology, but by our failure to examine our premises. The experts aren't doing this. As Herman Kahn said, "It is the hallmark of the expert professional that he doesn't care where he is going as long as he proceeds competently!" Herken calls for a new debate, not by the experts but by the American people, a debate on the question, "just where are we heading and do we want to go there?" Judging by the polls, many citizens are ready for such a debate.

Many persons would argue that the experts have lost sight of another important factor: morality. Have the people who are computing "throw weight" and "yield" and "deterrent effect" lost their way spiritually? Are we so involved in counting bodies that we've lost our souls? Has conscience abdicated? What is the morality of inventing weapons designed to destroy millions of people whom we have never seen and who have never wronged us?

When the scientists who invented the A-bomb returned to Los Alamos for a reunion in 1983, Isidor Rabi sadly remarked that "nations are now lined up like people before the ovens of Auschwitz, while we are trying to make the ovens a little more efficient." And he dismissed the experts by saying that today's arms controllers have "lost human sympathy. They lost an understanding of their own selves—of their own meaning. There has been an atrophy of the imagination, a decline of the moral sense."

Traditionally scientists have said, "Our task is to create something in our laboratories that has a practical application. We're not moralists. We leave ethics to others." Coupled with the lure of the "technically sweet problem," arms invention becomes irresistible to many. Years ago the inventor of dynamite, Alfred Nobel, discussing his work on munitions, remarked to a friend, "Well, you know, it is rather fiendish things we are working on, but they are so interesting as purely theoretical problems and so completely technical as well as so clear of all financial and commercial considerations that they are doubly fascinating."[8]

Time passes, but the lure is still there. Helen Caldicott describes a conversation she had with Joe Weitzenbaum, professor of computer science at MIT. When she asked him why men work on systems of genocide, he said, "Do you know why? It's incredible fun."[9]

Of course, many of the scientists who did the early work on the A-bomb were spurred by their hatred and fear of the Nazis, but as the moment of truth arrived, several prominent physicists begged President Truman not to use the Bomb, or at least to warn Japan first that an enormous weapon would be used on them. And Einstein confessed to Linus Pauling that he had made one great mistake in his life "when I signed the letter to President Roosevelt recommending that atom bombs be made." Others felt guilt. Boyer reports:

> In a February 1950 manifesto, twelve prominent physicists, all Manhattan Project veterans, declared: 'No nation has the right to use such a bomb, no matter how righteous its cause. This bomb is no longer a weapon of war, but a means of extermination of whole populations. Its use would be a betrayal of all standards of morality.[10]

Scientists are still divided. The enormous number of physicists hired to work on defense projects suggests that many still see this work as compatible with moral values, or that they have put moral values aside; other scientists disagree, and many refuse to work on nuclear weapons projects. Scientists associated with the Pugwash conferences and the Union of Concerned Scientists have fought the arms race for years; and some new organizations have emerged, such as High Technology Professionals for Peace in Boston, and the Engineers/Workers for Social Responsibility in California.

Admitting culpability on the part of his colleagues, those who designed the Bomb, Barry M. Casper makes an eloquent "Appeal to Physicists": "Physicists should grasp the opportunity to speak out about what was once our issue but has become *the* issue of our time."[11] To speak out means to oppose, in loud and clear tones, the perversion of science to manufacture weapons of mass destruction. In their celebrated pastoral letter, the American Catholic Bishops advocated a "moral about-face":

> The whole world must summon the moral courage and technical means to say no to nuclear conflict; no to weapons of mass destruction; no to an arms race which robs the poor and the vulnerable; and no to the moral danger of the nuclear age which places before mankind the indefensible choices of constant terror or surrender.[12]

What Has Changed in the Nuclear Age

Let us not inventory the whole terrible litany of facts again. Ground Zero, the Union of Concerned Scientists, Physicians for Social Responsibility, and many other groups have published graphic and carefully documented studies of nuclear weapons and the effects of nuclear war. By now we all should know that together the nuclear powers possess over 50,000 warheads, of which about 17,000 are *strategic,* or long-range weapons, as opposed to short-range or *tactical* weapons. Robert MacNamara, former Defense Secretary, said in the 1960s that about 400 warheads would suffice for deterrence. We have gone far beyond deterrence to overkill.

The 50,000-plus bombs in the world's arsenal represent a destructive force equivalent to over 1,000,000 Hiroshimas. The bomb dropped on Hiroshima was about 13 kilotons, or equal to 13,000 tons of TNT. That bomb killed an estimated 100,000 people outright and another 100,000 or more from radiation sickness, cancers, and other disease. Or, to put it another way, the 50,000 nuclear warheads we have today equal 6,000 tons of TNT for every man, woman, and child on earth.

But this is not enough. A 1983 study by the Center for Defense Information in Washington disclosed that the Reagan administration would build 17,000 additional nuclear warheads in the next decade and retire only 11,000; and that the US would spend $450 billion on nuclear war preparations in six years, representing 22 percent of the military budget and twice what the previous administration had spent. All of this in the name of deterrence, of course! But deterrence seems to be just a verbal smokescreen for the radical warplanners, those looking for a "counterforce" or first-strike nuclear strategy. (The Soviets have publicly rejected a first-strike policy, but the US has not.) These strategists indicated by their behavior that they have little faith in deterrence to keep the peace; instead they press desperately for newer, more accurate weapons, in pursuit of that elusive goal— nuclear *superiority*.

The Soviets, of course, race to keep up. This is our history, what MacNamara called the "mad momentum" of the arms race. Technology fuels the race; science is seductive, and some of our best minds are intrigued with the problem-solving involved in designing even more deadly means of destruction. Many technicians are incurably optimistic; if a weapon can be conceived, it will be built! No wonder the illness metaphor is being used these days to describe the runaway arms race. Indeed, the world is suffering from a disease that may prove to be fatal. David McReynolds of the War Resisters League writes,

> . . . there is something shadowy and unreal about our lives so long as we live only thirty minutes from the end of the world. If human life means less to us, if there is an ugliness to our politics, a random violence in the streets and seeping through society, this is inevitable in a world where the greatest possible violence has been given sanction by every major government and the best minds perfect the most terrible weapons.[13]

Einstein was right when he said that since the splitting of the atom, "everything has changed except our way of thinking." Psychologist Jerome Frank suggests that this is because our leaders' minds were shaped before Hiroshima, in the prenuclear age. They tend to think of war in prenuclear terms. They think about nuclear weapons as if they were conventional ones, even if, intellectually, they know they are not.

But we are not just making bigger bombs. The invention of nuclear weapons represents a quantum leap in weaponry, in mankind's ability to destroy. Political analyst Richard Barnet has said that it snaps the connection between weapons and politics. Previously one could add up the numbers and feel secure—*we* have more arrows—or cannonballs, grenades, or rocket launchers—than *they* do! Other things being equal, *our* side will win. Not so now. Having more weapons doesn't guarantee victory. It may be irrelevant.

One reason is that the offense has overcome the defense. Jonathan Schell contends that the history of warfare may be described as a long competition between offense and defense: "The invention of nuclear weapons gave the victory once and for all, it appears, to the offensive side."[14] It seems very doubtful—the way new offensive weapons spin out of the defense establishment think tanks—that the defense will ever catch up. There are the proposals for a Strategic Defense Initiative, or "Star Wars," but most credible scientists doubt its feasibility—the *Bulletin of the Atomic Scientists* called it a "science fiction pipe dream!"

Aside from the basic technical problems, the SDI is designed to shoot down intercontinental ballistic missiles—but already hundreds of *cruise* Missiles are being built, missiles that fly so low they cannot be detected by radar, much less shot down by lasers based in space. Any defensive system is bedeviled by the fact that delivery vehicles multiply. A missile launcher or a submarine is a delivery vehicle, and so is an airplane, truck, or brief case. Any ship afloat can be a delivery vehicle for cruise missiles, including an American PT boat or a Soviet fishing trawler. Jonathan Schell writes:

There seems little chance that all existing vehicles—not to mention all the vehicles that science will dream up in the future—can be decisively countered. And it is even more unlikely that the devices designed to attack all the delivery vehicles would remain invulnerable to devices that scientists would soon be inventing to attack *them*. The superiority of the offense in a world of uninhibited production of nuclear weapons and their delivery vehicles, therefore, seems to be something that will last for the indefinite future.[15]

With nuclear weapons, defense has to be virtually *perfect*. During World War II the British tried very hard to shoot down the German V-1 rockets aimed at London. On their most successful day, August 28, 1944, they destroyed 97 of 101 rockets, according to the Harvard Nuclear Study Group.[16] Successful? Yes, but consider . . . if those four rockets had been nuclear weapons, Britain would have been decimated, possibly destroyed as a functioning society! Which is one reason why the US and USSR agreed to the Anti-Ballistic Missile Treaty in 1972. Both sides saw ABMs to be an impractical idea; and if it *were* practical, destabilizing. The Reagan "Star Wars" defense would supposedly rely on particle beam or laser beam space weapons to shoot down incoming ICBMs. The system will lack the ability to deal with low-flying cruise missiles or submarine-launched missiles off the coast. Again, the offense prevails.

With nuclear weapons we have superlative force; indeed, *superfluous* force. Normally one's idea of victory is based on the assumption that the amount of force each side possesses is finite, and that one side will exhaust its force before both sides are annihilated. But, as Schell says, "nuclear doctrine begins with the premise that the amounts of force are so great that both sides, and perhaps all mankind, will be annihilated before either side exhausts its forces." And so we are talking not about a win-lose scenario, but about mutual or global suicide. No wonder Admiral Mountbatten said that "the nuclear arms race has no military purpose. Wars cannot be fought with nuclear weapons. Their existence only adds to our peril because of the illusions which they have generated."

Challenging Assumptions

All of which means that we need to challenge three assumptions. Number one, the idea that *wars may be just*. Historically, some religious people have been pacifists; others have believed that God may commission "holy crusades" in which the enemy may be dealt with harshly because they are God's enemy; and a third group, basing an argument on ancient Christian doctrine, would legitimate only those wars which meet the requirements of God's *justice*. The Second World War was widely believed to be a just war because it met these basic criteria: it was waged (1) under legitimate authority (2) as a last resort (3) and for a just purpose; and it conformed to the notions of (4) proportionality, (5) discrimination, (6) and a reasonable hope of victory. Some of these principles are embodied in international law, and we shall detail them later. Here, a brief application of these criteria to a potential nuclear attack or retaliation.

(1) The US constitution provides that only Congress shall declare war, but a nuclear strike would almost certainly not involve Congress because decisions will have to be made within minutes, if we are to respond to a first strike *against us;* and if *we* are making a first strike, because of the secrecy involved; hence no *legitimate authority* in terms of consulting Congress, much less the popular will. (2) The nuclear strike might be a *last resort* but most likely would not be, since there are many options short of using nuclear weapons for resolving disputes—have they all been explored? (3) Some would argue that the only *just cause* is self defense, or in the case of nations, that the proper occasion for a just war is invasion by an adversary; thus the purpose of the war is to repel invaders and restore peace. But if we are talking about retaliation we have already been attacked by the other side, and virtually destroyed; so there will be little to defend. How can one ascribe any reasonable goal to a nuclear attack, whether it be first-strike or retaliation? What purpose can possibly justify millions of deaths and perhaps the extinction of the species?

(4) *Proportionality* is the question of whether the benefits of the nuclear strike would exceed the damage caused by the means

being used. This is doubtful—the destruction would be incalculable. The Northern Hemisphere would almost certainly be obliterated by a nuclear exchange, wrecking Eastern and Western civilization; we would be eradicating our past as well as our future—museums, libraries, opera halls, theaters, botanical gardens, archives, all culture as well as all history gone, evaporated in an instant. One has to wonder if even the death of an "evil empire," using President Reagan's phrase, would be worth the result.

The medical effects of nuclear war have been graphically depicted in the literature of Physicians for Social Responsibility and in the books and movies of Dr. Helen Caldicott. The radiation effects would in time even spill into the Southern Hemisphere, encircling the globe for weeks and even years, and with enough explosions—Carl Sagan's educated guess is that the threshold might be 1,000—usher in the dreadful "nuclear winter." The sun's rays would be screened from earth by tons of radioactive dust, the globe would become extremely cold, and the arctic weather combined with an irradiated soil would make it impossible to grow crops.

(5) There is also the principle of *discrimination* in just war theory, the idea that the damage should only be inflicted on the enemy's military forces, not on the civilian population. This principle was violated by the saturation bombing of World War II, and it would be totally violated by nuclear war; indeed, the standard deterrence strategy involves the threat of a "countervalue" response to a first strike, which is to target the enemy population centers. Even if "counterforce" strategy is used, or the targeting only of military facilities, there is no way to prevent thousands or even into the millions of civilian deaths, as a result of military targets centered within urban areas, missed targets, and the radioactive airflow. The fallout will drift beyond the boundaries and over neutral nations, and beyond our species to other life-forms.

(6) All of which suggest that the final criterion for a just war is violated too: that a war is just only when there is a *reasonable hope of victory.*

Clearly, there is no such hope with nuclear war, which requires us to challenge another traditional assumption, that *wars are winnable.* Certain of Reagan's people have been quoted as saying that America can wage a nuclear war and win it—Secretary Weinberger proclaimed, "we shall prevail"—but the average citizen knows better. The Public Agenda Foundation discovered that 89 percent believe there can be no winner in an all-out nuclear war, and 81 percent don't think it is possible for one side to win a *limited* nuclear war because it would escalate into an all-out war. Sane heads, including some retired military personnel, are telling us that nuclear wars are not winnable and must never be fought.

The third assumption that we have always made is that *war is survivable.*

This was always true in the past. Someone survived. But now, for the first time, humankind has the potential to destroy itself, and not only itself, but all life. People are talking about biocide and *omnicide.* Even if we haven't put all life at risk, or if there is a chance that the "doomsday prophets," as they are called by such people as Edward Teller who see no danger in nuclearism, are wrong—doesn't the chance of their being right make it a very grave matter? Doesn't even the slimmest possibility that humankind can exterminate life make it imperative that steps be taken to rid the world of the means of doing so? If a mental patient were suicidal, no sharp objects would be permitted. If you saw a friend playing Russian roulette—even though you knew there was only one chance in six to be killed—surely you would try to take that revolver away!

A New World View

Clearly we need a new world vision in order to escape from the deadly result of our folly. There is such a vision: it is the mindset that supports the Nuclear Free Zone movement. One element, of course, is the conviction that something must be done, and quickly! We live in the shadow of extinction—not just death. "Evolution was slow to produce us," Schell writes in *The Fate of the Earth,*

> but our extinction will be swift; it will literally be over before we know it. And so we must match swiftness with swiftness. Because everything we do and everything we are is in jeopardy, and because the peril is immediate and unremitting, every person is the right person to act and every moment is the right moment to begin, starting with the present moment.[17]

We must be risk-takers. We are at risk now, of course; to continue our present course will enhance the risk. Surely the risk to our persons and reputations in opposing nuclearism is nothing compared to the risk of doing nothing, of letting matters take their course.

But what is the essence of the new world view? It is the conviction that we are planetary citizens first and Americans—or Soviets, Chinese, Italians—second. After a Vienna convention on the role of women in world peace, Patricia Mische wrote of "the transformation already slowly in progress among individuals and groups who, in a deep probing of their own humanness, are discovering the bonds they have with people everywhere." Can attitudes be changed? The Vienna participants seemed living testimony that the answer is "Yes." At the close of the congress one participant asked, to tumultuous applause, that at future conferences speakers not be required to identify themselves by nationality. "I am here as a planetary citizen," she said, "and these problems belong to all of us."

Today our paramount obligation is to our planet. This is not to renounce patriotism—I do not love America less, I love the world more! Nor is it necessarily an appeal for world government, although in the long run some international controls and constraints will be necessary. It is to say that our individual destinies are inextricably bound to that of the human race. It is the conviction that this world does not exist for me alone, nor for Americans alone; therefore, my nation has no right to threaten others or to impose its will on them. It is to say that no nation, including mine, has the right to jeopardize the lives of millions of people on this globe, even the citizens of nonaligned nations, those who haven't chosen sides and want only to be left alone.

Labels like "conservative" and "liberal" go out the window, as well as "radical," as in "radical fringe," the tag so often tied to peaceminded people. The real conservatives are the people working to conserve nature; indeed, to *preserve* the planet earth. Those whose actions put it in jeopardy are the real radicals.

It may help to use the word, *conservator*. Webster: "Conservator: a protector, guardian, or custodian." "Conservatory" is defined as "a room enclosed in glass," as a greenhouse. This is an apt description of the spaceship earth enclosed in a fragile atmospheric envelope. We live in a glass globe in which, for us to be secure, everyone must be secure. To throw stones in this greenhouse—to even threaten people with nuclear weapons—is intolerable. It is time for the new conservatives, or *conservators*, to let the radicals know this.

To live on a fragile spaceship means that we are caught in a web of life of which *homo sapiens* is only one element, though an important one. An awareness of this web of life, of life's interconnectedness, gives dignity to every living thing, every organism from the simplest to the most complex. Chief Seattle, who befriended early settlers in the region around the city that bears his name, said this in 1854:

> The earth does not belong to man; man belongs to the earth. This we know. All things are connected like the blood which unites one family. All things are connected. Whatever befalls the earth befalls the sons of the earth. Man did not weave the web of life. He is merely a strand in it. Whatever he does to the web, he does to himself.

When we learn that nuclear explosions could tear gaping holes in the earth's atmospheric envelope and permit the sun's rays to blind living creatures, we tremble. This means that all the bees and pollinating insects in the area impacted by an explosion—possibly within 500 miles of it—would be blinded and unable to pollinate the plants; and our vegetation dies.

As we become aware of how connected we are, we also begin to value the crudest, rudest organisms for their intrinsic merit, their *worth,* and not just because they keep *us* alive; and we assume that reverence for life of which Albert Schweitzer spoke so eloquently. We come alive to the world, and to the world's marvelous beauty, as we escape from the prison of subjectivism, that spiritual myopia that has blinded us to the rich fabric of life. Einstein said, "Our task must be to free ourselves from this prison by widening our circle of compassion to embrace all living creatures and the whole of nature in its beauty." In terms of our human companions on this spaceship, we know the truth of John Donne's "no man is an island," and, in Martin Luther King, Jr.'s words, "We are caught in an inescapable network of mutuality tied in a single garment of destiny." Joanne Rogers Macy captures this spirit in a fine work on healing and empowerment:

> In each of our lives we have tasted that mutuality. Even though we have been conditioned in our culture to have a conception of ourselves as separate and competitive beings, striving at each other's expense for a place in the sun, we know at a deep level of our existence that we belong to each other, inextricably.[19]

As we reconnect, she writes, we know the real meaning of religion: it is "to bond again, to re-member."[20]

The Failure of Governments

So how do we start a *peace* race? Or rather, how do *we* start? As wars are too important to be left to generals, so nuclear war is too important to be left to presidents and prime ministers. Eisenhower said, "One of these days the people are going to want peace so much that their governments are going to have to step out of their way and let them have it." But why can't the governments do it? Why don't they negotiate arms reductions? *Why?*

A James Margulies cartoon in the *Houston Post* had Secretary of State Shultz talking to a reporter at the airport: "Efforts to meet the Soviets face to face are stalled over various technical issues." "Such as . . .?" "Chernenko's pacemaker causes static on Reagan's hearing aid." (When pacemakers interfere with peacemaking we're all in trouble!)

There are, of course, serious reasons why negotiation is difficult and why meaningful arms agreements are scarce. Political scientist Herbert F. York reviews the history of US-USSR arms talks and treaties, from the Limited Test Ban to the recent ASAT dialogue, and he draws some conclusions.[21] York observes that both sides operate from a political context which makes it hard for the negotiators to sell an agreement to their own people, apart from any problems involved in reaching an accord with the other side.

For example, it is difficult to sell an arms agreement to the American Congress without a means of verification. The Soviets have less need for verification since the US is an open society and any cheating—building or exploding a nuclear device on the sly—would no doubt be leaked to the press. But with the tremendous amount of secrecy in the Soviet Union, and its severe limitation on the flow of information, Americans are suspicious; and so, American negotiators have always sought on-site inspections whenever arms control accords were discussed. Soviet diplomats tend to reject this demand as a pretext for spying or for Western interference in their internal affairs.

The development of highly sophisticated "national technical means" of verification, including seismic instruments and satellite surveillance systems so sensitive that it is possible to read something the size of a license plate in Moscow, makes on-site inspection almost irrelevant—but American diplomats continue to demand it as a matter of principle, or in order to undermine an accord they don't really want anyway.

Other aspects of American government make arms negotiations problematic. American presidents have short terms, and very few are elected to a second four years. A president really has only two years for serious negotiations, since he has to spend his first year getting organized and his last year campaigning for himself or someone else. American negotiators, appointed by each succeeding president, spin like revolving doors while Soviet diplomats go on forever—Andrei Gromyko lasted several decades.

Along with the discontinuity of American foreign policy, there is the problem of ratification. The American constitution provides that the president must secure a two-thirds vote of approval from the Senate for any treaty—rather unusual among the industrialized nations—and so a treaty will often fail even though more than two-thirds of the public want it. It only takes a couple of obstructionists in the Senate to delay a treaty with the infamous filibuster! History is rife with the wreckage of treaties derailed in the Senate. President Wilson failed to secure approval for the League of Nations: President Carter was unable to secure the ratification of SALT II, and even a relatively noncontroversial issue, the Genocide Convention, took decades to ratify.

Arms negotiators are conservative. They know they will have to justify every move, everything they "give away," not only to the Senate or to political rivals, but to the public. Consequently, conferences billed as disarmament talks often result only in some insignificant limitation on arms testing or on arms production in a particular category. So we had the Partial Test Ban Treaty of 1963 which halted nuclear testing in the atmosphere but resulted in a much intensified underground nuclear testing program—and, sadly, induced the peace movement to relax.

In terms of arms production, if you negotiate an agreement to freeze a particular category—say cruise missiles—the research and development of another type of weapon—Trident II, perhaps, or Star Wars or bacteriological warfare—will quicken. Trying to stop the production of all weapons by means of arms talks is like trying to squeeze the air out of an air mattress: wherever you sit, it balloons up somewhere else!

As Richard Barnet explains in *The Giants*, negotiations fail because the military establishments on both sides think alike. They follow two principles: (1) "Don't negotiate when you are behind. Why accept a permanent position of number two?" and (2) "Don't negotiate when you're ahead. Why accept a freeze in an area of military competition where the other side has not kept up with you."[22] This mentality tends to reduce the likelihood of any significant results.

BY AUTH FOR THE PHILADELPHIA INQUIRER

Arms accords are often used merely to win time and justify armaments, as Secretary of State Henry Kissinger admitted in discussing his reasons for making the SALT I agreements. SALT I froze the number of strategic ballistic missiles for each side and permitted an increase in submarine-launched ballistic missiles to a ceiling. Marek Thee quotes Kissinger as saying, "our strategy was to agree on a five year freeze—the interval we judged would enable us to catch up by developing cruise missiles, a new submarine (Trident), a new ICBM (MX), and the B-1 bomber. We froze a disparity we inherited in order to gain time to reverse the situation."[23]

Kissinger's perceptions of an imbalance were probably wrong, but the point is that, like most negotiators, he did not see dialogue as a means of making the world safer but as a way of producing a strategic advantage for the United States. With this attitude little can be accomplished in terms of arms reduction.

The Reagan administration's sincerity about arms control or reduction is highly suspect. Congressman Thomas J. Downey said of the president: "His major arms control appointments—Eugene Rostow, Edward Rowny, Paul Nitze, Richard Perle, and Richard Burt—were chosen because of their opposition to the most comprehensive arms control yet negotiated: SALT II. It is not realistic to expect other than unremitting opposition to arms control from the US government as long as the Reagan administration remains in power."[24] Gerald C. Smith, a former head of the Arms Control and Disarmament Agency, says that our proposals are often designed to demonstrate Soviet stubbornness. He adds, "Some of our national security managers are probably not heartbroken when the Soviets reject our proposals."[25]

The US Arms Control and Disarmament Agency was founded in 1961, and Gerald C. Smith was the director, 1967–73. The Agency was to develop, negotiate, and implement international agreements to control and reduce arms, and in Smith's terms, "It should inform the public and Congress about the need for arms control just as the Pentagon does about the need for arms." Senator Clairborne Pell, one of its original sponsors, wanted the Agency "to play the role of an advocate for arms control . . . an agency that would more often than not counterbalance what was coming out of the Pentagon."

It has done this occasionally, but often not. Smith doubts whether it can or will be done under Reagan. The fact that the Agency's budget is less than one-hundred-thousandth that of the Defense Department, whose projected 1986 budget approached $300 billion, makes the government's priorities clear. How important is arms control and disarmament to our national leadership?

So there are lots of factors that mitigate against an agreement—both in terms of reaching an accord and selling it to one's own people. Some of the Soviets problems are different but many are the same. We see in their conduct the same mistrust, the same looking over the shoulder, the same game-playing to gain advantage, the same manipulation, the same reluctance to take any political risk for fear of repercussions. David McReynolds of the War Resisters League, takes a cynical view that may be close to the truth: "Governments prefer the stability of the arms race to the dangers of disarmament. They are aware of the long range risks . . . but they fear the short range impact of disarmament on their own power more." So governments *talk* a good game without playing it. They "give their allegiance *in words* to disarmament even as they give their allegiance *in deeds* to instruments of war." As Anders Thunborg, Swedish Defense Minister, points out: "Strategies or approaches for arms control are certainly not lacking. They are abundant. What is lacking, and sadly lacking today, is the *political will* to reach solid agreements on terms acceptable to both sides."[26] (italics mine)

We cannot therefore rely on governments.

But Nuclear Free Zones ignore governments. Ignoring the politicians, NFZ organizers take their appeal directly to the people: to the neighbors across the hall or in the laundromat or library, on the other side of the hedge or at MacDonalds. This kind of local initiative, as it multiplies, produces two major results. First, the emerging mosaic of nuclear-freedom will liberate whole sections of the earth from nuclear domination. The nuclear nations will have to think more carefully about where their weapons can be designed, manufactured, stored, or transported, and how they can dispose of waste without running afoul of local restrictions. This is a powerful political shove in the direction of disarmament.

Second, the movement will impact the spiritual climate of the age, the *zeitgeist*. As NFZs proliferate instead of weapons, more people will adopt the World Citizen world-view. They will think differently about life and interconnectedness, interdependence and *inter*national security. As these attitudes percolate up from the grassroots they will affect the political climate too, modifying the jingoism of hawks who begin to realize that the business of peace transcends national boundaries. Our national leaders may be emboldened to take some risks—offer unilateral initiatives as the Soviets did with their 1985 test moratorium—and even make treaties to reduce arms. If that happens, however, it will be a *popular* victory. The *people* will have done it, with the help of a few sympathizers in government, and the leaders will formalize it with their treaties.

Exactly how the weapons themselves will be destroyed is open to question; but that is a minor matter, once the will is found. Some members of the Union of Concerned Scientists support the following plan, which I paraphrase here: Build a dismantling plant somewhere in a neutral zone, outside of the boundaries of the United States and the Soviet Union. Both sides will bring to it large numbers of nuclear weapons, selected independently by each country. Under the joint supervision of a Soviet-American commission, inspect the weapons and measure the amounts and composition of the fissile isotypes present to ensure that both sides are turning in equal amounts of fissile materials. Dismantle the weapons. Stop the production of weapons-grade material in both countries. Subject all nuclear power plants in both countries to regular international inspection to guard against the division of plutonium from spent fuel.

The UCS scientists' aim is not to get to zero nuclear weapons, only to some "minimum invulnerable deterrent," but the same method could be used to get to zero.

Surely the political effect of this process, as the weapons are destroyed in front of the world's cameras, would be to create a momentum difficult to reverse, even as the present situation carries with it a different sort of momentum, fearful and grim. The UCS plan needs refinement, and there may be other ways of actually dismantling nuclear weapons, but it can be done. It *will* be done *if we want it done!*

Is the Goal Safe?

We have been discussing the means. What about the end, the goal of *zero* nuclear weapons: is the goal safe? Will the political scene be more stable or less so? The skeptics say less.

Serious questions have been raised by those who point out that you cannot "disinvent" the bomb, you cannot remove the knowledge of how to build nuclear weapons. Indeed, someone said that a world without nuclear weapons is "an unimaginable global state of grace." Skeptics argue that if we get down to zero there will be the chance of someone secretly rebuilding an arsenal—an aggressive nation, or perhaps a single terrorist using a bomb and threats to get his way. This, then, will put a disarmed nation at a disadvantage. Although some NFZ advocates call this argument a "red herring" or "fantasy," it needs to be addressed.

One answer is *transarmament,* moving from an offense-based system to a purely defensive one. Jonathan Schell argues rather eloquently for such a move in *The Abolition.* He claims for it the traditional middle ground between unilateral disarmament on the one hand, and world government on the other. He would, by mutual agreement, remove all offensive nuclear weapons from the earth, permitting nations only conventional defensive weapons and, in addition, anti-nuclear defensive systems, just in case someone secretly makes a few bombs. Also, nations would have the *capacity* to rearm with nuclear weapons should another nation do so. This would be a "weaponless deterrence": "factory would deter factory, blueprint would deter blueprint, equation would deter equation."[27] The result would put the world's military planners "on the same side: the side of defense. Their aim would be to equip every army with steel shields and rubber swords."[28] Lewis Bohn, a Los Alamos scientist in the early days, argues similarly for weaponless deterrence. Unlike our present system of Mutual Assured Destruction,

> it could not escalate in minutes to global catastrophe. There would be no poised missile systems to cause or permit global disaster by accident, crisis miscalculation, madness or treachery in high places or low, or by hope of successful preemption or surprise attack.[29]

Swiss political analyst Dietrich Fischer makes an intelligent case for transarmament in *Preventing War in the Nuclear Age.* He urges the nations to move from offensive strategies and weapons to purely defensive ones so that they can no longer threaten each other. "The most desirable characteristic of a country in terms of contributing to international peace," he writes, "is neither to be 'militarily superior' over others, nor to be militarily weak, but to be strong in terms of defense and weak in terms of offense."[30] Nuclear weapons would go, as well as conventional offensive weapons. (Tanks, for example, are "offensive" but not anti-tank artillery.) In addition to a defensive military system, Fischer suggests various forms of nonmilitary defense: economic, social, and moral sanctions against threats and invasion.

Many Nuclear Free Zone activists, of course, would not want to rule out total disarmament, whether unilateral or universal. Nor would some rule out a world federation, perhaps a strengthened United Nations, with the power to police a disarmed world. To be sure, we cannot "disinvent" nuclear weapons—but this does not mean that a world without nuclear weapons would be in a precarious position. Removing the incentive to build nuclear weapons, or creating a world where their presence is so onerous that any nation having them becomes a pariah, would do the trick. Albert Donnay, Director of Nuclear Free America, counters the disinvention argument in a letter to the author:

> There is no shortage of examples of things which, although not disinvented, we no longer build, use, or practice. The guillotine, gas ovens, the cross, the hanging rope, and biological weapons (not to mention virgin sacrifices) are just some of the ways nation-states used to kill people in great numbers. These technologies have not been disinvented any more than slavery or colonialism or the divine right of kings . . . What is politically safe? A world with 50,000 nuclear weapons in the control of a dozen geriatric fools or a world with no nuclear weapons and the possibility that someone (with a great deal of time, energy, resources, and the infrastructure of a "warring state" to back it up) might build one, two, ten, or even one hundred nuclear weapons? No contest.

There is some risk in reducing the world's arsenals of nuclear weapons to zero. It has never happened. Anything that innovative, like finding a northwest passage or putting a man on the moon, involves risk. But, obviously, such a "state of grace" would be safer than a world thirty minutes from omnicide and, if we won't risk nuclear disarmament, we shall have to risk nuclear war.

Coexistence or No Existence

The Public Agenda Foundation voter survey suggests that there is significant popular support for the goal of getting to zero nuclear weapons. One-third—a strong minority—agreed with the statement that "by the 1990s, it should be American policy *never* to use nuclear weapons under *any* circumstances." Respondents indicated an awareness of the need for political accommodation. 67 percent agreed with a "live and let live" philosophy: "Let the Communists have their system and we ours. There's room in the world for both."

But the new world-view is more than simple accommodation. It requires cooperation. It involves a shift in thinking from the we-versus-them mentality to an us-and-them-versus-the-Bomb mentality. The real problem for us is not the Soviets, or for them the Americans, but (for both) the Bomb and whatever keeps it alive, whatever forces and factors keep the arms race humming. Greed. Self-perpetuating defense contracts. Intense nationalism. Xenophobia. Machismo politicians.

There are precedents for international cooperation. Often old adversaries become working partners, if not allies. Consider the happy relationships we've developed with Japan and Germany, former enemies, to say nothing of Communist China. Marek Thee, Swedish Defense Minister, writes:

> . . . there seems little reason why there should exist basic in-
> compatibilities beyond the clash of two great military machines.
> Both the US and the Soviet Union are satiated great powers, at the
> apogee of their might, with vast lands rich in natural resources.
> They have no common border and no territorial feud. They have
> never fought directly against each other; indeed, they were allies
> in World War II. Barring imperial compulsions and the propensity

to be guided by the military rather than by the political imperative, it should be possible to find a feasible base for peaceful coexistence.[31]

The issue is coexistence or *no existence*. This is not to deny the real ideological differences. The Soviet Union is a closed society, Marxist and doctrinaire. The United States is an open, capitalistic, disputatious society, with a representative form of government quite different from Soviet totalitarianism. But the contrasting ideologies should not prevent us from cooperating to ensure our common survival. We must learn a *modus vivendi* that is much more comfortable than the present nervous terror. Together we must conserve the earth and make it secure.

There are ways of building mutual understanding and trust, including cultural and scientific exchange, twinning, and various forms of dialogue. And there are *political* confidence-building steps on the road to mutual disarmament: a comprehensive test ban, a ban on the production of fissionable materials, a no first-use policy, and other measures.

These are all disarming measures, as is the creation of a vast global mosaic of Nuclear Free Zones.

3

Americans Opt Out:
Cases and Consequences

"Our citizens are worried about potholes. A nuclear bomb makes the world's biggest pothole!"
> former mayor Sam Abbott, Takoma Park, MD.

ASK YOURSELF: WOULD JESUS MAKE A NUCLEAR WEAPON-EVEN A SMALL PART OF ONE?
Vote YES on No. 56!
> Advertisement, Ashland (OR) Citizens for Measure 56

Opting out of the arms race is becoming popular. Americans are declaring homes and garages, shops and offices, schools and colleges, churches and synagogues nuclear-free. In a related effort, Louis Kousin of Cranford, New Jersey is promoting "Peace Sites," places dedicated to peace education—again, a symbolic witness to the need for nonviolent alternatives in this nuclear age. Over sixty international YWCAs were declared Peace Sites by February, 1986, with over 150 Peace Sites overall. Generally, Peace Sites do not engage in political action but are, sometimes, associated with NFZ activity.

In terms of Nuclear Free Zones, the idea begins with an individual, or just a handful of people daring to declare their living space or work space nuclear-free; then it may spread to churches and schools, where it is often begun by students; and finally to towns and village councils or to the ballot box where, in good democratic tradition, citizens vote to declare their turf "off-limits" to the bomb and its makers.

Often it begins with children who are too wise to accept the legacy of terror bequeathed to them by their parents and grandparents. The children, too, are afraid and angry. Studies show that children are more anxious about the bomb than they appear to be. They say little even to parents, but fears and worries occupy their dreams and daydreams. This concern carries into secondary school and college where opinion surveys tell us that young people are pessimistic about the fate of the earth. Arthur Levine, President of Bradford College in Massachusetts, found a strange paradox in his analysis of college students, their philosophies and values. In campus group interviews conducted by the Carnegie Studies (1979), 91 percent of the college students were optimistic about their professional life and future financial security, but only 41 percent were optimistic about global affairs. Levine concludes that most of them are optimistic about their *personal* futures but pessimistic about their *collective* future, in light of pollution, acid rain, etc., as well as the bomb.[1] They don't expect the world to survive the nuclear sword of Damocles for long but, meanwhile, they want to make money and live as comfortably as possible. Levine calls it a "Titanic mentality." Although the ship is sinking, young people are saying, "If it's going to sink anyway, I guess I owe it to myself to go first-class!"

Not all of our student population has succumbed to the materialist vision of expensive suburban homes and fast-track business or professional careers. Some are restoring an ethical dimension to the campus that it had in the 1960s. Many are active in the battles against pollution, racism, sexism, poverty, and hunger—consider how the Ethopian tragedy activated thousands! And some are fighting the bomb. The STOP network (Student-Teacher Organization to Prevent Nuclear War) has energized many high school students in the 1980s, and UCAM (United Campuses Against Nuclear War) and other groups have supported newly-active college youth.

Schools as diverse as Windham School in Madison, Wisconsin, Our Lady of Lourdes Catholic Boarding School at Pine Ridge Indian Reservation in South Dakota, Oakwood High

School in Poughkeepsie, New York, and West High School in Davenport, Iowa, have been declared NFZs. Michael Bradley wrote the Nuclear Free Zone Registry,

> Our fourth hour Comparative Government class started the ball rolling. The students in that class voted to make Room 158 between the hours of 11:00 and 11:55 A.M. a Nuclear Free Zone. There was only one "no" vote.
>
> Why stop there? A student senator in the class presented an NFZ bill to the student senate of West High, where it passed by a healthy margin. The law then passed by a two-thirds majority of the junior and sophomore classes. Our letters to the appropriate governments should soon reach their destinations and we will anxiously await their replies.

The process took longer at Oakwood School. Oakwood is a Friends' boarding and day school in Poughkeepsie, NY. Students, faculty, and staff together declared Oakwood nuclear-free after a five-month period of education, discussions, and debate. There were questions. Some of those involved felt that it would be hypocritical for Oakwood, whose students and faculty enjoyed a relatively high standard of living, to declare itself nuclear-free. After all, much of the school's equipment is made by nuclear weapons-related firms. Some persons believe that the high standard of living is protected by our government's weapons "muscle" or the threat it poses to other nations. The majority at Oakwood, however, felt that nuclear disarmament would provide money to be used for improving the living standard of the "have-nots" without sacrificing the security of the "have" nations.

Interestingly, the school did not avoid counter-arguments but welcomed them. A chemical engineer who had testified against the freeze in the Dutchess County legislature was invited to present the "peace through strength" case. He was heard politely, questioned vigorously, and then the school community voted against his position and for nuclear freedom.

According to Jeanne Moucka of the Nuclear Free Zone Registry in California, fifty-one schools and colleges had registered as nuclear-free by March 1, 1986. (There may be others that have not registered.) She told me that many campaigns are initiated by students, often in collaboration with a faculty member. The campaign helps educate the school personnel on the nuclear issue but also provides students with insights into the democratic process as they write a resolution, lobby for it, and carry it through the system to a vote.

The list of NFZ colleges includes Marquette, Tufts, Grinnell, Hampshire, three branches of the University of Wisconsin, Tacoma Community College, the University of Scranton, and the University of Oregon at Eugene. The Eugene campaign climaxed in April of 1983 when about one-third of the university's 14,000 students voted 79 percent approval of a resolution sponsored by Students for a Nuclear Free Future. SNUFF members collected over 900 signatures to place the issue on the ballot.

Usually a campus campaign begins with a core group of students who form a sponsoring committee, draft a resolution, plan the educational process and petitioning, and place the issue before the student government or the student body for a vote. At the same time, students may seek the help of sympathetic faculty members to have the issue brought before the faculty senate. Once the issue has been approved by students and/or faculty, the next step is to meet with the President or members of the college administration and request that it be placed on the agenda for the Board of Trustees. The sponsors should attempt to secure a binding vote of the Board of Trustees. Often the trustees will refuse to ratify such a policy, but that should not deter young activists. Educating their fellow students and a faculty that is often naive on political issues makes the process extremely valuable.

Nuclear Free America offers these suggestions for campus organizers: A) *Build coalitions*. Seek the support of faculty, employee groups and unions, sororities and fraternities, clubs, religious groups, and similar organizations. B) *Set clear goals*. The goal might be to just ban nuclear weapons from the campus, however, some of these items might be included in a declaration:

1. Prohibiting nuclear weapons-related research. The University of Michigan, for example, will approve "no research the clearly

foreseeable and probable result of which, the direct application of which, or any specific purpose of which is to destroy human life or to incapacitate human beings." (The wording of which could be more clearly discernable, but they had the right idea!) Princeton, MIT, Harvard, and Columbia have regulations prohibiting classified (government-made-secret) research on campus. Of course, not all weapons research is classified and professors may do consulting work off-campus for the Departments of Energy or Defense. But a university could be asked to dismiss faculty engaged in such research or to adopt a non-contract policy for such persons in the future.

2. The withdrawal of all university investments from nuclear weapons-related companies. As a first step, consider demanding that the university submit and report shareholders resolutions opposing involvement in the arms race. Another creative approach comes from Harvard where members of the "Class of '83" have established an excrow account in which all of their future donations to the university will be held until the university agrees to divest from corporations involved in South Africa. A similar step could be taken with regard to weapons industries.

Nuclear divestment campaigns have been conducted by students at Notre Dame, Tufts, and Hampshire College. When students at Tufts did their homework, they discovered that in its original charter Tufts was founded to promote peace and justice. They found a clause in the university bylaws that prohibits Tufts from investing in weapons firms. This boosted the NFZ drive on campus and helped persuade the board to divest. At Hampshire College, a student sit-in at the administration building helped convince the trustees to divest their holdings in the companies of the top one hundred defense contractors.

3. The banning of nuclear weapons contractors on campus during the annual recruiting drives when big business signs up its new crop of college graduates—echoes of policies adopted during the 1960s that kept ROTC recruiters off campus.

4. Other tactics would include civil disobedience in support of a nuclear-free policy, such as removing all of the civil defense signs on campus (or adding, "There is No Defense Against Nu-

clear War"), or collecting student pledges not to work for the nuclear weapons industry upon graduation.

The University of California is deeply involved in the arms race, managing the two major research laboratories for the Department of Energy, at Livermore, California, and Los Alamos, New Mexico. Livermore is the world's largest weapons research laboratory. From it have come the designs for 90 percent of the nuclear warheads in the American arsenal. Some of the nation's huge antinuclear demonstrations have been held there, and on one occasion in the early 1980s over 1,000 people were arrested. In January, 1983, Berkeley students formed a nonviolent blockade around University Hall to protest the military research conducted by university faculty. Meanwhile, students at nearby Stanford had collected thousands of signatures to petition for an end to the military research being done at Stanford's atomic linear accelerator. Despite rebuffs, many students are still actively opposing weapons research.

The Pentagon octopus, its tentacles brandishing lucrative contracts, seduces one university after another. According to sociologist Howard J. Ehrlich, there are more than 250 colleges and universities involved in military-related activities. What are they doing with the government largess? Ehrlich provides some examples from 1984:

> A project at the University of Wisconsin is measuring how wind currents carry chemicals or bacteria for use in chemical or germ warfare. University of Washington scientists are developing ultrasound detection devices for anti-submarine warfare. Researchers at the George Washington University Medical Center are studying chemical agents for a nerve gas. A University of Michigan research team is working on firebombs that detonate clouds of fuel vapor to create an explosion that approximates in intensity the fireball of an atomic bomb. At Johns Hopkins University and MIT, two of the largest university military contractors, scientists are developing new weapons systems.[2]

The size and strength of the military-academic connection is appalling. Disconnecting the links is a difficult task but NFZ campus organizers can help it happen. By doing their homework and by demanding full disclosure of the university's military contacts, NFZ campaigners will be doing a service to the public. The ethical commitments and values of the university's Board of Trustees and staff will be exposed to the community at large, for good or ill.

Churches Opt Out

On May 30, 1984, the Religious Task Force of Mobilization for Survival called a news conference to announce the declarations of the first fifty religious Nuclear Free Zones in the United States. This was the beginning of a grassroots network that was to extend throughout the United States and connect with the global religious peace network.

Since that news conference, the number of declared Nuclear Free Zones in the religious community has increased to over 190. These are churches and synagogues, religious schools, convents, conference centers, monasteries, and denominational offices. The movement was boosted by the American Catholic Bishops' Pastoral Letter and by the action of three Protestant denominations in declaring their headquarters' premises nuclear-free. In so doing, the Church of the Brethren, the Unitarian-Universalist Association, and the Christian Church (Disciples of

Christ) encouraged their local congregations to follow suit. The Union of American Hebrew Congregations (Reformed) also has passed a resolution supporting NFZ action by its member temples.

The Church of the Brethren, with its long tradition of peace-making, has sent the national declaration to its member churches, encouraging each congregation to imitate the parent body. Over fifty churches had declared by March 10, 1986, according to Charles Boyer at the national office. Many Brethren see this as a uniquely positive action, unlike draft resistance, for example, which is important but rather a negative action.

Many NFZ churches have also rejected FEMA plans. The Federal Emergency Management Agency (FEMA) designated thousands of religious buildings as fallout shelters. Many Jews and Christians deny FEMA's basic assumption that nuclear war is survivable. "The idea of using churches as a shelter against nuclear attack is a joke," said pastor Robert B. O'Connor of the church of Holy Name of Jesus, on New York's West Side.[3] He removed the black-and-orange Fallout Shelter sign. Other churches have done the same. John Donaghy, a lay minister at St. Thomas Aquinas Catholic Church in Ames, Iowa, told his county civil defense disaster coordinator that "we'd be most happy to cooperate in cases of disasters where our building might be needed, but we stated we will not be an officially designated fallout shelter."

The space redeemed from nuclearism needs to be given over to worthy purposes. In addition to weekly worship, many of the nuclear-free churches are providing space to meet human needs—nursery schools or day care centers, soup kitchens, shelter for the homeless or for refugees. Some provide office space for peace or social justice groups.

For example, the Wellington Avenue United Church of Christ in Chicago, and the La Mesa Community UCC in Santa Barbara, California, are sanctuary churches. First United Methodist of Reno, Nevada, offers space to AA and Meals on Wheels for the elderly, and sponsors an Indian tutoring program. Presbyterian Camp Highlands, near Allenspark, Colorado, has an outreach to Spanish speaking children, low income people, and senior citizens. Notably, Camp Highlands became the first NFZ in Colorado when, one summer, ninety junior high young people petitioned the Boulder Presbytery to declare the two hundred acres nuclear-free. Happily, the Presbytery agreed unanimously.

A number of Catholic orders have declared their facilities nuclear-free. Some of them run conference centers where hundreds of guests annually are treated to the gentle persuasion of Nuclear Free Zone signs; or hospitals, where patients have their consciousness raised along with their health! Others operate schools, whose facilities carry the same designation, giving the sisters the opportunity to awaken young minds to a global attitude and a nonviolent philosophy.

Seeking information, I developed and sent a survey to fifty NFZ-declared religious bodies in February of 1986, with twenty-three returns. The results were interesting. For one thing, in over half of the cases the NFZ proposal was initiated by a woman, although it often came out of a committee such as Social Concerns or a Witness or Peace Commission. Then it would either go before an official board of the church for a decision, or to the congregation for a vote, or both. Church polity varies from one communion to another, and sometimes from one congregation to another. In a few cases, notably the Friends, there is a consensus decision instead of a vote.

When the Convent Immaculate Conception of the Sisters of St. Benedict (Ferdinand, IN) declared itself a nuclear-free zone, more elaborate steps ensued: (1) discussion among Peace Committee members; (2) drafting of a proposal for the Religions Community Council; (3) presentation of that statement to full community membership; (4) education of the community over a span of several months; (5) proposal brought to full community membership for hearing, discussion, and vote.

In the questionnaire I asked if there were any significant opposition, and all but two said no; whether anyone from the body was involved in community or regional NFZ campaigns, and about half said yes; and whether individuals were involved in other empowerment activities. The twenty-three contacts cited the following activities: political lobbying (11), tax resistance (4), boycotts (9), vigils (12), civil disobedience (5). Work for the "pledge of resistance" and letter-writing to congress were mentioned, and two congregations reported "twinning" with nuclear-free churches in New Zealand. The Religious Task Force is trying to encourage more twinning for American congregations, and they have a long list of New Zealand churches for whom no twins have yet been found.

This survey suggests the following profile: a nuclear-free religious body is typically one that is involved with a number of social issues, often provides space for social relief programs, contains activist individuals, and is quite "together," that is, united on an antinuclear position. Of course, activists in churches that are divided on the issue may not want to bring it up and, if the issue is raised, it may fail to pass.

Finally, respondents were asked to complete the sentence, "Church or religious Nuclear Free Zones are important because . . ." A few answers follow:

. . . It has to start somewhere.

. . . One more sandbag against the flood of militarism.

. . . Our ultimate security cannot rest in that which ultimately kills. God offers Shalom and Abundant Life. To trust in Fear and Nuclear Death is heresy.

. . . They are one visible and unequivocal way that the religious community can oppose the life-threatening arms buildup. It is one way that committed Christians can say yes to life and no to death. Ideally, it is the first step to more active ways of working for peace.

. . . They witness in our communities to a different understanding of patriotism and to our belief that we must destroy our nuclear arsenals before they destroy us.

Verily, the movement grows. Tributaries from the academic and religious nuclear-free communities feed into the main stream, that of the cities and towns bravely and boldly making their declarations, opting out of the arms race at risk of federal disfavor, asserting their right to keep the bomb-and-missile industry away from themselves and their children.

What follows are four case studies of Nuclear Free Zone communities designed to show the diversity of the movement and showcase some of the creative tactics used by local organizers. Lest we be one-sided, I shall discuss two relatively unsuccessful campaigns toward the end of the chapter.

Two other successful campaigns, those in Amherst, Massachusetts, and Takoma Park, Maryland, are covered in other chapters. Here we examine the Ashland, Oregon; San Juan County, Washington; Hoboken, New Jersey; and Evanston, Illinois, campaigns.

Ashland, Oregon: A Socially Conscious Community

Ashland, population 15,000, a college town nestled in the verdant valleys of southern Oregon, was a likely prospect for a nuclear-free campaign. Ashland is a pleasant town, carefully manicured, with quaint antique streetlamps and tudor-style storefronts. A local "sunshine law" prohibits any building over a certain height. Many artists live in the region, and Ashland has a nationally acclaimed Shakespearian theater. "Tourism is a big industry," the Ashland organizers have written in a campaign manual,

> so economics dictate preservation of scenic and cultural values. Healthful living, demonstrated by regard for natural foods and regular exercise, is a large concern with many people. The community is largely white and middle class, with a strong Christian bent. Ads for the NFZ stressed protection of the quality of local life, and found support from churches and the wide variety of health-oriented businesses. It is probably important to note that the local college has no facilities for nuclear experimentation, nor does business or the military have any current local interests. We, therefore, emphasized *keeping* Ashland a nuclear free zone rather than making it into one.

And so the campaign flyer read, "Keep Ashland a Nuclear Free Zone: Vote YES on 56." A full-page advertisement read, "Peace is Everybody's Business. Keep Ashland a Nuclear Free Zone, Vote YES on 56," and it was signed by some 70 individuals and local businesses. Another full-page ad carried the names of fifteen local clergy: "Ask Yourself—Would Jesus Make a Nuclear Weapon—Even a Small Part of One? Vote YES on 56," and in italics, *"Blessed are the peacemakers for they shall be called the children of God." (Matthew 5:9)* Merchants and professionals were courted for financial support. This advertisement appeared:

The seven Ashland organizers decided to take the initiative route, which meant securing the signatures of 15 percent of those voting in the previous mayoral election. "The basis of this decision," they said, "was our desire to have the ordinance emerge from community participation and awareness. Having the city council pass the measure may prove easier, but an initiative drive can help the NFZ idea to sink in at the grassroots level."

It did—but not without considerable debate, even in this community of professionals, artisans, and academics. First, the measure's constitutionality was questioned by a member of council during an open meeting; others argued that the council legally had to place an initiative on the ballot without ruling on its appropriateness. NFZ proponents testified to the potential reality of a nuclear holocaust and their fears about it. One resident, Jim Selleck, described modern times as "the diciest, the chanciest of eras," and added, "This is heel-digging time. We must stop this nuclear juggernaut."

The debate spilled into the public press. In an editorial titled, "Don't Dock Ships on Main Street," the *Daily Tidings* editor snorted, "This proposal is sort of like Ashland deciding it does not want to become a deep-water port for ocean-going shipping." (Ashland is landlocked, miles from the Pacific.) But activist John Stahmer, in a letter to the editor, said that was exactly the point. Component parts for Trident subs and missiles "are manufactured in many towns and cities—like Ashland—all across the country. Nuclear weapons are not made in 'nuclear weapons development centers,' but only finally assembled or deployed there. They are, in fact, made in Everytown, USA." Others raised the red herring of medical use of nuclear technology, but NFZ supporters countered by saying that it was not anyone's intent to ban radiology. (Other communities have incorporated a clause specifically excluding the medical uses of radiation from their NFZ.)

Later in the campaign, without warning, the mayor showed reporters a letter from the Oregon attorney general indicating that the proposed ordinance was "overbroad" and "fatally defective." The next day NFZ organizers held their own press conference. They said that in their view it was citizens, not mayors or attorneys general, who made laws, and if the measure seemed overbroad, certainly the proliferation of nuclear weapons could be seen as overbroad, and their destructiveness as "broad beyond belief."

On November 2, 1982, the public voted 53 percent to 43 percent to become a nuclear-free community. It was the fourth in the nation and the very first on the west coast; also, the first NFZ produced by a citizen ballot initiative. The Ashland experience spurred several other Oregon communities and counties to go nuclear-free, and by the end of 1985 Portland's city council had passed an NFZ resolution.

The Ashland campaign had taken exactly one year. Not content to rest on their laurels, the Ashland activists produced an excellent manual (see appendix for address) for NFZ organizers, "How to Make Your Community A Nuclear Free Zone." In it they stress the importance of controversy:

> In the final analysis, we decided that our opposition did us more good than harm. If there had been no opposition, the measure would have gone quietly to the voters, and may even have passed. But without the opposition, there would have been no debate. The public debate is what matters, perhaps even more than actually passing the NFZ ordinance . . . Welcome the opposition: they will provide a forum for you to develop the reasons for becoming a Nuclear Free Zone.

The Pig War and San Juan County, Washington

A dispute arose between American and British settlers in the mid-nineteenth century, over the ownership of one of the lovely islands dotting upper Puget Sound and the Straits of Georgia. Those islands in the Northwest Territory had been named by Spanish explorers: San Juan, Orcas, Guemes, Lopez. These islands lie between the two main channels: the de Haro's Channel to the west, by Vancouver Island, and Rosario Strait to the east, by the mainland. British traders related to the Hudson's Bay Company and American settlers intermingled without either nation having clear right to the islands. An Anglo-American agreement of 1818 had provided for joint occupation of the area but left the issue of which of the channels actually divided American and British territory in doubt. Both sides were discontented and there was growing tension waiting for an incident to ignite into open warfare.

The British operated a sheep farm on San Juan Island, and added other livestock. By 1859 there were about 25 American settlers on the island whom the British considered illegal squatters. One Lyman Cutlar, an American, shot a British-owned pig on June 15, 1859 because it was rooting in his garden. The British were upset. Tempers flared. The flamboyant, hotheaded American General, William Harvey, landed an infantry company under Captain George Pickett on the island. Soon the British had three armed warships threatening to bombard Pickett's encampment from Griffin Bay.

The situation took a long time to resolve. Hotheads on both sides demanded military action but, fortunately, cooler heads prevailed. British Admiral Robert Baynes advised the provincial governor that he would not "involve two great nations in a war over a squabble over a pig," and General Winfield Scott, dispatched by President Buchanan to investigate the matter, removed Harvey from the scene and secured a temporary agreement for joint occupation of San Juan Island. Ultimately, the issue was given to arbitration. In 1872 scholars appointed by the Emperor of Germany to settle the geographical issues determined that the proper boundary should be established as the "Canal de Haro," so the United States took the disputed islands.

So in one celebrated case, at least, two nations demonstrated that reason, patience, and arbitration would settle a dispute instead of war. This independent, enlightened attitude foreshadowed what happened over a century later when residents of San Juan County declared their islands a Nuclear Weapons Free Zone.

The Commissioners tipped their hand early by officially rejecting the government's Crisis Relocation Plan for civil defense: "We do not want to be part of strategies that are based on the assumption that nuclear war is survivable . . . Our nation's only real defense is to prevent nuclear war." Taking advantage of this spirit, organizers of the Islanders for Nuclear Arms Control (INAC) undertook a petition campaign in the fall of 1983, designed to demonstrate support for a Nuclear Weapons Free Zone to the County Commissioners. They collected 700 signatures on the five larger islands (the county includes 180), and organized an advisory ballot in which the concept passed public muster by a 61 percent vote on February 7, 1984.

Promotional tactics were creative. INAC collected 570 names countywide for a "Signature Ad" (with donations of $1 per signature to cover the advertising costs); individuals volunteered to write letters to the editor each week before the election; a member paid for a full page graphic ad; and a land developers' association independently passed a resolution supporting the NWFZ. There was some "muted opposition," but pro-NWFZ comments prevailed in the newspapers.

In a letter to the editor of *The Journal* (2/1/84), Katherine Scott condemned a national leadership "committed to a policy of nuclear militarization despite its costs," and praised the local NWFZ effort: "We are fortunate in San Juan County to have a board of commissioners and a conscientious citizenry willing to draw up an ordinance that will free us from complicity in the criminal folly and lessen our risk of peril." Organizer Amy Wing writes that "the county sheriff added to the momentum of our efforts by stating that if the ordinance were to prohibit the transportation of nuclear weapons through county waters, he would be more than willing to notify the Trident Submarine Commander, in the case of violation, by way of the sheriff of its home port." In a letter to me recently, Sheriff Ray K. Sheffer said that he had no report of any violation as of January 16, 1986, and if such occurred "the matter would be handled by contact between the Prosecuting Attorney of San Juan and the US Attorney's Office." He added, "I personally have no compunction about enforcing the provisions of this Resolution."

The ordinance passed by the Commissioners on April 3, 1984 included this language (Section 2): "It is unlawful for any person, firm, corporation, or governmental body to possess, use, test, deploy, or store nuclear weapons, or to manufacture components, whose sole purpose is use in the production of nuclear weapons, within county boundaries."

Activist Katherine Scott writes from Friday Harbor, Washington: "I am personally very happy with the declaration of the county as Nuclear Free as I feel the real work of peacemaking begins at home, and it's up to local governments to legislate for the kind of life quality, safety, and security the Federal government is unwilling to provide. To my knowledge, the Nuclear Free Zone designation has not affected business one way or another." Washington state representative Pat McMullen, who had testified in support of the ordinance, commented, "Passing this ordinance in San Juan County is like lighting the first candle in the darkness."

It was not the first, of course—San Juan County became the 44th American Nuclear Free Zone—but the first legally binding ordinance of its kind in the state of Washington. The cooler heads of 1859 had become the cool-headed peacemakers of 1984, on the islands lying between de Haro's Channel and Rosario Strait.

The NFZ Hustlers of Hoboken

Hoboken, New Jersey, is a small, gritty city hard by the Hudson River, directly across from the imposing Manhattan skyline. The city is bordered on the north by the Lincoln Tunnel, on the south by the Holland Tunnel, and on the west by Jersey City, which has also become nuclear-free. Hoboken's narrow, crowded streets are frequently double-parked, and its downtown gives the impression of a well-worn, working-class community, which it has been, for the most part. It has currently become, to a considerable extent, a bedroom community for yuppies, artists, and scholars who work in New York. Some of these young professionals engineered the successful NFZ campaign in Hoboken, culminating in the unanimous city council vote on September 20, 1984.

Hoboken's population of about 42,000 is racially mixed, with a strong Hispanic faction of about 40 percent—the Nuclear Free Zone ordinance is printed in English and Spanish. The housing is older—mostly row houses—with 79 percent of it having been built before 1939, according to information furnished me at City Hall. Minutes of HAND (Hoboken Action for Nuclear Disarmament) meetings indicate that the NFZ activists were well aware of their constituents, and made plans to reach the various Hoboken communities, from the poor to workingclass, merchants, yuppies, and artists.

Robert A. Ranieri, a councilman who admired their initiative, called the nuclear-free Hoboken activists "a lovely group of young hustlers," political amateurs who in nine months managed to collect 2,800 signatures on a petition asking city council to declare Hoboken a Nuclear Free Zone. Judith Karpova, the founder of HAND, is an energetic, bright, attractive woman who is disgusted with hypocrisy and politicians who prey on people's fears to generate funds for more expensive weapons and so-called defensive systems like Star Wars.

Karpova admits her roots are in the activism of the 1960s. "I don't know how many times I got arrested," she says, referring to anti-Vietman demonstrations. She became very involved in extremist actions that she regrets now: "We got carried away—calling people pigs and such—we got crazy!" Karpova sees much of that activity as destructive—though understandable, given the horrors of Vietnam. She wanted desperately to do something constructive for society, and in particular to prevent nuclear war. Ultimately, helping to make Hoboken nuclear-free became a very satisfying activity for Judith Karpova.

A turning point occurred when Karpova spent time at the Women's Peace Encampment at the Seneca Falls Army Depot, and she became fully aware—through educational experiences—of the terrible tragic results of nuclear war. "I was physically sick for days," she told me. In Hoboken she made contact with the Nuclear Freeze Campaign, then formed HAND in November 1983 after the television showing of *The Day After*. The Freeze and HAND complemented each other, both working for an end to the arms race. But Karpova felt that the NFZ concept generated a more positive response from the local press and public. "The freeze was something hard to explain," Karpova says, "and it wasn't something you could put into practice. But when people asked us what *we* wanted we could say it in three words—Nuclear Free Zone—and tell them it's something we can do right here!"

HAND activists used a number of educational events and other tactics to enlist support. Local merchants were approached. On a certain weekend HAND received a percentage of the profits from local businesses which had pledged support. And there were rallies, advertising, the showing of a movie, *The Atomic Cafe,* followed by discussion, a public debate. At a benefit Valentine Party for OXFAM to aid the Ethiopian famine victims two antinuclear films were shown: a documentary, the *Video Disarmament Survey,* and Stanley Kubrick's monumental movie, *Dr. Strangelove, or How I Learned to Stop Worrying and Love the Bomb.* Live music followed the film.

HAND's efforts even extended to school children; after all, they have a right to express themselves, and we adults need to hear them! HAND circulated news of an essay contest through the elementary schools: "My Feelings About Living in the Nuclear Age." Chris Woehrle (first place tie) wrote, in part:

> Whenever I hear about nuclear missiles I wonder if I'll live to be 20. I would very much like to have a family and raise children. But then I wonder, what kind of a world is this to bring them into? Do I want to take the risk of them being deformed or having brain damage because of some nuclear power plant leakage?
>
> They say missiles are for peace. What kind of peace is having to worry if you'll have a world to wake up to in the morning? . . .

And from Nadhim Frangul (first place tie):

> I am totally for nuclear disarmament, for it is a sure-fire way to prevent nuclear war . . . The American government could save billions of dollars of resources on missiles and silos. They could make hundreds of housing projects or something more important. The government also uses trillions of taxpayer's dollars on nuclear preparation and arms. This could be used for welfare and unemployment. Also, if an area of the United States has missile silos it is a potential or definite target of other countries . . .

Carrie Kilmer (second place):

> When I think about war I get very scared. A couple of days ago I was lying on my bed and looking at a lamp. For some strange

reason I thought the lamp turned into a bomb. I turned the lamp on and I thought it exploded. I thought about all my brothers and sisters dead and my mother and father and all the people I cared about . . . I wrote a letter to President Reagan about war. This is some of the things it said: War is terrible. The people who die aren't dolls and the people who die never did anything to the people who killed them. If you don't stop war, you'll die too . . .

All of which was a boost for the movement, educating and preparing the community for the passage by city council of Hoboken's Nuclear Free Zone Ordinance on September 19, 1984. The local press was favorable. Other good results followed. Two HAND members attended the Second International Conference of NFZ Local Authorities in Cordova, Spain, in March 1985, proudly representing Hoboken and the American NFZ movement.

The HAND campaign in Hoboken was capped by a stirring Hiroshima Day Commemoration on August 3, 1985, planned and staged by the NFZ organizers. Sahomi Tachibana, the celebrated Japanese dancer, was featured, along with her dance troupe, as well as speeches, poetry, an art exhibit, and the film, *No More Hiroshima*. Special guests included members of the Hibakusha Peace Tour, consisting of survivors of the first nuclear attacks in August, 1945. The mayor and city officials were present and played host to the visitors. HAND activists considered Hiroshima Day a marvelous educational finale to their activities over the past two years. It was a sobering reminder from 1945 but also a victory celebration for HAND. Well attended, the affair demonstrated the extent of community support for the ordinance and for an end to the nuclear arms race.

There are questions about Hoboken's ordinance. It contains a non-nuclear purchasing clause: (2e) "The mayor and the Council of the City of Hoboken shall not do business or award any municipal contract to any person, firm, or organization engaged in the production of nuclear weapons or components." This is a broad policy statement without the specifics in the Takoma Park and Amherst ordinances, which also specify non-nuclear purchasing. "What do we do about light bulbs, or AT&T telephone systems?" the city administrator, Edwin Chius, said to me. More significantly, the city is about to contract for a new radio system, and non-nuclear manufacturers are difficult to find. But Chius seemed anxious to implement the ordinance, and said that within a year he thought he would be comfortable with the purchasing process. Another clause in the Hoboken ordinance seems admirably ambitious:

> (2d) The Mayor and Council of the City of Hoboken shall request the United States Department of Transportation and the New Jersey Department of Transportation to provide the city with advance notification of any radioactive waste shipment through the city limits. Upon such notification, the Mayor and Council shall act to prevent transportation of radioactive waste through the city by seeking an exemption from preemption by Department of Transportation regulations or using other legal means at their disposal.

There have been several spin-offs from the Hoboken action. Prodded by the Hoboken councilors, an identical ordinance was passed in Jersey City, a neighboring community, on September 12, 1985. Passage of a Union County, NJ, ordinance followed on October 30. And the Hoboken city council has been active in support of New York activists' campaign for a Nuclear Free Harbor.

The next step? "Perhaps a Hudson County NFZ, or a statewide campaign?" I asked Judith Karpova. "Maybe," she said, "after we recover from this one." The long struggle continues.

Nuclear Freedom in Mid-America

Evanston, Illinois on Lake Michigan is a northern suburb of Chicago. In Evanston a five-and-a-half month whirlwind campaign resulted in a 13 to 4 vote by city council to declare Evanston, by resolution, the first Nuclear Free Zone in Illinois. The Nuclear Weapons Freeze organization was the dynamo that propelled the nuclear-free Evanston campaign. A summary of events by a member of the community tells the story:

The idea of Nuclear Free Zones began in Evanston in 1982 when a local activist Methodist Church declared itself a Nuclear Free Zone and erected a sign on its grounds as a public statement about it. Several other religious institutions followed suit within the year and the Unitarian Church organized an informal network to combat the theft and vandalism of NFZ signs that plagued the group. A local businessman donated wood and a local sign painter offered his services at a nominal cost, so that within weeks after a given sign was stolen or damaged, it was replaced.

Last spring (1985), the local Freeze campaign decided that the logical extension of the movement within the religious community was to mount an active public campaign to petition the elected officials of the city to declare Evanston itself a Nuclear Free Zone. Based on the successful canvassing activities during the last election, the group knew that a great many residents had strong feelings about stopping the nuclear threat. The campaign was officially launched at a Mother's Day music concert held in Evanston to benefit the Freeze.

The group solicited sponsors from organizations and individuals of influence in the community. Names of present and former city council members, religious groups, faculty members from Northwestern University (which is in Evanston), and leaders of groups representing interests as diverse as the local democratic party to the black community were listed on the petitions as sponsors.

People were organized to gather petition signatures at the weekly farmers' market, at numerous art fairs and other outdoor events, and through churches and community organizations. In five months, over 5,000 signatures were collected in this city of 74,000 people. Public sentiment was overwhelmingly in favor of making Evanston a Nuclear Free Zone.

One of the highlights of the Evanston campaign was a Nuclear Free Zone float constructed for the annual Fourth of July Parade. Over 40,000 paper napkins were used in the float, which carried a lighthouse—an Evanston landmark—and a sign: "A Beacon of Hope: Make Evanston a Nuclear Free Zone." The car pulling the float sported 150 helium balloons with the slogan, "Make Evanston Nuclear Free," and the balloons were given to children along the route.

The float was built in ten days with over twenty people involved in its construction—an excellent way to increase citizen involvement and provide interesting media fare. There were 140 entries in the parade, with an estimated 80,000 spectators. The Evanston NFZ float won first place in the "organizations" class, beating out the Right to Life float and the Marine Corps First to Fight float!

Organizers decided to petition city council at one of their October meetings. In Evanston, October is Peace Awareness Month. Activists ran a full-page ad in October in one of the local newspapers, which carried the text of the petition and the names of many of its sponsors. The media was given information regarding the issue prior to the council meeting: all major area television stations covered the story, as well as a dozen radio stations, one of the two major Chicago newspapers, and the local weekly paper. Proponents held a candlelight peace vigil at Civic Center on the eve of the council meeting, which helped to draw the media.

The measure passed the council easily, 13-4, on October 28, 1985, with none of the alderman opposing the resolution publicly. An editorial in the Chicago *Sun-Times* (11/85) noted the difficulty in attaining a nuclear-free world, but added:

> If civilization ever reached that plateau, then it probably could use its collective knowledge and will to abolish poverty, disease, mental illness, and totalitarianism of all sorts. If nothing else, Evanston's action in declaring itself a nuclear-free zone makes one ponder remote possibilities we all dream of.

When the vote was announced, one city council member rose to ask the body to draft and vote on a Nuclear Free Zone ordinance. This seems to be the critical next step for Evanston, in light of the fact that a new industrial research park is to be constructed in the city, heavily supported by federal funds. Will some of the research done there compromise Evanston's brave stance against the bomb?

NFZ Campaigns "Defeated"

The local opposition to a campaign seems to be directly related to the extent of nuclear arms work done in the region. In the vast majority of communities where Zones have been proposed, there are no such facilities. But in Santa Cruz County, California; Cambridge, Massachusetts; and Ann Arbor, Michigan, NFZ referenda were defeated by voters bombarded with literature from the weapons industry.

Santa Cruz, in fact, had an NFZ campaign before anyone else in the nation. The Santa Cruz facility of Lockheed Missile & Aerospace Co., a small factory and test site that employed 300 workers to the north of town, was the primary target of NFZ activists. The Lockheed facility in Santa Cruz tests engines that come from the larger Lockheed plant across the mountains in Sunnyvale. Lockheed sought a use permit. One of the proposed new buildings was to be used for manufacturing "confined detonating fuses," the explosive devises that separate the submarine-based Trident II missile into fourteen independently targeted warheads, each one five times as powerful as the bomb that destroyed Hiroshima.

One campaigner described the intense opposition to Measure A, as the NFZ statement was called:

> Lockheed threatened to pull out its $11,000,000 payroll. The Chamber of Commerce President called the measure 'disastrous' for the local economy, a threat to the light, 'clean' industry the county sees as an important economic base. A county supervisor called it 'bordering on treason.' Letters to editors were fast and furious. At least one family separated over the issue. Ten tires were slashed, and several houses and car windows shot among activists involved with People for a Nuclear Free Future.

The Lockheed Corporation spent over $220,000 to defeat Measure A on June 3, 1980, but NFZ campaigners took pride in getting 36.7 percent of the vote. Perhaps it is amazing that so many people voted yes since jobs affecting some 300 families were involved. One campaigner concluded that the challenge this issue presented was "to engage teachers, doctors, attorneys, psychologists, parents of many sorts, labor people and more in the quest, "How are we to live in the nuclear age? How are we to live out our passion that nuclear terror must end?"

The Nuclear Free Cambridge campaign also demonstrates that the nuclear weapons industry takes this movement seriously. Weapons companies around the nation, including Lockheed, General Electric, AT&T, Sperry, and Honeywell contributed $290,000 to "CARB" (Citizens Against Research Bans), formed to fight the Cambridge initiative. Including money borrowed from local banks, CARB spent over $507,000 which, at $18.97 per vote, stands as one of the most expensive political campaigns in American history! CARB outspent the NFZ proponents by 20 to 1.

The Cambridge ordinance would have banned research and development of nuclear weapons within city limits:

> The purpose of this Act is to establish Cambridge as a city which is Nuclear Free in that work on nuclear weapons is prohibited within the city, and that the citizens and representatives of Cambridge are urged to redirect the resources previously used for nuclear weapons towards endeavors which promote and enhance life.

The proposal was defeated by a vote of 59.7 percent to 40.3 percent. Again, jobs were an issue, as was academic research. The campaign was targeting Draper Laboratory, a research facility that receives some $120,000,000 per year in defense contracts. In forming the CARB alliance Draper attempted to shift attention from local involvement in the arms race to the sacred cow of academic freedom.

The proposed ordinance, like Amherst's resolution, specifically excluded from the ban all research that was unrelated to nuclear weapons, but CARB contended that the ordinance would put kindly professors and blue collar workers in jail and would even make it illegal to teach college students about the arms race! Harvard professor Stephen Jay Gould called the issue of academic freedom a red herring: "It's predicated on the idea that we have 'freedom of research' now, and that notion is just nonsense." Nobel Laureate George Wald and fifteen other illustrious Harvard professors endorsed the campaign, scoffing at the idea that it would curtail academic freedom.

But the proposed ordinance was defeated. Why? A post-election analysis showed an interesting paradox. Nuclear Free Cambridge polls found that 63 percent of the electorate believed there was a good chance of nuclear war in their lifetimes and 73 percent thought that NFZs were an effective way to slow the arms race; and yet, 30 percent of those persons accepting both propositions voted against the Cambridge initiative! For them it was a case of conviction without the attendant action. To explain such personal inconsistency one has to consider the anxiety-producing factors, especially the fear of what one's neighbors would say and do, particularly those friends who worked at Draper Lab or had family members who did. There was also apprehension about what the closing of Draper Lab would do to the entire community. Conclusion: it is very difficult to convince some people that a nuclear holocaust (which may seem *likely* but not *imminent*) is a greater hazard than the immediate threat of unemployment for them or their friends.

As a result of Cambridge, some NFZ organizers may think twice about whether to include a research ban in their legislation, or even propose legislation for a community where research is ongoing. The organizers of the Nuclear Free Chicago campaign decided not to include a ban on basic physics research to avoid a confrontation with Chicago's academic community, a staffmember with Clergy and Laity Concerned told me. However, applied research on nuclear weapons is prohibited by the Chicago legislation.

Cambridge and Santa Cruz, you may say, were losing battles. Perhaps, but the campaigners agreed that it was not time wasted. People were energized, stirred, and prodded. Others trained in social change techniques, and the campaigns had a strong educational impact on their communities.

And there is a notable footnote to the Santa Cruz story. On November 28, 1984, the Santa Cruz County Planning Commission voted 3-2 to deny Lockheed's request to build a new plant to manufacture parts for the Trident II missile. The deciding vote was cast by a former Lockheed supporter on the commission who surprised everyone. His decision to help slow the arms race may have been influenced by that "losing" campaign of 1980. And on January 8, 1985, following the commissioners' lead, the Santa Cruz Board of Supervisors voted 3-2 against Lockheed. Minds can be changed as a result of the educational fallout from NFZ campaigns.

Finally, after some failed attempts, Chicago provides a breakthrough long sought by NFZ advocates. A city harboring some nuclear weapons-related industry has passed Nuclear Free Zone legislation. Let the military-industrial-academic-political complex that produces the Bomb take notice! Others will follow.

4

The Abolitionist Connection

"Nuclear weapons are now, as slavery was two hundred years ago, a manifestly evil institution deeply embedded in the structure of our society."
—Freeman Dyson, *Weapons and Hope*[1]

"Our control lies—as it always has done whenever it's been tried—in the force of public argument and public anger. It was public opinion in this country which forced the ending of the slave trade—opinion marshalled then as it can be now by pamphlets, speeches and meetings in every village hall."
—Nicholas Humphrey, "Four Minutes to Midnight"[2]

These statements suggest a connection between eras and between two major movements. Antinuclear campaigners today often describe themselves as abolitionists. Significantly, Jonathan Schell's latest book is titled, *The Abolition*. The founders of Nuclear Free America, the Baltimore-based clearinghouse for the Nuclear Free Zone movement, titled their newsletter *The New Abolitionist*. In Senator Mark Hatfield's office one day, an aide shared the Senator's conviction that the abolition of nuclear weapons is the paramount issue of this century, parallel to the abolition of slavery in the last.

Today, antinuclear spokespersons are using bondage and liberation imagery similar to the abolitionist discourse of the pre-Civil War period. Psychologist Robert Jay Lifton speaks of our "nuclear entrapment" and political scientist Richard Falk writes of "liberating our planet and our species from the nuclear curse," language which echoes Linus Pauling's 1963 Nobel speech in which he referred to the arms race as a "prehistoric barbarism" and "curse." The word curse was a favorite term applied by nineteenth century abolitionists to slavery. And Jacob Bronowski asks, at the end of his essay, *Science and Human Values,* "Has science fastened on our society a monstrous gift of destruction which we can neither undo or master, and which like a clockwork automation is set to break our necks?"[3]

In a Biblical treatment of nuclearism, *Darkening Valley,*[4] Brethren theologian Dale Aukerman uses a number of metaphors that suggest human bondage. He refers to our nuclear madness as a kind of alcoholism, suggests that we are marionettes in the grip of some diabolic force, and identifies adoration of the Bomb as comparable to the worship of the pagan god Molech, who demanded human sacrifices. Many prominent Protestant and Catholic theologians have written of nuclearism as sin, and Episcopalian layman Howard Webber even argues that the *preparation* is sin: "Readiness for nuclear war is as destructive as nuclear war itself . . . To construct the means of annihilation is sinful, and because we have done that, sin is impairing and *enslaving* us" [italics mine].[5]

David McReynolds of War Resisters League draws a tighter parallel between the centuries: "Just before the American Civil War Abraham Lincoln observed that no nation can long endure half slave and half free. He was right then and the political reality is that the world cannot remain 'half prepared to kill, half willing to live.' "[6]

Many of those currently involved in civil disobedience use abolitionist language in explaining their actions. Typical are the direct actionists who poured blood and damaged a Trident submarine's missile tubes at Groton, Connecticut on July 4, 1982 (The "Trident Nein"). Their flyer proclaimed, "With our hammers we ring out a new freedom; freedom from nuclear arms; freedom for life." Nuclear Free Zone advocates are using similar language in promoting their cause. During the Amherst campaign, activist Fran Fortino wrote: "Like the rejection of slavery by the Free States of the past, Nuclear Free Zones will shake the conscience of the nuclear powers."[7]

But are there parallels beyond language between the two eras and movements? Yes! We shall consider some intriguing parallels, discuss certain paradoxical differences as well as some real ones, and suggest some caveats or lessons to be learned by modern abolitionists from their counterparts in the nineteenth century.

Distinctions That Matter

First, there is an important distinction to be made between the general attitude of being opposed to slavery/nuclear weapons and working for its abolition. In the nineteenth century almost everyone was against slavery, at least outside the South, and even many Southerners before 1830 were willing to admit to its faults; but not all were abolitionists. In the 20th Century almost nobody but Dr. Strangelove "loves" the Bomb, but many people accept nuclear weapons as a "necessary evil"; not everyone is an abolitionist. In this chapter I am comparing the two abolitionist movements, rather than antislavery and antinuclearism, as they relate to a contextual understanding of the two eras.

There is great diversity in modern abolitionism, as well as in the nineteenth century variety. But we must not confuse means and goals. Despite considerable overlapping and interaction between strategies, let's posit three main "wings" of the antinuclear movement of the 1980s: (1) the Bilateral Nuclear Freeze proposal, which would halt all testing and production of nuclear weapons, if agreed to by the superpowers; (2) our Nuclear Free Zone movement which, I will show later, is a strategic "middle ground" between the Freeze Campaign and (3) direct action campaigns, which typically involve a commitment to the breaking of law in order to register a protest or to interfere with the operations of those engaged in manufacturing or installing nuclear weapons. Actions include trespassing at military installations or defense industries, blockading entrances to nuclear plants, damaging the weapons themselves, etc. Although many individuals are involved in two or more of them, these three approaches are somewhat discrete and can be usefully compared.

All three are *means,* or strategies. Within each as well as between the three, people have differing goals. In the Freeze movement, not everyone is an abolitionist. Some want the Freeze to be a first step towards reducing nuclear weapons to zero; others want to reduce down to some minimum deterrent. Still others may see the Freeze as an end in itself, stabilizing the political scene at present levels of arms. Nuclear Free Zone campaigners and direct actionists are also divided, but are much more likely than the Freeze people to see zero nuclear weapons as their ultimate goal. Certainly the hope expressed often by Nuclear Free Zone proponents, in this country and abroad, is that they shall make the world ultimately one big Nuclear Free Zone, so the means prefigures the end, and each local Nuclear Free Zone foreshadows the ideal world that its proponents desire.

Contexts and Parallels

Let us consider the contexts from which the two abolitionist movements arose. A *first* major parallel is that both slavery and nuclear weapons were initially seen as connected with human progress, considered to be blessings or boons for humankind. For three thousand years there was hardly a major figure—writer, philosopher, statesman—who questioned the institution of slavery. Slavery was legitimate, part of the natural order of things. Aristotle said that "from the hour of their birth some are marked out for subjection, other for rule." In *Slavery and Human Progress,* noted historian David Brion Davis adds that from the sixteenth to the nineteenth century "the African slave trade was sanctioned by international law as well as by the highest clerical and temporal authorities in Catholic and Protestant states alike . . . The most revealing connection between slavery and national progress is the eagerness of the most 'progressive' peoples to join the system. To refrain from acquiring slaves or from engaging in the triangular trade was almost as unthinkable *as spurning nuclear technology is in the world of today"* [italics mine].[8]

Similarly, the invention of atomic weapons was heralded by many as a blessing for the United States, if not for the world. When Harry Truman was handed the bulletin announcing the successful drop on Hiroshima he exclaimed, "This is the greatest thing in history!" Truman went ahead with research and development, despite the call from a group of physicists for a moratorium on the development of nuclear weapons. According to Sidney Lens in *The Day Before Doomsday,*[9] the consensus of the Truman cabinet was that the Bomb would make the Soviets more pliable, especially more manageable in Europe. American atomic power appeared to be absolute and it would deny the Soviets any territorial advantage. There was rejoicing in the Western capitols! The *London Observor* observed:

"It is we who hold the overwhelming trump cards. It is our side, not Russia, which holds atomic and post-atomic weapons and could, if sufficiently provoked, wipe Russia's power and threat to the world peace from the face of the earth."[10]

In America, Senator Brien McMahon was especially fulsome in his praise of the Bomb:

We must have atomic weapons to use in the heights of the sky and the depths of the sea; we must have them to use above the ground, on the ground, and below the ground. An aggressor must know that if he dares attack he will have no place to hide . . .

Mark me well: massive atomic deterring power can win us years of grace, years in which to wrench history from its present course and direct it toward the enshrinement of human brotherhood.[11]

Gradually such elation gave way to a realistic sobriety, but the initial exuberance fostered a number of justifications for the Bomb, as well as for slavery.

Second: both slavery and nuclearism were rooted in economics, a fact making them hard to eradicate. In *Time on the Cross: The Economics of American Negro Slavery,* Fogel and Engerman argue strongly that American slavery was economically viable in the South and was not about to fall of its own weight—as some contended—on the eve of the Civil War.[12] Slavery was well integrated within the Southern experience. Most planters were prosperous and feared economic ruin should their slaves be taken away. Many debate the notion that slavery would have continued to be, in the long run, economically viable, but there is no question that the individual planter's economic investment in slavery was real and this created an enormous resistance to change.

Perhaps slavery as an economic investment is best illustrated by a quote from an anonymous nineteenth century anti-abolitionist:

> "The abolitionists, in advocating emancipation without compensation, do not forget, do not regard, the fact that the slaves have fallen into the hands of their present owners as *property,* that the laws of the Southern states, and the laws of the General Government, and even the laws of the Northern states, regard them and respect them *as property.*"[13]

We should note that the British slaveholders in the West Indies were offered the inducement of compensation for their "property" but most were still reluctant to give up their slaves when emancipation took place in 1833. Compensation was never seriously offered by Northern leaders in the ante-bellum period, although abolitionist Elihu Burritt campaigned for it.

If the economics and the defense of private property made slavery difficult to eradicate, the same applies to nuclear weapons. There has been an increasing investment in nuclear weaponry, and when there is financial gain people are reluctant to change direction. They refuse to give up what they have, even to make the world safer. Robert Aldridge, a former Lockheed engineer, comments on this materialism: "As I look back on my 16 years with the nation's largest defense contractor, it seems to me that the reason for all these new weapons and weapons systems is the profit motive, a matter of keeping business going rather than protecting the country."

This statement may seem unduly cynical, but consider this. The "military-industrial complex" that Eisenhower warned

America against has grown into a multibillion-dollar military-industrial-scientific-academic-political complex. Thousands of contracts are let out each year by the Pentagon, with the blessing of Congress, to manufacturers and to private and university researchers. By spreading the contracts the Pentagon has sunk its tentacles into virtually every congressional district.

Members of Congress, for the most part, encourage this. Sidney Lens reports that when Mendell Rivers of South Carolina was chairman of the House Armed Services Committee, "he boasted that he had brought to his district some 90 percent of its lush defense facilities—including a Marine Corps air station, an Army depot, a shipyard, a Navy training center, two Navy hospitals—a payroll, all told, of $200 million a year."[14]

The defense industry works hard to sell its weapons to the military and to members of Congress. Recently a Common Cause study found that the top 13 defense contractors working on the MX donated $2.1 million to candidates in 1983–84. And the linkage between private industry and the military is demonstrated by Gordon Adams, in *The Iron Triangle*, who says that between 1976 and 1980, nearly 2,000 persons moved through the "revolving door" between the Pentagon and NASA and their eight largest corporate contractors.[15]

Third: there is a geographical similarity. The base for both abolitionist movements in America seems to have been New England, Massachusetts in particular. William Lloyd Garrison, supported by the brilliant attorney, Wendell Phillips, began his famous *Liberator* in Boston; and there, Channing's Federal Street congregation fired Unitarian abolitionist sentiment as Lyman Beecher fostered it in the Hanover Street Church. Soon the evangelical abolitionism of Beecher and others spread West from its New England base—along with the efforts of the Tappans in New York State—through the zeal and devotion of transplanted New Englanders like Theodore Weld, Beriah Green, Elizur Wright, and Henry Stanton.

In our time Massachusetts remains a domain of liberal political thinking, if not evangelical Christianity. Massachusetts was the only state that McGovern captured in 1972. More recently, the Nuclear Freeze movement essentially began in New England town meetings, and the Nuclear Free Zone movement was spurred by its early success in Massachusetts: by 1985, 25 percent of the towns and cities that had declared themselves NFZs were in Massachusetts.

Fourth: both abolitionist movements have been staunchly religious at the core. Although in both eras some Christians have used the Bible to defend the status quo—weapons or slavery—the abolitionists have generally been deeply committed Christians. A few writers have called them misguided—indeed, the revisionist historian Avery O. Craven branded them "irresponsible fanatics"—but most authorities cite the nineteenth century abolitionists for their devotion and sincerity. Virtually no one joined the movement for personal gain, and David Donald writes that "in all truth, the decision to become an antislavery crusader was a decision of conscience."[16] Indeed, before 1830 abolitionists were roundly ridiculed. This was not a popular cause. Even in Boston, New York, and Philadelphia, according to Frank Thistlewaite, "to be an abolitionist . . . meant courting social ostracism, business ruin, or physical assault."[17] Garrison and other early activists were mobbed and beaten. On October 21, 1835, a mob led Garrison (reported to be serene and smiling!) through Boston streets with a noose around his neck. Elijah Lovejoy's presses were destroyed first, and then he was lynched by an angry Illinois mob. William Whipper praised the faithfulness and courage of these early abolitionists in 1837:

> There have been many faithful advocates of peace since the apostolic age, but none have ever given a more powerful impetus to the cause of peace than the modern abolitionists . . . They have been beaten and stoned, mobbed and persecuted from city to city, and never returned evil for evil.

Many of the abolitionists were Quakers, some Unitarians. Although the Great Awakening of 1856–7 did not seem to stimulate much antislavery sentiment, there were several evangelical leaders in the abolitionist camp. One of the most influential was Charles Grandison Finney, the fiery revivalist. Just as influential as Finney was the dynamic and dedicated Theodore Weld, who organized an army of abolitionist apostles at Lane Seminary in Cincinnati in 1834, despite the opposition of their faculty. Weld and Finney had their hands in the founding of Oberlin College, which was from the start an abolitionist haven.

Slavery was a sin. William Lloyd Garrison and Theodore Weld—together wielding tremendous influence in the movement—came to the same conclusion. Slavery constituted rebellion against God. When someone claimed ownership over another he was claiming a right to control which only God could claim—he was making his slave accountable to himself instead of to God. Weld wrote Garrison in January, 1833:

> That no condition of birth, no shade of color, no mere misfortune of circumstance, can annul that birth-right charter, which God has bequeathed to every human being upon whom he has stamped his own image, by making him a *free moral agent,* and that he who robs his fellow man of this tramples upon right, subverts justice, outrages humanity, unsettles the foundations of human society, and sacriligiously assumes the prerogative of God.[18]

The nineteenth century abolitionists were largely devout Quakers, Unitarians and evangelicals. To these three factions today, add Roman Catholics. Such individuals as Dorothy Day and Philip and Daniel Berrigan have, in our time, pressed the Roman Church for a more radical peacemaking, and have personally led in that direction. The stance taken in the 1983 American Catholic Bishops' Pastoral Letter, *The Challenge of Peace: God's Promise and Our Response,* is a bold one given that church's traditional conservatism. Roman Catholics, especially priests and nuns, are figuring prominently in today's peace movement and, increasingly, Jewish people are to be found in the front lines of the battle against the Bomb.

Appeals vary, and many biblical sources are cited—we noted several in chapter one. Prominent arguments are based on the commandment, "Thou shalt not kill." Other scripture warnings include: Jesus' "love thine enemy" and the rest of the Sermon on the Mount, his warning that "those who live by the sword will die by the sword"; the prophets' call for justice in Old Testament times; the visions of Micah and Isaiah of a day of peace when men "shall beat their swords into plowshares." There are arguments likening obeisance to nuclearism with an idolatry similar to the worship of Molech, and comparing the "gods of metal" (psalm 135) to modern missiles.

Just as the language of sin and guilt failed to move the slave-holding South, so these modern appeals for a change of heart seem to fall on deaf ears. Very few nuclear advocates are moved, and few in the nuclear industries leave their work. In both eras, of course, the abolitionist "preachers" have been pretty much insulated from the "sinners"; Garrison and his type railed against Southern slaveholders without having any real contact with them. This is true also of much of the antinuclear debate which consists largely of arguments shouted over a distance or within the legal confines of a courtroom, where authentic, human interpersonal exchanges are unlikely.

A final note on the religious nature of both abolitionist movements: the appeal to a higher law. During the ante-bellum period, Southern states had laws forbidding emancipation, and the laws of most states recognized slaves as property: the federal government seemed to establish this with the Fugitive Slave Act of 1793 and the Dred Scott decision. But the crusaders against slavery appealed to a "higher law" and to the rule of conscience. Similarly, many direct actionists now claim that what they have done (trespassing at defense plants or military bases, blockading doorways, damaging nuclear components, pouring blood on corporate logos) is not simply civil disobedience, but *divine obedience*. They appeal from the local, state, and federal laws on which they are convicted to international law and, more importantly, to the laws of God, or moral law. They argue that God affirms life, that God disapproves of the preparation for nuclear war which is taking place, and that they have a sacred obligation to obey God and the gospel as opposed to governments or human beings.

Fifth, many of the arguments used *against* crusaders in both eras are similar. "There are many issues," the nineteenth century abolitionists were told, "so don't be preoccupied with this one!" The same is true now. In the nineteenth century the other issues included temperance, miners' rights, child labor; current issues include hunger, poverty, racism, ecology, abortion. "Don't be single-minded," the argument runs, "broaden your horizons!"

Another argument, which begs the issue of the means to be used, is the argument from time. "Don't be in such a hurry," the abolitionists are told, "it can't be done all at once (or tomorrow)—these things take time!" It was the South that pled for time in the nineteenth century; today it is the federal government that says, "trust us, good people, we're negotiating with the Soviets, or attempting to negotiate, or talking about negotiating—but world politics are very complicated and these things take time!"

Abolitionists reject the time argument. Antislavery crusaders saw that slavery had not diminished in centuries and they saw no "give" on the part of their generation of slaveholders—they weren't willing to wait. Now anti-nuclear protesters cite the 6,000 arms control talks since World War II, with the concomitant escalation of the arms race, and they won't wait either. Time is often used by those who oppose change to stall and delay progress. With an entrenched evil, change doesn't happen automatically, it has to be fostered or forced.

The question of time leads to a *sixth* parallel, the debate over a *gradual* or *immediate* abolition. Once the goal of abolition was established, antislavery activists began to debate the means. Typically the "gradualist" faction argued for Negro freedom "by slow degrees, and in a course of years," as Thomas Buxton proposed in Britain, and included the idea of Negro education—to prepare them for their freedom—as well as laws preventing mistreatment by slaveowners.

There was no consensus among gradualists, and the term itself was subject to diverse interpretations, but some gradualists favored the expatriation of slaves to Liberia. Others argued for laws that would emancipate Negro women or infants born after a certain date, thus achieving total emancipation in the end.

Immediatists, on the other hand, demanded a general emancipation, but they were vague as to how that would be accomplished prior to Lincoln's edict. Some of them nourished the vain hope that the slave states would give up slavery of their own accord, but most of them knew this was impossible. Interestingly, Garrison himself seems to have at one point become resigned to slow progress, despite his immediatist sentiments: "Urge immediate abolition as earnestly as we may, it will, alas! be gradual abolition in the end. We have never said that slavery would be overthrown by a single blow; that it ought to be, we shall always contend."[19]

Actually, immediatism was more of a state of mind and will than a demand for a sudden, unconditional emancipation. A letter from a certain Vigornius in the Boston *Recorder and Telegraph* (1825) put it this way: *"The slave-holding system must be abolished:* and in order to accomplish this end, *immediate,* determined measures must be adopted for the *ultimate* emancipation of every slave."[20]

Presently, the nuclear establishment argues gradualism: "Our diplomats are negotiating with the other side and in time we'll reduce these huge nuclear stockpiles! Have patience, we can't give away the store! It has to be *quid pro quo!"* In response, immediatists argue that negotiations are useless, as recent history shows, and often they serve to escalate the arms race. These activists have lost faith in the national leadership, or at least the ability of governments to harness or halt the arms race. They seek a more drastic remedy than the bargaining table offers. Yesterday's immediatists are today's unilateralists: they want their own government to take unilateral initiatives toward disarmament that would, hopefully, become multilateral as other nuclear nations follow suit.

Two Paradoxes

So we have found similarities. Both slavery and nuclearism were associated with human progress and deeply rooted in economics, both movements were New England-based, and both were influenced by deeply committed Christians using strong moral and Biblical arguments. The arguments used against them by their opponents were similar, and the issue of means split both movements, especially the question of immediacy and gradualism. Now I want to consider two paradoxical issues, paradoxical because they seem to represent differences between the two eras, but can also be seen as parallel. These are the questions of who is enslaved, and whether anyone is suffering.

In terms of who is actually enslaved, the slaveowners had put African blacks into bondage. Apparently, Negroes were enslaved and everyone else was free, but today's abolitionists contend that everyone is held in bondage by the Bomb, not just its makers or those empowered to use it. This appears to be a difference. Some nineteenth century abolitionists, however, also argued that *slavery reduced everyone's freedom,* a point made later by Gandhi, Martin Luther King, Jr., and others—as long as anyone is captive everyone's liberty is jeopardized. "The contest is becoming," James Burney wrote in 1850, "nay, has become—one, not alone of freedom for the *black,* but of freedom for the *white.*"[21]

As to suffering—obviously the slaves were suffering. The nineteenth century abolitionists cited case after case of Negroes suffering in the South. They built their case with lurid tales of Southern white brutality, horrifying earnest Christian audiences. Theodore Weld's *American Slavery As It is,* a devastating indictment of slavery, was a collection of the "testimony of a thousand witnesses." This piece and similar literature were circulated by the thousands of copies, inflaming Northern passions. Perhaps a few of these grim and lurid tales were exaggerated, but as an institution slavery was oppressive and people suffered under it.

By contrast, modern abolitionists seem to have no victims to use in building a case against the Bomb. To be sure, there was Hiroshima and Nagasaki, but no one is suffering now. The Bomb is not killing anyone *now.* Pro-lifers have urged me to join their movement because, they say, abortion's the critical issue! Infants are dying *now* at the hands of those "butchers," but no one's dying from thermonuclear explosions!

Abortion is clearly an important issue, but we have to discount the argument. The evidence is that the Bomb *is* taking its toll, decade by decade. Radiation from thousands of nuclear tests since 1945 have had their effect on human health. Dr. Rosalie Bertell has researched the effects of low level radiation, and she estimates that "the past 40 years of weapon production have caused some 2.3 million radiation victims." These are the "early victims of World War III," beginning with the Japanese survivors and their genetically-damaged descendants and continuing through generations of genetically injured Polynesians, Nevadans, Native Americans, Lapps, Siberians, and others who have been in close proximity to thermonuclear tests. Even now dozens of people working in defense labs or nuclear power plants are being subjected to low-level radiation. One study shows that the cancer rate is between 50 and 500 times as great for those working near radioactive materials.

Further, today's activists claim that the arms race is killing people even without nuclear research or explosions. Resources being devoted to weapons could be diverted to hunger projects and the alleviation of drought and disease. Millions die, the argument runs, while the nations of the world spend a million dollars a minute on their military systems. Millions suffer because of our venal global preoccupation with the machinery of death and destruction. The argument has a strong emotive appeal, but there is no guarantee that money not used on weapons would be devoted to humanitarian work. To the extent that the argument can be accepted there is another historical parallel.

Important Differences

We have looked at some parallels, and at some paradoxical "differences." There are three very real differences between eras: one of means, one of public response, and perhaps most important, the issue of urgency.

First, means: the question of violence. Nineteenth century abolitionists were double-minded on violence; twentieth century abolitionists seem comparatively single-minded.

The antislavery crusaders were, for the most part, and certainly in principle, committed to nonviolence. Many of their leaders condemned violence as a means and called for only nonviolent resistance. In many attempts to desegregate local facilities, such as the attempt to open the Massachusetts railroads to blacks, campaigners offered no physical resistance to the taunts and blows of an irate public. Earlier, in the 1730s, the Quaker Benjamin Lay became an abolitionist. He spoke out, fasted, and once spattered delegates at a Quaker meeting with the blood of an animal to awaken their consciences—foreshadowing the throwing of blood on corporate logos, missiles, and bombers by antinuclear protesters today!

Lay and others modeled nonviolence for the nineteenth century abolitionists, including the bold John G. Fee of Kentucky. Fee became an agent of the antislavery American Missionary Society, working quietly within Kentucky to establish integrated churches, and by 1859 he had founded eleven. This work did not make him popular. Fee was mobbed twenty-two times, twice being left for dead by ruffians who ambushed him on route to preaching engagements. They dragged him out of a pulpit in Rockcastle County, took him to another county, and warned him not to return on peril of death. Fee returned, only to find that the churches in which he had preached had been torched! He spoke in a private home, and after he left it, too, was burned. Fee never carried a gun and never offered to retaliate. Often he spoke to his captors and defused their anger with kind words and prayers for them.

John Fee's friends wanted to protect him but he refused their help. "He said that people who win a struggle by violence are praised for their skill in violence, not for their principles; such people do not affect conscience."[22]

Certainly the abolitionists wanted to awaken, arouse, and *deeply affect conscience.* Many felt that violence was not a proper means. But there were times and places, and especially when aroused by such events as the killing of Lovejoy in Alton, Illinois, when abolitionists countenanced violence—for self-defense, not *offensive* violence. Some conceded that in the attempt to save runaway slaves from capture, and especially after the Fugitive Slave Law was strengthened, violence was justified. And so Henry C. Wright, a Congregationalist pastor and a member of the nonresistance wing who had said that killing another human being was the greatest crime one can commit, became disturbed by the volatile condition of the 1850s—and felt it was time to inflict "instant death" on the slave-chasers. "Every man . . . is bound by his own principles (not by mine)," he said, "to arm himself with a pistol or a dirk, a bowie knife, a rifle, or any deadly weapon, and inflict death with his own hand on each and every man who shall attempt to execute the recent law of Congress . . . and return to bondage fugitive slaves."[23]

Other abolitionists who did not condone violence on the part of whites even found it possible to *encourage* violence on the part of slaves in revolt. Actually, black abolitionists predated Garrison. *Freedom's Journal,* as early as 1827, provides evidence of black militancy and, in 1829, the black abolitionist David Walker wrote a leaflet calling on slaves to revolt. The leaflet was described by a contemporary as "the most inflammatory publication in history"! The Garrisonian abolitionists declared themselves against violence but their rhetoric became more and more abrasive as time went by. Howard Zinn describes this verbal violence in his essay, "The Tactics of Agitation":

> There is no denying the anger, the bitterness, the irascibility of the abolitionists. William Lloyd Garrison, dean of them all, wrote in blood in the columns of the *Liberator* and breathed fire from speakers' platforms all over New England. He shocked people: "I am ashamed of my country." He spoke abroad in brutal criticism of America: "I accuse the land of my nativity of insulting the majesty of heaven with the greatest mockery that was ever exhibited to man." He burned the Constitution before several thousand witnesses on the lawn of Framingham, calling it "source and parent of all other atrocities—a covenant with death and an agreement with hell" and spurred the crowd to echo "Amen!"[24]

Wendell Phillips responded to those who criticized the abrasive abolitionist rhetoric: "From Luther down, the charge against every reformer has been that his language is too rough. Be it so. Rough instruments are used for rough work."[25]

Perhaps such violent rhetoric, combined with increasing frustration at the lack of progress, spurred some abolitionists to violent acts, and others to condone those acts. Among those who believed that the means (violence) was justified by the ends were Nat Turner, who led a slave revolt in Virginia; Cassius Clay, an aristocrat who used guns and knives in protecting himself while speaking against slavery; and the guerilla fighter John Brown of Harper's Ferry fame. Brown's raid was condoned by some abolitionists who had previously condemned violence. Henry David Thoreau virtually placed Brown in a hero's hall of martyrs. Garrison declared himself still a "peace man," but when he was asked if Brown's action was justified Garrison said, "Yes, if Washington was in his."

Stephen Foster graphically demonstrates the abolitionist ambivalence toward violence. A confirmed "nonresistant" for most of his life, Foster became more and more enamored of using physical force to free the slaves. Once the Civil War began he was deeply torn—if the war were the agent of emancipation he could support it, but if not . . . Nonresistant in methodology, yet Foster's voice was strident and his spirit militant. In December, 1863, he addressed the American Anti-Slavery Society's third decade celebration in Philadelphia:

> Proclaim emancipation to the slaves, to the men whom God appoints as true soldiers of this land; then, if they fail to do the work, I will volunteer, non-resistant as I am; and I will go down to Carolina and face the rebel armies; with the sword of the spirit, however, and not with the sword of steel . . . Place me between you and the enemy. Only let me have an army of liberators, and that is all I ask.[26]

So the abolitionists were ambivalent. For the most part the head said no but often the heart said yes. The vast majority were against war, however, and when the Civil War came they saw it initially as a defeat for the cause. Most of them had rejected coercive methods of freeing the slaves, and they saw war as the ultimate coercion. Garrisonians, at least, preferred schism to civil war; indeed, some had suggested that the *North* should secede to hasten the demise of slavery! Before the war ended most of the abolitionists had come to see it as either a blessing or a necessary evil, but only because they had convinced themselves that it was God's instrument for ending slavery.

By contrast, today's antinuclearists seem totally committed to nonviolence. Within the American peace community there is practically no interest in tactics that could threaten human life. Violence is seen as tactically useless. It can alienate the public, destroying any sympathy for one's cause. More importantly, violence is thought to be immoral—it is the ultimate violence of the Bomb that we struggle against—and if one uses immoral means to achieve even a noble end, the perpetrator will be contaminated, and the end as well.

Civil disobedients, therefore, have been careful not to give even the appearance of threatened violence. The vast majority of what are called "direct actions," resulting in arrest, are carefully designed to be nonthreatening to persons and property. In those few cases—like the "Plowshares" actions—where direct actionists have damaged property (missile cases, for example), the actionists made it clear that they were not threatening anyone and they offered themselves for arrest. These guidelines for civil disobedients which were distributed to activists at the June 20, 1983 blockading action at General Dynamics (which makes Trident submarines in Groton, Connecticut), are typical: "Participants will be nonviolent at all times, even if provoked. No weapons or instruments that could be construed as weapons shall be carried."

Clearly, the absence of violence in twentieth century abolitionism marks a difference from the nineteenth century. As the struggle continues, however, with the inevitable frustration resulting from a lack of apparent progress, will some protestors resort to violence against persons, or be less discriminating in regard to property? Possibly. But today's peacemakers have the benefit of Gandhi, A. J. Muste, and Martin Luther King, Jr.

Despite this advantage over their nineteenth century counterparts, one finds frequent and passionate cases made for nonviolence in the literature of that era, and many of the abolitionists foreshadowed our Civil Rights Movement of the 1960s with 1830s and 1840s tactics. Sit-ins, pray-ins, railroad ride-ins, and church speak-ins were used not only to demonstrate the indignity of slavery but to desegregate facilities in the North!

In sum, nineteenth century abolitionists had mixed feelings about violence while their modern counterparts are more single-minded.

Second, there is a difference in terms of public response. The general public seems not to be as "exercised," to use a good nineteenth century word, by twentieth century abolitionists. This generation does not seem to be overly concerned about ridding the world of nuclear weapons. The modern abolitionist has had less impact on society than his or her nineteenth century counterpart. (On *American* society, that is—in other parts of the world, as we know, the peace organizers are able to call out thousands for their demonstrations!) The tempestuous debates and strident controversies provoked by the antislavery crusaders are largely lacking in American forums where the nuclear threat is discussed. This, of course, is my own perception, and impossible to prove. But consider the following possible explanations for what I perceive as a lack of protest against nuclear weapons.

One explanation is that American materialism tends to choke and stifle individual action against the Bomb. Few in the nineteenth century enjoyed the affluence that Americans enjoy today—even the working class—and this has something to do with risk-taking. The more possessions one has, the more one fears the loss of those "things" that are prized. So . . . one works to preserve the status quo and save wealth, avoiding risk. The individual will avoid espousing unpopular causes. We have seen how Americans everywhere stand to gain something materially from defense contracts, since they are spread about the nation so widely; yet in the ante-bellum period very few in the North gained very directly from Southern slavery.

Today religion seems to play a less important role in shaping the social conscience. There is the Moral Majority, to be sure, but since the 1960s American religion seems to have lost much of its social activism. This is due, perhaps, to a renewed recognition of "original sin," the inherent propensity for evil that humans possess. Freeman Dyson, in *Weapons and Hope,* cites it as a major obstacle in the way of a solution to nuclearism. Certainly the increased popularity of premillenialism following the Civil War hastened the demise of evangelical "liberalism." More recently the liberalism of the early twentieth century lost ground as we lost whatever innocence we had—whatever belief in the perfectibility of human nature we enjoyed—with Buchenwald, Auschwitz, Hiroshima, Nagasaki, and My Lai.

Another explanation has to do with the fact that the target of protest, slavery, was a more tangible reality for many people than nuclear weapons represent. Fugitive slaves and freedmen were physically present in the North, and even pro-slavery people were often moved by their stories of suffering and courage. But today the missiles are hidden away in the earth, below the surface of the oceans, and on high-flying bombers. We seldom see them. Even the results of nuclear blasts are classified: the film footage taken by the US army within two months of the bombings of Hiroshima and Nagasaki was shut away in archives for years because the government was afraid that the American people would not support the ongoing development of atomic weapons if they had actually seen the carnage. Today this material has been declassified, and some of us have read or heard the dreadful stories from the Japanese atomic survivors. We have been jaded and numbed, however, by constant exposure to Vietnam and to local media brutalities and we cannot feel the pain or develop an outrage appropriate to our nuclear peril.

Third, there is the issue of time and urgency. The demise of slavery, one may argue, happened very quickly in light of that institution's long history. Political action and war brought to an end an institution that had stood above criticism for three thousand years. But do we have that kind of time today? Indeed, we argue, the nuclear threat is imminent, and eminently possible.

Viewed in this light we have an *urgent* issue. We must eliminate nuclear weapons before they eliminate us.

Some Cautious Conclusions

Our study yields some caveats and advice for the antinuclear abolitionists, including those who support Nuclear Free Zones.

The argument that everyone's liberty is endangered by the actions of a few should be pressed today, as it was in the nineteenth century. As several military leaders have admitted, nuclear weapons have no real military value. Having them is self-defeating and paradoxical. The more of them we have, the less secure we are on this globe. Abolitionists also need to argue that people are suffering *now* from nuclear arms: Bertell and others have substantiated this point.

Our look at the nineteenth century abolitionist movement underscores the folly of making *ad personam* attacks on the adversary. Zealous nineteenth century abolitionists abused the slaveholders in numerous speeches, editorials, and tracts. The result was to drive a great wedge between North and South, to eradicate what antislavery sentiment existed below the Mason-Dixon line, and completely alienate the regions. We are not by any means opposing confrontation tactics, only suggesting that abolitionists need to attack nuclear weapons and the ridiculous rationales for them—but not question the sincerity of the nuclear proponents themselves.

Somehow, antinuclear abolitionists have to engage the adversary in dialogue—despite the adversary's reluctance. Peacemakers need to convince those who work in the nuclear establishment that it's in their best interest, as human beings, to end the arms race and remove this "blight" or "curse" from the world. It will require a new way of looking at nationalism, to be sure.

In *Weapons and Hope,* Freeman Dyson cites the Quakers as pioneers in the battle against slavery. For him, the ingredients of the Quakers' success were a moral conviction, patience, objectivity, and the willingness to compromise. Modern abolitionists certainly have a moral conviction. It is more difficult to be patient in the face of countless frustration, and often hard to maintain objectivity—one is often tempted to fudge the facts or pinch the truth in making one's arguments as strong as possible—but these are qualities worth cultivating.

What of a "willingness to compromise?" Dyson does not mean by this that we should give up our goal of zero nuclear weapons. His example is that many of the earliest antislavery actionists (mainly in England) set a manageable goal for themselves:

> They decided to concentrate their efforts upon the prohibition of the slave trade and to leave the total abolition of slavery to their successors in another generation . . . They were able to mobilize against the slave trade a coalition of moral and economic interests which could not at that time have been brought together in the cause of total abolition.[27]

Dyson says that today's crusaders have made this sort of wise compromise by focusing on the elimination of nuclear weapons, rather than waging a general war against war. The abolition of war is a more formidable task which may best be left to our successors in the twenty-first century!

In plotting strategy, today's peacemakers may find the concept of *suffocation* useful. "Once the abolitionists had given up hope of converting the South," Thomas Harwood writes, "they worked to place the slaveholding area in a kind of moral isolation."[28]

This isolation, or moral embargo, complemented some economic and political tactics whose effect might have been to suffocate slavery; that is, to eliminate whatever nourished and sustained it. An example was the campaign to boycott slave-produced goods, such as cotton. Most abolitionists favored the boycott but it failed because it lacked anything close to total support. Many thought that slavery would be suffocated when slaves could not be sold from state to state, or when slavery was removed from the territories and the District of Columbia, or if no new slave states were permitted. It was thought, also, that slavery would be stifled if the powers delegated to the federal government, such as the power to tax and distribute mail, were directed against slaveholding.

Consider the arms race. Here *suffocation* may be seen as a middle road, strategically, between gradualism (diplomacy and laborious negotiation) and immediatism (unilateral, leading to multilateral disarmament). Consider the three strategies again: the Bilateral Nuclear Freeze, Nuclear Free Zones, and direct action involving civil disobedience. The Nuclear Freeze Campaign is essentially gradualism and federalism. To be sure, achieving a Freeze on the manufacture of arms would be a positive step, but the Freeze is still an attempt to work through channels. Reaching the goal depends on the political whims of our national leaders and their willingness to negotiate. Even if there should be a bilateral freeze on present levels of arms, that is still a long way from nuclear disarmament.

At the other end, direct action campaigns (involving mass arrests) are an immediatist, personal strategy. The actionists want to provoke the powers-that-be and precipitate a radical change in policy or, through suffering and moral suasion, convince the bomb-makers to quit their work.

Nuclear Free Zones represent a combination of means, a middle way, a kind of *immediate action begun now* by citizens at the local level, unwilling to wait for their leaders in Washington. NFZs are suffocating. Since they fence off areas that cannot be used by or for the Bomb, they remove much of what sustains the nuclear establishment. Suffocation increases when local NFZs prohibit the investment of municipal funds in nuclear weapons industries or prevent the giving of municipal contracts to firms engaged in nuclear work.

Nuclear Free Zones within a nuclear power, coupled with attempts to boycott the products of nuclear industries, represent suffocation by *internal* pressure. But the suffocation strategy requires *external* pressures also. These come from the non-nuclear nations. In addition to regional NFZs, ceasing to export weapons-grade fissionable material and denying one's ports to nuclear warships are ways that non-nuclear nations may act. Together, internal and external methods of suffocation will take their toll on the arms race. But the question again is how much time is left?

Wendell Phillips said of his contemporaries that abolitionists "are taking this country by the four corners, until you can hear nothing but slavery!" Abolitionists are now similarly occupied with nuclearism. Their detractors say they're *preoccupied* with it but, in light of the nuclear peril, such a preoccupation seems warranted. Surely nuclear arms as an issue are as important to our time as slavery was to its. Freeman Dyson, who is probably not an immediatist, is none the less hopeful: "We shall not be finished with these weapons in a year or in a decade. But we might, if we are lucky, be finished with them in a half century, in about the same length of time that it took the abolitionists to get rid of slavery."[29]

Dyson seems to be optimistic about time. Sagan and many others are not. But clearly, nuclear weapons can be abolished. History offers encouragement. By 1852, antislavery measures were widely embraced by political and religious leaders who had scorned them twenty years before. Garrison, in fact, seemed taken aback when he addressed the Massachusetts Anti-Slavery Society in 1860: "Whereas, ten years since, there were thousands who could not endure my lightest rebuke of the South, they can now swallow John Brown whole, and his rifle into the bargain."[30]

Perhaps this would not have happened without the pioneering work of "radicals," as James Russell Lowell argued in 1849:

> . . . the simple fact undoubtedly is that were the Abolitionists to go back to the position from which they started, they would find themselves less fanatical than a very respectable minority of the people. The public follows them step by step, occupying the positions they have successfully fortified and quitted, and it is necessary that they should keep in advance in order that people may not be shocked by waking up and finding themselves Abolitionists.[31]

Will we wake up tomorrow and find Americans by the thousands totally committed to the battle against the Bomb? Will scores of people risk arrest by refusing to pay war taxes or by trespassing at nuclear weapons facilities? Will thousands of communities or dozens of states declare themselves Nuclear Free Zones?

If so, present-day abolitionists, fighting nuclear numbness, burnout, public apathy, and the power of the entrenched establishment, will have made it possible.

5

Declaring Interdependence

*"HAVE A PEACEFUL WEEK IN BRADFORD . . .
VISIT BRADFORD . . . BEFORE BITS OF BRADFORD VISIT
YOU!"*
    —Advertisement produced by the Bradford, England, Council

*"If you want to live in a nuclear-free world, start right here on this
street."*
                                            —Ulli Kohler, West Germany

*"People who develop the habit of thinking of themselves as world
citizens are fulfilling the first requirement of sanity in our time."*
                                            —Norman Cousins

At Darwin, Australia, longshoremen refused to load uranium
ore onto ships. In Germany, a ship's captain and two union representatives were fired for demanding that the union "resist by
all means" transporting American nuclear missiles to Europe. In
Kobe City, Japan, foreign military vessels entering the harbor
must certify that they are not carrying nuclear weapons. In
Auckland, New Zealand, a visiting US nuclear submarine was
greeted by fifty boatloads of protesters. In Sicily, peace campaigners fasted for two weeks after gathering one million signatures opposing deployment of 112 cruise missiles in Comiso.

Throughout Europe, hundreds of thousands marched, sang,
and denounced the deployment of 572 American cruise and
Pershing missiles that NATO began to deploy in December,
1983, ostensibly to counter the Soviet SS20s aimed at Europe. In

1985, year of the fortieth anniversary of the bombing of Hiroshima and Nagasaki, hundreds of events were held around the world to protest the arms race. In the United States, 17,000 gathered in Washington on August 4 to surround the Capitol, the Pentagon, and points in between with fifteen miles worth of banners fashioned by 25,000 people from every state in the union. Some 500 took part in the August "Desert Witness" at the Nevada test site near Los Vegas. Globally, on Hiroshima Day, 1986 some 125,000 human "shadows" were painted on streets and sidewalks as a grim reminder that people were vaporized on Japanese streets in August of 1945.

The first half of the 1980s—particularly in that part of the world beyond America—was marked by an increasingly strident antinuclearism. During this decade the last-ditch battle against the bomb is heating up. People are beginning to understand that *national* security is dependent on *inter*national security. Citizens are calling on governments to issue a Declaration of *Inter*dependence. In the United States apathy still reigns, but more and more Americans are hearing the call, awakening to a new world-consciousness, responding to a vigorous and committed trans-Atlantic activism.

It may be fear that motivates the Europeans who have crowded the streets in this decade and the desire to save one's own skin and one's family—but who is to argue with the natural instinct for self-preservation? And there are many other motivations: altruism, compassion, the conviction that the planet's marvelous biology, its elaborate and wondrous ecosystems teeming with life, must be protected. In some ways these concerns are captured in the political creed of the European "Greens" parties, whose "Beyond the Blocs" campaign in 1986 included a determination to promote NFZs as a part of the peace process.

Governments are hard of hearing and pleas are often ignored. The move to stop the emplacement of Euromissiles seems to have failed—despite mass protests and petition campaigns in several countries—with the final capitualization of the Dutch government to NATO pressure on November 1, 1985. During the previous week the Dutch activist committee, Cruise Missiles No (KKN), organized a closing rally for the national citizens petition campaign (*volkspetitionnement*) against deployment. The campaign, which had been conducted in September-October, produced 3,743,455 signatures from a population of 14.5 million. The Dutch prime minister Ruud Lubbers and the heads of both houses of parliament were present at the rally. In his speech Lubbers congratulated KKN for the result, but many of his 10,000 listeners had turned their backs on the prime minister to protest his plans. Events in the Netherlands demonstrate the strength of local opposition to the nuclear missiles along with the intense determination of NATO officials to keep them rolling.

But the people have had some victories. Responding to public opinion, New Zealand's Labour government in 1984 moved to fulfill its campaign promise to make New Zealand nuclear-free. Several Pacific island nations made similar determinations. Hundreds of new local zones are annually declared around the world. Angry street protests continue and peace groups grow. The Campaign for Nuclear Disarmament (United Kingdom) reports a membership increase from 75,000 in 1983 to over 110,000 in 1985. Although British missile deployment continues, the authoritative *Jane's Defense Weekly* conceded that the Greenham Common demonstrators had prevented American cruise missiles from being wheeled out of the base to their launching positions during 1984. Women were camped at the American Air Base there from September 1981 to April 1984, when they were forcibly removed, but have returned since.

Working people around the world are taking a much closer look at the morality of handling nuclear materials. Scotland provides an example. In November 1982, both the shop stewards and the rank-and-file at the Rolls Royce plant in Hillington voted overwhelmingly to reject a $30,000,000 contract to build parts for Trident submarine missiles. "We refuse to work on such weapons which could be used against humanity," they said. "What we want is work which accomplishes some form of social need."

Regional Nuclear Free Zones

Five major treaties have theoretically freed vast global areas from nuclear tyranny: (1) The ANTARCTICA TREATY, entered into force on June 23, 1961 and which will be reviewed in 1991, specifically prohibits the deployment or testing of nuclear weapons and the disposal of nuclear wastes in Antarctica. Also it forbids the signatories to establish any military bases on the frozen continent and proscribes any military maneuvers or the testing of weapons of any kind.

The original twelve parties negotiated the Treaty while their scientists were cooperating at the South Pole during the 1957–58 International Geophysical Year. The Treaty has twenty-one signatories currently, including the US and USSR. By working together in scientific research, rival nations demonstrate that adversaries can cooperate for their mutual benefit.

(2) The OUTER SPACE TREATY was unanimously approved by the UN General Assembly on December 19, 1966, and was entered into force on January 27, 1967, with ninety-three signatories—now over one hundred—including the US and USSR. The Treaty forbids the deployment of weapons of mass destruction in space:

> Art. 4: States parties to the treaty undertake not to place in orbit around the earth any objects carrying nuclear weapons or any other kinds of weapons of mass destruction, install such weapons on celestial bodies, or station such weapons in outer space in any manner. The moon and other celestial bodies shall be used by all states parties to the treaty exclusively for peaceful purposes.

Both the Outer Space Treaty and the 1972 US-USSR Anti-Ballistic Missile Treaty may well be undermined by the Reagan administration's plan to develop an exotic Star Wars defense system involving particle-beam and nuclear-fired laser beam weaponry.

(3) As a result of the Cuban Missile Crisis of 1963, several nations clamored for the UN to secure an agreement for "The

Prohibition of Nuclear Weapons in Latin America." This became known as the TREATY OF TLATELOLCO when finalized in 1967. Virtually every Latin American country has signed the Treaty, although Cuba refused to join until the United States removes its military base at Guantanamo Bay; Argentina has signed but not ratified; and Brazil and Chile hedged their signing with qualifications.

Guaranteed by the five nuclear nations, the Treaty of Tlatelolco was mainly the work of a tireless reconciler, Alfonso Garcia Robles, who was awarded the Nobel Peace Prize in 1982. Robles saw great hope in the emerging mosaic of nuclear-free regions. Ultimately he saw it expanding globally to the point where "the powers that still possess these terrible weapons of mass destruction will be something like contaminated islets subject to quarantine."

Did Great Britain violate the Treaty of Tlatelolco during the 1982 Falklands conflict when it sent its warships into the South Atlantic? As a matter of policy, the United Kingdom refuses to say whether or not any particular ship carries nuclear weapons; the question is whether such warships sailed through Argentina's territorial waters or those of another treaty state.

(4) The SEABED ARMS CONTROL TREATY was originally signed by the US, USSR, and the UK on February 11, 1971, and entered into force on May 18, 1972, with thirty-nine signatories. The parties agreed not to place on the ocean floor "any nuclear weapons or any other types of weapons of mass destruction as well as structures, launching installations, or any other facilities specifically designed for storing, testing, or using such weapons."

(5) On August 7, 1985, eight Pacific nations including Australia and New Zealand marked the 40th Anniversary of the bombing of Hiroshima and Nagasaki by signing a treaty declaring the SOUTH PACIFIC NUCLEAR FREE ZONE. Five additional countries were expected to sign; the pact must be ratified by eight eligible states to enter into force. However, the prime minister of Vanuatu said that he might not sign because the treaty

was not strong enough. For one thing, it left open the issue of whether treaty states would permit the warships of nuclear states to dock at their ports.

The treaty, signed by members of the South Pacific Forum meeting at Raratonga, will ban the testing, manufacture, and presence of nuclear weapons in the region. The five nuclear powers, including France which has been testing nuclear devices at Mururoa in French Polynesia, have been asked to sign protocols including commitments not to use nuclear arms against treaty nations, and not to conduct nuclear tests in the South Pacific Zone.

Other Proposals

Many regional zones have been proposed. One comes from the indigenous people of the North Pole. A resolution calling for a nuclear-free Arctic was unanimously passed by the fifty-four delegates of the Inuit Circumpolar Conference, at its Third General Assembly in July, 1983. The Conference represents over 100,000 people native to Greenland, Alaska, and Canada—often called Eskimos. The Inuits know that the North Pole is the route most ICBMs will take if and when the superpowers launch their missiles. The missiles will travel at supersonic speed over the pole, entering space and re-entering the earth's atmosphere in a grim and perilous arc. "We are afraid that the Canadian, Alaskan, and Greenland Arctic is going to be used as the highway to hell," said Arqaluk Lynge, who is a member of Greenland's parliament.

Many other proposals have been advanced. In 1959, Ireland proposed a plan for a global Nuclear Free Zone that would take shape region by region. In 1968 the USSR proposed the creation of a Nuclear Free Zone in the Mediterranean: it would not deploy nuclear weapons in Mediterranean waters provided other states would say the same. And in 1974 the Shah of Iran proposed a Middle-Eastern NFZ. The proposal was supported by several Arab states but opposed by Israel, which insisted on bilateral negotiations with each nation instead of a multilateral agreement.

In 1960, fourteen African states proposed a trans-Africa NFZ in reaction to French atmospheric testing in the Sahara. In November 1961 the UN General Assembly adopted resolution 1652 (XVI) entitled "Consideration of Africa as a Denuclearized Zone. The resolution requested member states:

(a) To refrain from carrying out or continuing to carry out in Africa nuclear tests in any form.

(b) To refrain from using the territory, territorial waters or air space of Africa for testing, storing, or transporting nuclear weapons.

(c) To consider and respect the continent of Africa as a denuclearized zone.

The idea of an Africa Zone—in large measure to forestall South Africa's nuclear weapons program—has been consistently endorsed by the Organization of African Unity but opposed by the United States, the United Kingdom, and South Africa. In its resolutions of December 1979 the UN General Assembly denounced the South African nuclear program as a "dangerous threat to the security of the African states" and appealed to that nation to open its nuclear installations to inspection. To this date, that has not happened, nor is it likely, and the fact that South Africa would remain outside of a treaty is one factor inhibiting the formation of an African Nuclear Free Zone.

Many regional proposals involve Europe—predictable since Europe is the region often voted most likely to succeed as a nuclear battleground! In 1956 Adam Rapacki, foreign secretary for the Polish People's Republic, proposed that Poland, along with Czechoslovakia and the two Germanies, form a Nuclear Free Zone. The Zone would be ratified by unilateral declarations of each of the four states and enforced by a commission of nonaligned, NATO, and Warsaw Pact countries using a system of inspection posts. Rapacki cited benefits going beyond the denuclearization of the area. He wanted to facilitate the limitation of conventional weapons as well, and to expedite the removal of foreign troops sanctioned in those nations.

Initially Belgium and Canada welcomed the Rapacki Plan, and France and Denmark expressed interest. But West Germany and the United States, led by the aggressive anti-Communist diplomats Konrad Adenauer and John Foster Dulles, rejected it. So did Great Britain's Conservative government. One might think that since three of the four nations to be denied nuclear weapons were Soviet bloc countries, the West would applaud. Not so! Adenauer and Dulles argued that the Rapacki Plan would threaten the European military alliance, lead to a withdrawal of American troops from Europe, and delay the reunification of Germany.

Revisions of the Rapacki Plan were submitted in 1958 and 1962 and again rejected by the West. Meanwhile, other proposals were made. Romania proposed a Balkans NFZ in 1957. The Soviets proposed both a Balkans and a Nordic NFZ in 1959: the latter would include Sweden, Norway, Denmark, and Finland. President Kekkonen of Finland also proposed a Nordic NFZ, in 1963; a revised proposal was offered in 1978. Sweden supported the general idea. Norway in 1981 proposed yet another plan for a Nordic NFZ, and it was endorsed by powerful groups: the Norwegian Labor Party and the Trade Union Congress, as well as by the Social Democratic Parties in all four nations. Scandinavian campaigners collected over 2,500,000 signatures supporting the idea in 1981–82.

Representatives of six independent peace organizations (from Denmark, Finland, the Faroe Islands, Iceland, Norway, and Sweden) met at Reykjavik on April 24, 1983, to formulate a concrete Nordic NFZ proposal. The Preamble of the proposal suggests that there are two competing defense policies in the world, *deterrence* and *confidence*. The first contributes to a constant erosion of security; the second, if practiced by nations willing to cooperate in *trust* (my insertion), will lead to less tension and increased global security. Nations adhering to such a treaty would agree not to "(a) develop, test, or produce nuclear weapons; (b) acquire, accept or possess nuclear weapons; (c) allow other countries to introduce, deploy, or store their nuclear weapons in the zone."

The delegates admitted that sticky questions would involve air space and water surrounding the treaty nations. The proposal would declare the airspace up to and including the earth's atmosphere part of the Nuclear Weapons Free Zone, meaning that bombers and cruise missiles would be banned from overflights. The treaty nations would seek pledges from the nuclear powers on this. There is also the problem of keeping the bays and oceans adjacent to the signatories nuclear-free. A pledge, for example, would need to be secured from the USSR to restrict its warships to narrow shipping lanes between the Danish Straits and Soviet harbors and shipyards in the Baltic and the Bay of Finland—keeping the Baltic nominally free of nuclear weapons.

The proponents also expressed the hope that such a Nordic Zone would provide impetus to create a North Atlantic Nuclear Weapons Free Zone and eventually a European Zone.

Like the Nordic nations, Austria and Switzerland have no plans to produce or procure nuclear weapons. Prominent diplomats have called for a Central European Nuclear Free Zone, with the Nordic and Baltic states linked through the two Germanies and neutral Austria and Switzerland. In 1982, the Independent Commission on Disarmament proposed a non-nuclear "buffer zone" 300 kilometers wide that would, in effect, straddle the Iron Curtain. This zone would exclude all nuclear weapons both ways, 150 kilometers from the border into the two Germanies and into part of Czechoslovakia (based on this distance as the maximum range for battlefield nuclear weapons). The Commission was chaired by the eminent Swedish Prime Minister Olof Palme and included seventeen members representing the three political blocs: East, West, and Nonaligned.

For years the Western allies, or NATO, have been committed to a "limited" battlefield nuclear warfighting strategy. This means that nuclear landmines and artillery, if not air strikes, could be used to slow an invasion by the Warsaw Pact nations—if it could not be slowed by conventional armed forces. The American public is misinformed on this policy, as the Public Agenda Foundation discovered in its 1984 voter survey. By 69 percent to 22 percent their sample denied that "it is current US policy to use nuclear weapons if the Soviets invade Europe or Japan with soldiers or tanks . . . if they don't use nuclear weapons," and 77 percent said it should *not* be our policy to do so.

The Palme Commission proposal would minimize the "use them or lose them" dilemma—the hard choice between firing the weapons or losing them to an advancing enemy—and it would preclude the possibility of an early use of nuclear weapons in the event of border hostilities. Palme described the Commission's proposal as "an exercise in peaceful coexistence," and suggested that the Commission was unique in that

> for the first time, and under difficult international circumstances—prominent people from both Warsaw Pact and NATO countries were able to agree with people from neutral countries on a factual description of the military situation . . . and on a broad program of action to avert these dangers . . . Our discussions over two years—and above all, I believe, the moving and shattering experience of our visit to Hiroshima—convinced us of the urgency of working together for common interests.

The Palme Commission plan was criticized by those who thought it went too far, and those who didn't think it went far enough. Among the latter, Prime Ministers Andreas Papandreou of Greece and Nicolae Ceausescu of Romania stand out. They issued a joint letter on December 19, 1983, asking that the US halt its deployment of Euromissiles, asking the Soviets to refrain from any countermeasures, and they asked the superpowers to bargain for arms reductions in good faith.

The idea of a Balkan Nuclear Free Zone had been proposed before. The State Council President of Bulgaria, Mr. Zhivkov, had said in 1981: "We warmly support the idea of turning the Balkans into a Nuclear Free Zone . . . It would be a substantial contribution to the improvement of the international climate, to the gradual transformation of Europe into a continent free of nuclear arms; it would be one more victory for peace."

Greece's Prime Minister Papandreou boosted the notion of a Balkan NFZ to a new level of credibility when in early 1983 he announced that Greece would order the removal of all NATO nuclear weapons from its soil if a regional Nuclear Free Zone could be arranged. Evidently Greece is willing to risk its NATO connection to promote regional security. In 1984 Greece refused a request from the NATO Supreme Commander to replace old nuclear weapons stored in Greece with modernized ones.

Advocates of a Balkan NFZ contend that once the Zone is established it will influence the formation of a Nordic Zone. It, then, may be possible to denuclearize the two Germanies, producing a viable Central European NFZ, much stronger than the original Palme proposal. Perhaps even Poland and Czechoslovakia would join, creating something like the Rapacki Zone, and Belgium and the Netherlands, where strong antinuclear movements have emerged, might join as well. The Soviets offered to remove some of their missiles targeted on Europe if a Northern European Zone developed and if this were to happen—who knows?—even Britain and, yes, France, might be persuaded to give up their dangerous toys.

Visionary? Of course. But what a grand step toward a nonnuclear world! We would at least have a Nuclear Free Europe, "a calm space between the superpowers," in the words of Britain historian E. P. Thompson.

Western Objections

The NATO governments on the whole, dominated by the United States, refuse to consider such a scenario. Washington has rejected time after time any plan for a regional European Zone. A kind of knee-jerk rhetorical response occurs: "Soviets Attempt to Sow NATO Discord" is the typical headline for a piece about an NFZ idea emanating from the East. Western diplomats argue that the Soviets want to split the NATO alliance and that is why they propose Nuclear Free Zones. If the region were to become nuclear-free this would leave NATO without sufficient nuclear weaponry to defend Western Europe from a Soviet invasion. Morton Halperin, former US Assistant Secretary of Defense, put it baldly: If the Soviets invade, "The NATO doctrine is that we will fight with conventional forces until we are losing, and then we will blow up the world."

The contention that nuclear weapons are required for a defense of Europe is based on three shaky assumptions: (1) The Soviets intend to invade Europe, probably at the earliest opportunity; (2) A military-based defense is the only way to resist an invasion; (3) The Soviet bloc possesses superior conventional (nonnuclear) forces compared to NATO. If these assumptions are granted, the only way to bar the door to the Russian bear is to threaten it with nuclear retaliation—and some of these weapons must be placed in the path of an invasion.

All three assumptions are dubious. In *Soviet Power,* the well-traveled British journalist Jonathan Steele contends that the Soviets are not about to invade Western Europe. They have internal domestic troubles, the old ideological fervor has cooled, and they really would like to return to détente. "It seems inconceivable," he writes, "that Moscow would prefer the unknown consequences of attack and the problem of occupation" (of Western Europe).[1] Steele cites both Soviet and Western sources in support of his view. Even in the Third World, says Steele, the Soviets have shown a remarkable restraint in containing their mischief to just a few nations. Steele writes elsewhere:

> I don't think the Soviet system is one which is prepared to take risks. The good side of that is that I don't think they are risk-takers in the direction of war and I think the history of recent Soviet policy, since the Brezhnev period began, has been relatively cautious. However they're not, unfortunately, prepared to take risks for peace either . . ."[2]

Even if we were to concede that the Soviets have designs on Western Europe, we must question the assumption that a military-based defense is the only way to resist military aggression. History is a record of battles won and lost, Tours and Hastings, Gettysburg, Dunkirk, and Guam—but historians largely ignore times and places when nonmilitary defense was used to counter repression or repel an invader. Gene Sharp, a

Harvard historian, cites 198 methods of nonviolent political protest and persuasion in his monumental work, *The Politics of Nonviolent Action,* cited previously. Sharp has developed the idea of a nonmilitary or *civilian-based defense,* particularly in a subsequent work, *Social Power and Political Freedom,*[3] and applied it to Europe in *Making Europe Unconquerable.*[4]

With a national conviction and careful planning, civilian-based defense can thwart a dictator or deny any foreign power that has designs on one's country. Total noncooperation with the invaders would bring the nation's economic and social system to a standstill—officials refusing to do their work, laborers striking, media refusing to broadcast the conquerors' statements, police refusing to arrest their countrymen and women, shippers refusing to transport goods. The invaders would be baffled, confused, frustrated, and at best, psychologically befuddled; at worst, wanting desperately to get out without losing face.

Civilian-based defense worked in the case of the Danish resistance to the Nazis, when even the King of Denmark adopted the Star of David. It worked in Norway, where teachers went on strike against the Nazi indoctrination scheme and the Quisling regime, and in the celebrated campaign of Gandhi against the British rule in India. It worked less well in South Africa in the 1960s and with Polish Solidarity in the 1980s; that is, there was less than total success. Sharp might argue that nonviolent resistance was, in those cases, not systematically planned, or that it failed to achieve near total participation. When properly engineered, given time, it can bring down a repressive regime. There will be some brutality; government troops may kill some people. There would be fewer deaths, however, and much less destruction than would result from taking arms.

This, you may say, is visionary too—some persons would argue, much too visionary for this war-torn world. But civilian-based defense offers a great deal of faith, hope, and sanity as an alternative to guns, missiles, and armed conflict.

For the sake of argument, let us concede the second point—that a military defense of Europe is necessary. There remains the third point: do the Soviets and their allies possess conventional forces superior to those of NATO? If the answer is yes, then perhaps a nuclear defense or threatened defense is necessary to deter invasion. We hear a loud *yes* from the Pentagon . . . but others differ.

American political scientist Richard Falk in a fine work, *Indefensible Weapons,* cites British defense analysts Mary Kaldor and Dan Smith who "argue that Europe is currently quite capable of defending itself at present levels of expenditure without reliance on nuclear weapons."[5] Other independent analysts (authorities unrelated to the Reagan administration) agree.

In *Beyond the Freeze,* members of the Union for Concerned Scientists argue that the difference in conventional forces between the two sides is exaggerated. They argue (1) that the United States and NATO are together stronger than the USSR and its Warsaw allies in terms of economic and technological abilities; (2) that the two sides are closely matched in military manpower (4.9 million troops against 4.7 million, with one-fourth of the Soviet army tied to the Chinese border); and (3) there is a rough equality in terms of conventional military hardware. Quoting the *Annual Report of the US Department of Defense for 1982,* they state that "the Warsaw Pact seems to have numerical leads in most categories but 'NATO still retains its overall qualitative edge.' "[6]

The main offensive land weapon is the tank. Do the Soviets have an invincible tank armada, as some fear? Actually, the Eastern bloc has twice as many tanks as NATO but NATO has the edge in anti-tank weaponry. In fact, new developments in anti-tank missiles could make tanks obsolete! Certainly NATO has no need to match the Warsaw nations tank for tank. Also, NATO has a clear advantage in naval forces, according to the UCS writers, and although the Warsaw Pact has more tactical aircraft, NATO planes are equipped with highly sophisticated radar and with Sidewinder heat-seeking missiles.

"In short," according to *Beyond the Freeze,* "forces deployed in Europe are roughly equivalent. According to a recent NATO study, the West has the defensive capability to prevent the Warsaw Pact, despite its emphasis on offensive weapons, from gain-ing a decisive edge. No deficiency in NATO's strength invites a Soviet attack."[7]

Apparently Western fears of a huge Soviet military advantage in Europe are overblown. There is some risk of a Soviet attack perhaps, but the risk of moving to a Nuclear Free Europe would be significantly less than the risks involved in nuclear posturing or nuclear combat.

European Local Initiatives

Handa, Japan, in 1958, was, to my knowledge, the first community to declare itself nuclear-free. Other Japanese communities followed: 240 NFZs were declared in 1984 alone. Australian communities began declaring in 1975, stirred by the Movement Against Uranium Mining. For many other nations the pivotal year was 1980. Since then, local activity has escalated, and by April 1, 1986, there were over 3,000 zones in seventeen nations, including over half the population of Ireland, the United Kingdom, Australia, New Zealand, and nearly half of Spain.

The First International Conference of Nuclear Free Zone activists was held in Huddersfield, England, March 30–April 1, 1983, and the First International Conference of Nuclear Free Zone Authorities was held in Manchester, England, a few days later. (*Authority* refers to local governments or officials. In Britain, authorities may be county, borough, or district councils.) The Manchester Conference attracted some 200 delegates from twelve nations. A Second Conference held in Cordoba, Spain, in March 1985, drew delegates from ten countries and observers from seven others. A Third Conference was planned for Bologna, Italy in 1986.

Manchester, the location for the First Conference, had become the first British Nuclear Free Zone, on November 5, 1980. Wales in 1982 became the first "Nuclear-Free Principality" when all seven county councils passed NFZ declarations, and by January 1, 1986, Great Britain boasted 160 Nuclear Free Zones.

Vigorous protests from British activists forced the government to cancel its September, 1982, "Hard Rock" Civil Defense exercise. NFZ authorities countered with "Operation Hard Luck," an educational program based on a hypothetical "limited nuclear attack" scenario. All British NFZs were advised of the nuclear targets in their areas and were provided with computer calculations showing local casualty figures for blast and radiation—an effective way of bringing the dangers home to people! Press conferences and promotional tactics developed by the NFZ authorities and the Campaign for Nuclear Disarmament fueled the "Hard Luck" project and focused public attention on the hazards of nuclearism.

In December, 1982, the Southwark, England, Council decided to purge from their list of approved contractors those involved in construction of the cruise missile base at Greenham Common. The Campaign for Nuclear Disarmament has been encouraging other NFZs to take action similar to Southwark's: the idea is to put the economic squeeze on people doing business with the nuclear weapons establishment. If British firms want to retain their local contracts, they will have to listen to what people are saying about the morality and politics of nuclear defense.

British local authorities often combine NFZ declarations with other political action. This may involve opposition to civil defense plans sent from London or the attempt to promote peace art exhibits and festivals, or peace education in the schools. Local authorities often form peace committees. Sometimes they promote *twinning*, meaning that a village or city connects itself with a foreign community. For example, joint nuclear-free declarations have been signed between Sheffield, UK, and Donetsk in the USSR, and between Manchester, UK, and Karl Marx Stadt in the German Democratic Republic. The mayor of Camden, England, Barbara Hughes, sent a peace appeal to the mayors of twenty-one American cities named Camden. The Camden Peace Groups Steering Committee supported the project by writing to peace groups, churches, and newspapers in the American Camdens to let them know of British peace activities.

Many European nations have local Nuclear Free Zones. The movement began in West Germany in 1982; by January 1986, there were 154 NFZs. Hundreds of West German children voted their schools nuclear-free in October 1983, despite a warning from the Ministry of Education that schools were becoming places of "strife and political polarization." Teachers departed from their usual topics to discuss whether American Pershing missiles should be deployed in Germany, and politicians—not always treated deferentially by the young—were invited into the schools to debate the issue. One youth spoke frankly to an official defending government policy: "You say we're defending democracy, yet 75 percent of the people say they're against deployment, so where is the democracy?"

In the Netherlands, 400 communities had declared themselves nuclear-free by January 1986. Amsterdam has nuclear-free signs at its borders, provides grants to peace groups, and pursues peace education programs. The Rotterdam council has banned shipments of nuclear weapons through its port, the world's largest. Council members feared the city was a prime target for attack in the event of nuclear war.

Despite government opposition, 170 Italian towns had declared themselves NFZs by January 1986. Spain had 350 Zones, and communities in which American bases are located have been asking whether nuclear weapons are being stored on Spanish soil. The Spanish passed their referendum on NATO in March, 1986, but specified that Spain would not accept nuclear weapons. Political parties in Spain and Portugal have introduced an initiative for an Iberian peninsula NFZ. There were 86 NFZs in Portugal by January 1986.

There were 9 NFZs in Denmark as of January 1, 1986. On November 1, 1984, a majority of the Danish government requested the government to work actively towards a Nuclear Free Denmark—but under pressure from NATO the government has decided to accept American missiles. The Faroe Islands and Greenland, which are theoretically defended by Denmark, have declared themselves nuclear-free. Iceland has a policy against the presence of nuclear weapons on its soil, but does not refuse port access to NATO warships.

By January 1, 1986, Norway had 107 Nuclear Free Zones and Belgium 281, including the towns of Evere, the European headquarters for NATO, and Florennes, targeted for Euromissile implacement. Ireland had 117 Nuclear Free Zones including Dublin, the world's first capitol city to make the declaration. Approximately one fourth of Norway's 430 municipal councils and 11 of its 19 county councils had adopted resolutions by January 1, 1986, asking parliament to ban nuclear weapons from Norwegian territory and to support the establishment of a Nordic NFZ. Several coastal communities have ruled that nuclear weapons-capable warships will be denied port access unless they declare that nuclear weapons are not on board. The first such law was adopted by Horten, a navy shipyard about ninety kilometers south of Oslo, on April 22, 1985, and several others followed—lending support to similar activity in Japan and, more significantly, New Zealand.

In Sweden, incidentally, it is not legally possible to declare a community nuclear-free. But there is great interest in Sweden, and a campaign to declare schools, shops, and other locations nuclear-free has been launched as a way of stimulating discussion on the issue. Stockholm hosted a seminar on the Nordic NFZ concept in February, 1986.

Canadian Activity

The northern neighbor to the US boasted 86 Nuclear Free Zones by March 1, 1986, representing over 23 percent of the population and including the cities of Toronto and Vancouver, and the province of Manitoba. Vancouver erected signs at fourteen access points, "Welcome to Vancouver—A Nuclear Weapons Free Zone," a slogan also used in cancelling mail. Several NFZ bills have been introduced in the federal parliament as well as in provincial legislatures. Project Plowshares, a church-related antinuclear group, has been pursuing a campaign to make Canada nuclear-free. And on November 10, 1986, after a year of planning and consultations, the Canadian Peace Alliance was formed in Toronto. Over 250 peace groups are covered by this "peace umbrella." The founding statement of unity affirmed the delegates' desire to make Canada nuclear-free.

But Canada, you say, has no nuclear weapons. Indeed, Canada will have none by the end of the decade, when its nuclear-tipped Genie missiles have been removed from its CF-101 aircraft, which are being retired. If Canada became a Nuclear Free Zone, restrictions on the storage and transit, manufacture and support of nuclear weapons systems would actually constrain US defense strategy.

In terms of (1) *transit,* it's not likely that American nuclear weapons would ever be carried across Canada by land. In the case of an alert or emergency, American B-52s might conceivably overfly Canadian airspace. US Trident submarines based at Bangor, Washington, will need to pass through Canadian waters in the Strait of Juan de Fuca to reach the Pacific—a clear violation of Canada's proposed nuclear-free status.

In terms of (2) *manufacturing,* Canadian companies are being urged to bid on American defense contracts, and Canadian firms have landed jobs to make components for the Lance and MX missiles, Trident subs, and other systems. The Litton Corporation makes the guidance system for the air-launched cruise missiles that are being attached to B-52 bombers. This new weapon is to be flight-tested in Alberta and the Canadian arctic.

In terms of (3) *support,* Canadian defense commitments to NATO and NORAD (North American Aerospace Defense Agreement) involve the government in various surveillance and warning systems designed to support nuclear war. These include the AWAC system (Airborne Warning and Control); the Canadian Aurora airplanes designed to assist US anti-submarine operations; NAVSTAR, a surveillance, detection, and missile-guidance satellite; and Loran-C, an international navigational system which provides information to American submarines which enables them to target their missiles. Canadian personnel also participate in joint training and testing operations involving nuclear weapons with Canadian allies. At Nanoose Bay on Vancouver Island, US nuclear submarine crews are given extensive training in torpedo operations and in using underwater detection devices, and the Canadian Forces Base at Goose Bay, Labrador, is used for flight training by NATO allies, including low-level flights by British Vulcan bomber crews.

If Canada became nuclear-free, some of these activities clearly would be proscribed. The presence of Vulcans with nuclear weapons almost certainly would be forbidden. Other activities, such as surveillance and navigational systems which have some nonmilitary uses, are difficult to ban outright. These are some of the issues that currently concern Canadian peacemakers.

Transatlantic Comparisons

Every movement needs pep rallies. Activists who are on a high from successful campaigns or who are suffering from burnout need a boost occasionally, the kind of boost provided by international conferences. Delegates to the First International Conference of NFZ Local Authorities (April, 1983) in Manchester, England, enjoyed themselves. They compared notes on what was happening elsewhere and exchanged ideas and opinions, as well as family photos. In addition, they discussed and distilled eleven key issues related to their NFZ activities. These included nuclear weapons manufacture, naturally, but also civil defense, uranium mining, nuclear power, nuclear waste, the transport of nuclear materials, public education and the public's "right to know," investing and contracting policies, economic conversion, public health and safety, and land use. Most NFZ campaigns address only two or three of these, perhaps five or six at most.

On his return from that first international conference, Albert Donnay made some interesting observations.[8] Comparing European and American NFZ campaigns, he noted that:

> In the United States, the declaration of a Nuclear Free Zone is usually accomplished through extensive grassroots organizing: public education, petition drives, hearings, rallies, and either a referendum or a council vote. There is little follow-up, however, and few public funds have been spent on Nuclear Free Zone programs or peace education. In many European countries (and Canada), however, Nuclear Free Zones are often declared at the initiative of local authorities (Labor-party controlled councils in England, for example) with little input from local peace groups.

While American peace groups generally have to scratch for money, European communities often expend public funds for NFZ campaigns and peace education. Sometimes councils publish official city postcards, brochures, and souvenir buttons with an NFZ theme, or display NFZ logos on public buildings or vehicles.

In England, local authorities may hire a peace (not police) officer full-time to promote NFZ policies and coordinate the city's policies with the programs of local peace groups. English councils often fund peace groups or provide access to public meeting rooms for them. In Sheffield the council gave local peace groups a downtown office with a store front and print shop, all rent-free, and established an NFZ Working Party with a $40,000 budget! The Sheffield council also considered sending the women camped outside the fence at the American air base at Greenham Common a Christmas present of Sheffield-made wire cutters. Sadly, the Sheffield legal department vetoed the idea.

Peace is considered a patriotic activity in much of Europe. Working for nuclear disarmament may be considered part of one's civic obligation. But in America, peace workers are often eyed suspiciously; peacework is still a resistance movement carried on by a dedicated minority. In Europe, elected officials are often the ones who initiate NFZ activity, or even declare a place nuclear-free without having to conduct a public campaign; in America, it is only due to intense public pressure that any community manages to get its officials to declare it nuclear-free . . . when they do.

Pressure On the Superpowers

Europeans are much more vocal than Americans on nuclearism, but Americans are beginning to scream louder than before. There is a powerful pressure directed at the superpowers from the nonaligned nations.

On May 22, 1984, the "Five Continent Peace Initiative" was launched. Six prominent leaders in Asian, African, European, and Latin American capitols issued a joint statement calling on the superpowers to halt the testing, production, and deployment of nuclear weapons: Indian Prime Minister Indira Gandhi, Mexican President Miguel de la Madrid, Tanzanian President Julius Nyerere, Prime Minister Olof Palme of Sweden, Greek Prime Minister Andreas Papandreou, and President Raul Alfonsin of Argentina. Leaders from these nations met again on January 28, 1985, to repeat their challenge to the superpowers.

The Initiative, which grew out of meetings of Parliamentarians for World Order, was presented to the United Nations mission chiefs of the United States, the Soviet Union, France, Great Britain, and China. In effect, the Initiative followed the lead of UN Secretary General Javier Perez de Cueller who severely criticized the superpowers years before: "They have to get the message that nobody has given them the right to decide our fate."

"We come from different parts of the world," the text reads, "with differences in religion, culture, and political systems. But we are united in the conviction that there must not be another world war. On this, the most crucial of all issues, we have resolved to make a common effort in the interests of peace."

The joint declaration insists that the first step is for the nuclear powers to "halt all testing, production, and deployment of nuclear weapons and their delivery systems, to be immediately followed by reductions in nuclear forces." Verification would be worked out, followed by negotiations leading to "general and complete disarmament, accompanied by measures to strengthen the United Nations system and to ensure an urgently needed transfer of substantial resources from the arms race into economic and social development."

Universal nuclear disarmament—the pressure mounts. But the superpowers seem to have "Eyes Only For Each Other," to use the title of an essay by David Albright: "For all their differences, the United States and the Soviet Union have always shared the opinion that nuclear disarmament is best left to them."[9] Others find this arrogance offensive.

The Nuclear Non-Proliferation Treaty, which entered into force in 1970 became—signed by 140 nations—the broadest-based arms control treaty in history. The bargain was that the non-nuclear weapons states would not seek to acquire the weapons if the nuclear nations would pursue negotiations to slow, stop, and reverse the nuclear arms buildup. The Treaty was subjected to its Third Review Conference in Geneva, in September 1985, and the non-nuclear nations deplored the lack of commitment and progress in arms control and reduction talks by the superpowers. By and large, the non-nuclear nations have kept their part of the deal, while the nuclear nations intensified the arms race. Indeed, a majority of delegates apparently supported the resolutions introduced at a plenary session by Mexico's Adolfo Garcia Robles, calling for immediate negotiations on a Comprehensive Test Ban, an immediate moratorium on nuclear testing, and a freeze on further arms buildups. American and British negotiators managed to produce a compromise declaration which avoided direct mention of the US and British stance while deploring the lack of progress towards a test ban.

Leonard Specter, author of *The New Nuclear Nations,*[10] cites the NPT as an important part of international controls and safeguards against proliferation, along with other agreements between nations, and the safeguards established by the International Atomic Energy Agency in Vienna. The IAEA was founded in 1957 and comprises over 100 member states.

But at least seven countries during 1984–85 took steps towards a nuclear weapons-making capacity. Under its new leader, Rajiv Gandhi, India seems to have new interest in building a nuclear stockpile, and Israel may have an arsenal of a hundred warheads or more. Specter cites evidence that South Africa's nuclear capability was boosted about 1980 and may have enough highly enriched uranium for 10–15 warheads. Horizontal proliferation seems, tragically, to be keeping pace with the mad vertical proliferation of nuclear warheads in the superpowers' arsenals.

The Superpowers and Nuclear Free Zones

In 1981 Leonid Breznev said publicly that "it would be a good thing if the nuclear-free status of northern Europe were formalized," but a year later the Soviet press service reported that Moscow would not accept a Nuclear Free Zone for northern Europe that included the Kola Peninsula, as West Germany had suggested. The Kola, bordering Finland and Norway, contains Soviet ground missile pads, and about two-thirds of the Soviet sea-launched missile force is homeported in the Murmansk area. Ellman Ellingsen, general secretary of the Norwegian Atlantic Committee, has charged that "there are more nuclear missiles per square mile in Kola than anywhere else in the world."

The Soviets are defensive about Kola. But the Soviet press release said that the USSR was willing to act "as a guarantee power for a Nuclear Free Zone in northern Europe." Just what "guarantee power" means is unclear; but the Soviets have said they would not target a nation which does not possess nuclear weapons.

Both superpowers, and probably most nations, will support Nuclear Free Zones when it is in their "national interest" to do so; that is, when it fits the leaders' political strategy. So far, the US has not publically endorsed Nuclear Free Zones; the Soviets have. In speaking to an audience of NFZ local authorities in Manchester, England, April 1982, Dr. Yuri P. Davydon of the Soviet Academy of Sciences said: "While it possesses nuclear weapons, the Soviet Union opposes these weapons on principle and consistently comes out for their abolition. Nuclear Free Zones are believed in the Soviet Union to be one of the ways whereby mankind can approach the complete liquidation of nuclear weapons."

Is this empty verbiage? Is it a smokescreen to disguise the Soviets' ambitious aims, as the hawks seem to think? The arms race continues. Neither side seems very willing to take any serious unilateral initiatives, although Secretary Gorbachev's August 1985 announcement of a Soviet moratorium on testing was important, and should have been welcomed by Washington. It was not. Hopefully, stubborn Uncle Sam and the defensive Russian bear will be forced to disarm together by the two pressures building simultaneously, the one from the grassroots within each nation (granted, more within the US than the USSR); the other from the nonaligned nations of the world.

It will happen none too soon. Activist David McReynolds wrote, "We may have entered the zone of the Third—and final—World War without knowing it, as the nations of Europe, like a leaf in a whirlwind, spun from Sarajevo into World War I." Let us hope not. We are living, however, in a twilight zone of history, caught in the limbo between darkness and light, uncertain whether the haze we see is the dawn or dusk of civilization, unwilling to trust, unable to reconcile and remove age-old political fears and suspicion, and holding in our hands the power to destroy everything but, perhaps, the insects and grass.

Is this temporal twilight zone the prologue to dawn, the coming of an age of enlightenment and justice, the Day of the Lord foretold by the prophets? We shall see. Working for Nuclear Free Zones is working to make it possible.

Ridding the world of nuclear weapons will not in itself guarantee a permanent peace. There are still too many gremlins lurking in the human psyche. But it will be a step back from the brink, from unreason—an intelligent step, a step demonstrating that we are, after all, a higher order of animal.

It is a step that humankind has not yet taken, and is long overdue.

6

Is a Nuclear-Free Pacific Possible?

"IF IT IS SAFE . . .
  DUMP IT IN TOKYO
  TEST IT IN PARIS
  STORE IT IN WASHINGTON
BUT, KEEP MY PACIFIC NUCLEAR-FREE!"
                    —Poster, the Pacific Conference of Churches

*"We the people of the Pacific have been victimized too long . . .
Our environment continues to be despoiled by foreign powers developing nuclear weapons for a strategy of warfare that has no
winners, no liberators, and imperils the survival of all humankind."*
            —from the People's Charter for a Nuclear Free Pacific;
                                            1975, Suva, Fiji

Ringed and spiked with American military installations,
cruised by American warships and buzzed by American
airplanes—in short, dominated by a military power as no other
body of water in the world—small wonder the Pacific Ocean has
been called an "American lake."

The United States, with its 160 military bases in the Pacific,
has dominated the region since the end of World War II. Its
bases may be found from Hawaii to Japan, from the Aleutians to
Australia. For example, Hawaii, South Korea, and Guam each
held 45,000 American sailors and soldiers by 1982. Guam is so
heavily militarized that one unsympathetic observer called it a
"floating aircraft carrier—with the people of the island being
taken for a ride!" Plans to increase the American armada worldwide to well over 600 ships will commit even more vessels to the
Pacific.

The United States depends for its political support in the region on bilateral defense arrangements with the Philippines and with Japan, and on the ANZUS alliance forged in 1951 between the US, Australia, and New Zealand.

The Pacific is becoming more militarized every year. As the decades changed, American vessels increased their ports of call in South Pacific waters. The number of US nuclear-armed and nuclear-powered ships visiting Cockburn Sound in Western Australia increased from 4 visits during 1976–79 to 35 visits during the first eight months of 1981. According to the Australian Strategic and Defense Studies Center, there is a nuclear-attack submarine docked at Cockburn Sound 25 percent of the time—making the nearby city of Perth a nuclear target.

The Pacific-area nuclear escalation involves both the cruise and Trident II missiles. America is equipping its Pacific surface ships with the Tomahawk cruise missile, a compact weapon that flies so low it cannot be detected by radar, yet with its 200 kiloton warhead possesses many times the destructiveness of the bomb dropped on Hiroshima. In theory, the computer-guided missile is so accurate that it will explode within 100 yards of its target on a 1500-mile flight. According to William Arkin, over 140 American vessels will carry Tomahawk missiles by the early nineties, with some 3,994 sub-launched Tomahawks planned for production.[1]

The US Navy also is planning to construct some 30 Trident nuclear submarines, with about half to be deployed in the Pacific and Indian Oceans. (The seventh was launched in early 1985.) Each of these subs will carry up to 24 Trident II multi-warhead missiles. Each missile will carry up to 17 independently-targeted warheads, with each warhead equivalent to 5 Hiroshimas. So each Trident will be able to destroy 408 targets and slaughter millions—and since these submarines are almost impossible to track it's no wonder that Congressman Tom Downey (D-NY) calls the Trident the "Prince of Darkness" and "the world's most destabilizing weapon."

Not to be outdone in the global suicide sweepstakes, the Soviets are proceeding with an equivalent submarine, the Typhoon.

Currently the Soviet presence in the South Pacific is minimal. The Soviets now have access to a naval base in Vietnam, however, and give evidence of a desire to increase their Pacific presence.

The American Presence Challenged

Challenges to the American nuclear presence have been mounted by two regional alliances: the South Pacific Forum and the Nuclear Free and Independent Pacific Movement.

The first of these is an alliance of thirteen nations: Australia, the Cook Islands, Kiribati, Nauru, Niue, Tonga, the Solomons, Tuvalu, West Samoa, Papua New Guinea, the Federated States of Micronesia, Vanuatu, and New Zealand. The last four named nations have nuclear-free laws or policies. In 1984, Forum delegates met in Tuvalu and agreed that the South Pacific should become a Nuclear Free Zone, with no nation permitted the right to make, store, or test nuclear devices in the region. The issue of port access was left open: "South Pacific countries retain their unqualified rights to decide for themselves . . . such questions as the access to their ports and airfields by vessels and aircraft of other countries." The Forum delegates met a year later in Raratonga and signed a Nuclear Free Zone Treaty with the basic provisions they had agreed upon. Only Vanuatu declined to sign, contending that the Treaty was weak without a commitment by the signatories to refuse port access to the nuclear powers' warships.

This removal of port calls by nuclear-weapons ships from the proposed ban on nuclear weapons in the area results from some intense political pressure applied by the United States to its ANZUS partner, Australia, the prime mover in the South Pacific Forum. Secretary of State George Shultz warned the Australians that denial of port rights would put the whole ANZUS pact in danger.

Australian and New Zealand Labour Parties have long held moderately antinuclear positions. In Australia the initial battle focused on uranium mining in the interior. In the 1940s the British government sponsored exploration for uranium to fuel its nuclear weapons program, and several nations who were developing nuclear power sought raw materials from Australia. Three Australian mines were opened in the 1950s. These mines have closed and others opened; two mines are functioning currently. With the discovery of the huge uranium deposit at Roxby Downs in South Australia in 1975, it appears that Australia has about one-third of the world's economically recoverable uranium.

Uranium is used for nuclear energy, but in splitting the uranium atoms a new element, plutonium, is formed. Plutonium is a long-lived and highly toxic material and the basis for thermonuclear warheads. Although the Australian government has signed "safeguard agreements" with nations to which it exports uranium, intended to ensure that it will not be used in weapons, in practice it is nearly impossible to monitor what happens to the material. Doubtless much of it winds up in warheads, to the dismay of Australian peacemakers.

Not only is uranium connected to the nuclear weapons industry, but uranium mining is hazardous and environmentally unsafe, according to information provided by the Movement Against Uranium Mining. Uranium is mined in two ways, open cut or underground, like coal. The former is more dangerous to the environment but the latter is not benign. Uranium wastes, or tailings, pose an enormous environmental threat. The tailings retain 80 percent of the radioactivity of the ore and this radioactivity will be emitted for thousands of years. Tailings can easily be dispersed by wind and rain; and dams, built to hold diluted radioactive waste, tend to leak.

Uranium miners may suffer a higher-than-normal mortality from lung cancer due to exposure to radioactive radon gas. Although miners' exposure to this gas is now more strictly limited, mining presents a serious health risk as the gas effects are cumulative over a period of years. Not only mine workers, but residents living near the mines are affected. A two-year preliminary study found an unusually high number of birth defects among Navaho Indians in New Mexico. The area is pockmarked by over 350 abandoned open-cut uranium mines. In Australia, aboriginal people have for a long time opposed uranium mining on their land, not only because of the radiation but because many of their sacred cultural sites would be destroyed. Vincent Forrester, Northern Territory Chairman of the National Aboriginal Conference, said in a June 1984 speech:

> Uranium is a threat to all people—radiation kills and bombs kill. I follow the culture of my people. We belong to the land. We are caretakers of the land. Our lifetime on this earth is only a blink in time, so our lifetime is spent protecting and caring for their land for future generations.

The aboriginals have combined with church people, union members, and peace groups in massive protests at Roxbury Downs, in the South Australian desert, potentially the largest uranium mine in the world. Actions in 1984 included dropping flowers on the mine shaft from a huge glider, people blockading trucks by chaining and supergluing themselves to gates and cattle grids, persons dressed as Snow White and the Seven Dwarfs dismantling the fence, and the nonviolent occupation of the offices of the British Petroleum and Western Mining Company—throughout Australia. These actions were an attempt to focus public opinion on the environmental hazards of uranium mining, especially the possible contamination of water in the Great Artesian Basin.

Australian unions are divided on the issue, but through the Australian Council of Trade Union's anti-uranium policy, some local unions have taken action against uranium exports. A national one-day railway strike was staged in 1976 to protest mining at Mary Kathleen. In 1981 the Waterside Workers Federation staged a blockade of uranium shipments at the Darwin Wharf for seven weeks. These are encouraging actions. In many countries organized labor has some clout. If the conscience of labor is aroused, the worldwide labor movement could make a strong contribution to the battle against the bomb.

The Australians elected a Labour Government in March 1983, and the Party had pledged to ban nuclear-weapons warships. Indeed, the Hawke government did deny access to the HMS

Invincible—but then backed off. Reconsidering, the Hawke government took a more conciliatory position *vis-à-vis* the nuclear powers. The Australian government still considers its American connection very important. However, the Hawke administration has expressed its objections to the US government policies regarding the Nuclear Freeze and Star Wars.

Fitzroy was the first local jurisdiction in Australia to declare itself nuclear free, in 1975, but the movement picked up after 1980. An Australian Secretariat was formed in April 1983, composed of elected local government officers. The organizations' function was to promote the involvement of every community in the nation, and a full-page advertisement promoting Nuclear Free Zones was published in *The National Times,* on the Anniversary of Hiroshima Day, August 6, 1983. By January 1, 1986, there were 96 Australian NFZs representing over 56 percent of the population.

Kiwis Take Courage

New Zealand deserves special attention in this study. With probably the strongest peace movement in the world, 65 percent of the population was living in 100 municipal Zones by January 1, 1986. New Zealand was attracting attention as one of the world's most vocal Nuclear Free Zone nations. When Prime Minister David Lange fulfilled the Labour Party's election promise to refuse port access to nuclear-powered and nuclear-armed ships, New Zealand surprised the world and shocked the Western nations.

No one who is aware of New Zealand history should have been surprised. Founded as a religious colony, New Zealand has often taken moral positions. The nation prides itself on being a remote island country with no enemies and no great strategic interests, despite its membership in the regional security pact with Australia and the US, ANZUS. When the United States reacted strongly to New Zealand's ban on nuclear ships—President Reagan was described as "furious" by a Washington observer—David Lange wondered publicly whether nuclear weapons had become "the whole character of the ANZUS alliance," and in a February 1985 speech asserted that "we live in a part of the world which does not have a strategic imperative for nuclear arms, and for us to be welcoming them is in fact an escalation."[2]

Lange, a Methodist laypreacher, is a devoted Christian. He spent six years as a criminal lawyer, often representing people who could not afford to pay—some estimate that his income, prior to entering parliament, was under $2500 annually. Lange has said he wants a more open government in a country where a citizen can actually reach the prime minister by phone at his home. Lange wants to provide more top jobs for women, and says he intends to frame a bill of rights for the nation.

Lange is passionately opposed to nuclear weapons. He demonstrated this passion and his rhetorical gifts in a debate at the Oxford Commons with Jerry Falwell, who, by all accounts, came off second best. (Students voted Lange the clear winner.) Lange's skill at debate was clear on ABC's "Nightline." Ted Koppel: "So what happens if New Zealand is attacked by nuclear weapons?" David Lange: "We'll burn. So what's your answer to that?"

Koppel had no answer, but in New Zealand concerned people have for years been seeking answers to the arms race. The peace movement is deeply rooted there. David Lange (referring to the Labour Party) told the "Nightline" audience, "We've been antinuclear for ten years. Now in government we're honoring our pledge not to permit nuclear weaponry." The movement's history begins in World War II and was spurred by Kiwi uneasiness about atmospheric testing conducted by the great powers in the Pacific in the 1950s, which France continues today at Mururoa, by concerns about Australia's mining of uranium and shipping it through New Zealand waters, and by the Japanese intention to dump "low-level" nuclear wastes in the Pacific.

In 1973 New Zealand took the French to the World Court on the nuclear testing issue and won. The French kept on testing, and New Zealand has acted in concert with Greenpeace to pressure the stubborn French. All of New Zealand was horrified at the sabotage of the Greenpeace ship, *Rainbow Warrior,* in the

Auckland harbor on July 10, 1984, killing the ship's photographer, and at the revelation of French government complicity. New Zealand's Chief Justice sentenced two French secret agents to ten years in prison for manslaughter and seven years for willful damage to the ship.

It was the French atmospheric testing that galvanized the movement, according to Owen Wilkes, a prominent New Zealand peace researcher. With the help of Greenpeace, New Zealanders in 1972–74 organized peace fleets of small boats to sail into the French testing zone. Ultimately these protests forced the French to go underground, but the tests went on.

US nuclear-armed warships had visited New Zealand ports since the 1960s, but about 1976 the new conservative government began to defy the peace movement by encouraging such visits. Peacemakers intensified their protests. In some cases activists deployed flotillas of boats to blockade the harbors when nuclear warships came in. Interestingly, this was not civil disobedience, it was legal. Again, Wilkes:

> We studied maritime law very closely and found that when one vessel overtakes another, the vessel being overtaken has to give way. So theoretically, if you overtake a nuclear warship, even if you're travelling quite slowly, they are supposed to get out of your way . . . . After about the third ship came in, it became impossible to stop them. It was too heavily policed. But it turned out that it didn't matter anyway, because we got just as much publicity by being there in the harbor, and it turned into a good-humored regatta, with about forty protest boats and an equal number of police boats."[3]

In 1980, a campaign to make New Zealand nuclear-free, "bit by bit," sprang up. The goal was to have 50 percent of the nation's people in municipal Nuclear Free Zones by 1983. The goal was passed, and by the time of elections in 1984 New Zealand was 64 percent nuclear-free. New Zealand therefore elected a Labour government and ousted the conservative National Party, whose prime minister, "Piggy" Muldoon, had treated antinuclear demonstrators roughly. Anne Clark Martindell, former US Ambassador to New Zealand, told the House subcommittee hearing,

> When I first arrived in Wellington my staff showed me a video-tape of the demonstrations a few months earlier at the time of a visit to Auckland harbor of one of our nuclear submarines. I have not been able to get out of my mind the frightening picture of a young woman protestor in a rowboat, holding a baby in her arms, with the slowly moving submarine bearing down on it and barely missing running over it. It was regarded as almost a miracle that no one was badly hurt that day.[4]

Muldoon, she reported, "thought it was good policy to encourage our Navy to visit New Zealand ports . . . and then to crack down hard on the inevitable demonstrations." This policy boomeranged, fostering pro-Labour sentiment and helping to elect David Lange in July 1984.

Owen Wilkes says the election was largely fought over the nuclear issue. "A Labour M.P. had introduced a private member's bill to declare New Zealand nuclear free, and Marilyn Waring, a member of the National Party, announced that she was going to cross the floor of the House to vote with Labour. The government only had a majority of one at the time, so that would have made the bill law."[5] Worried, Prime Minister Muldoon dissolved parliament halfway through the debate to call for an election.

After a whirlwind three-week campaign, Lange's Labour Party vaulted into office and the stage was set for a New Zealand—US confrontation. David Lange figured he had a mandate. Three of the four electoral parties were antinuclear; two parties, which were anti-ANZUS, actually garnered 20 percent of the vote. The congressman who suggested on the floor of the US House of Representatives that New Zealand's policy was the result of "a few activists who have a xerox machine and maybe access to a few editorial writers" was sadly misinformed.

Since it had been a Labour Party campaign promise, New Zealand's denial of port access to nuclear-capable warships was implicit policy when the party came to power in the summer of

1984. But the United States triggered a public test of the policy when it scheduled the USS Buchanan to visit New Zealand after a March ANZUS exercise. The US refused, as usual, to state whether the ship carried nuclear weapons. In testimony on AN-ZUS before the House Subcommittee on Asian and Pacific Affairs, the Deputy Assistant Defense Secretary James A. Kelley conceded that every American warship has the capacity to carry nuclear weapons and that:

> It would be unreasonable to expect the United States to ease an adversary's tracking and targeting problem by identifying which of our ships have the greatest capability. Identification or restriction of the area of movement and operations would increase the vulnerability of such ships and limit their usefulness. It would weaken deterrence and might increase our adversaries' temptation to resort to force, including the application of conventional military power.[6]

Interestingly, a Chinese official reported in April, 1985, that the United States had promised that its warships would not carry nuclear weapons when they visit China. If this is true, how paradoxical. Would the Reagan regime make such a deal with a former Communist enemy while treating New Zealand so rudely?

After deliberating for a month, the Lange administration refused port access to the USS Buchanan on February 4, 1985, and New Zealand became the first treaty member to deny port access to an American warship. Washington was outraged. Reagan, Weinberger, and Shultz expressed anger. Trade sanctions were considered in Congress and by the Chief Executive. The Reagan administration announced it would no longer share intelligence and surveillance information with its ANZUS partner. "It is time the Prime Minister [Lange] and his government face the realities of the situation," US Representative Molinari argued in the Subcommittee hearing,

> They say they made the gesture as a way of reducing the risk of nuclear war. Yet, do you reduce the risk of nuclear war by destroying a regional alliance that has kept the nuclear peace for four decades? Do you promote peace by denying military cooperation

to the one country in the world committed to, and most capable of, preserving that peace?[7]

The real concern seemed to be that a "ripple effect" would occur, with other nations following New Zealand's lead. Papau New Guinea and Japan have policies against port access for nuclear-weapons ships but have not strictly enforced them. Might they now? Considering the depth of antinuclear sentiment among the South Pacific island nations and even in Europe, would other bans be forthcoming? The resulting geographical patchwork would make it harder for American warships to pick their way through "protected" waters to "friendly" ports.

Is there a more devious strategy affecting US response to Lange's action? Retired US Navy Admiral Gene LaRoque, head of the Washington-based Center for Defense Information, told New Zealand in a television interview that "American strategy—and this is documented—is to keep the fighting as far as possible from the United States in hope that a 'limited' war can be fought and finished in a foreign theater without recourse to massive nuclear strikes between the United States and the Soviet Union."[8] One reason the US has overseas bases, especially in remote places, is to draw enemy fire from the US in the event of a nuclear exchange. New Zealanders know that any American bases—or warships in their harbors—make them a target of enemy fire.

Widespread support flooded New Zealand in the wake of the government's announced ban on warships. Support letters came from all over the world, and praise and approval sounded even in the Western bloc nations. A number of distinguished American clergymen contributed a statement approving New Zealand's stand to the record testimony of the House Subcommittee hearing on ANZUS. Other pro-Lange testimony was deposited with the Subcommittee, including a well-worded statement from the Friends Committee on National Legislation: "New Zealand's action is but one of many examples of the growing frustration around the world at the seeming inability of the superpowers to cure this addiction to more and more nuclear weapons."[9]

Within New Zealand support was widespread too. Three days after Lange announced the ban the administration received 7,000 letters and telegrams with nine of ten supporting the action. Polls conducted in February 1985 showed 65 percent national approval although 75 percent of the people wanted to remain in ANZUS. Clearly, New Zealanders like Americans. They want good relations with the United States. What they don't like is nuclear posturing and what they don't want is nuclear arms. A full-age ad in the *Washington Post* (11/5/84) titled, "A Letter to America from the People of New Zealand," referred to the Reagan administration's attempt to "undermine" New Zealand's nuclear-free policies:

> We believe such pressures are an affront to our status as a free and independent nation. They threaten the traditional friendship that exists between our countries. We call on the people of the United States to join us in working for a world free from the threat of nuclear war.

David Lange summed up the national mood in a speech before the United Nations Conference on Disarmament (Geneva, 3/5/85):

> My government will, indeed must, respond to the concern of New Zealanders about the continuing escalation of the nuclear arms race. We shall reflect, in our policies, their hopes and their determination that the nuclear weapons states will heed the calls which the international community has for so long made on them, and which in recent years have fallen on stony ground.
>
> The people and Government of New Zealand have rejected participation in the nuclear arms race. We do not say to any country in the world, do as New Zealand does; all we say is that when the opportunity is given to any country to pursue a serious and balanced measure of arms control, then that country has a duty to all of us to undertake that measure.

Where the Bombs Fell: Japan

The Japanese peace movement was galvanized by the March 1, 1954, "Bravo" hydrogen bomb test off Bikini Island. The American test irradiated the crew of a Japanese fishing boat, *The Lucky Dragon Five,* on that unlucky day and produced long-standing anger and resentment in Japan: the nation which had devastated Japanese cities in 1945 was at it again! This event coincided with the lifting of American military censorship on the films showing the horrible aftereffects and medical results of the Hiroshima and Nagasaki explosions. The resulting revulsion affected the Japanese government, which proceeded to draft the three non-nuclear principles of the Japanese constitution, banning the introduction, production, and storage of nuclear weapons in Japan.

Despite all this, and despite article nine of the Japanese constitution, which denounces war and prevents the development of a standing army, Japan's so-called "Self-Defense Force" is becoming a power in the Far East. The United States had discouraged the rearming of Japan after World War II. Now Washington wants to see a sizable increase in the Japanese military budget and is pressing Japan to assume a larger share in its defense. This approach is wrong. A sane approach would suggest that Japan poses no intrinsic threat to the Soviet Union. It is actually the 50,000 American troops stationed on 119 bases in Japan which make her a threat; indeed, a *target* for Soviet missiles! Without the American presence, Japan would be in a more secure position.

Japan's economy has grown by leaps and bounds since World War II, and Japan is looking for cheap labor and raw materials in the less developed countries. Her growing economic stake in the Pacific is threatened by anticolonial movements seeking autonomy for the island nations, especially Micronesia. Japan's uranium imports which are used in twenty-two nuclear power plants are challenged by the land use rights of indigenous peoples in Australia, South Africa, and the United States. Japan now gets 13 percent of her energy needs from nuclear power but shares the global problem of what to do with nuclear waste. She has alienated many Pacific people by proposing to dump "low-level" radioactive wastes in the ocean north of the Marianas Islands. The Pacific island peoples are opposed to the prospect of an increasingly contaminated ocean. There have been no "environmental impact studies," nor can there be any such studies, realistically, in such a vast area as the Pacific ocean. There is reason, however, to suspect harmful effects from the disposal of radioactive wastes anywhere.

By January 1, 1986, Japan boasted 638 Nuclear Free Zones—240 declared in 1984 alone—including Kyoto and most of the Tokyo districts. Kobe, Kiyose City, and Tokyo have declared their harbors off-limits to visiting military vessels thought to be carrying nuclear weapons. After Kobe City in 1975 required all foreign warships to certify that they were not carrying nuclear weapons, the number of visitors and tourists fell dramatically. Since this represents an economic loss for the city's merchants—when fewer American sailors shop in their stores—we must admire the Japanese commitment to peace. Actually, "working for peace in Japan is regarded as a civic duty," British historian E. P. Thompson writes. "In Nagasaki and Hiroshima the mayors regarded this work as the principle obligation of their office."

In June 1984, over one hundred leading citizens issued an appeal proposing that Japan adopt *five* non-nuclear principles: not to possess, produce, or permit the introduction of nuclear weapons on Japanese soil; but *also,* not to allow Japan to be used as a base from which to launch a nuclear attack, and to work for global disarmament. This came partly in response to the American decision to deploy 1,000 Tomahawk cruise missiles on ships and submarines over the next ten years. The cruise is easy to hide, practically undetectable, and could easily be carried on warships into Japanese ports. On October 21 and November 11, 1984, thousands demonstrated outside US bases.

The Japanese are very interested in peace developments elsewhere. When Stetson, Maine's Town Meeting voted on March 19, 1983 to become America's fourth Nuclear Free Zone (later revoked), the world's largest newspaper, *Asahi* of Tokyo (with 7,500,000 subscribers) sent its Washington correspondent to little Stetson for a first-hand account. And the Japanese have followed developments in Europe and the South Pacific wistfully. Many Japanese agree with Toshiyuki Toyoda, a Tokyo physics professor, who wrote recently, "As the only nation to have suffered nuclear disaster, what Japan needs to do is to recover its special influence on all nations including the United States, and thus to urge every country to pursue deliberate nonmilitaristic policies toward the abolition of nuclear weapons."[10]

Unfortunately, Japan is to a significant extent dependent on Washington, politically and economically. Time will tell whether Japan will follow New Zealand's lead and "tough it out" for peace; or, cave in to US demands and become a military partner in America's attempt to dominate the Pacific.

Life Among the Islanders

The South Pacific—these words evoke images of balmy breezes caressing palm-fringed atolls, happy native peoples, gentle warm waters lapping white beaches, mangos for the picking, inlets teeming with mullet and shellfish—a carefree idyllic existence.

This is no longer the case. These days one is just as likely to see a heavily armed warship docked near that palm-fringed island than an outrigger canoe. American military power is awesome and, some say, psychologically oppressive.

It is among the islanders that we find the second strong antinuclear force in the Pacific, the Nuclear Free and Independent Pacific Network. Unlike the South Pacific Forum, which is essentially an alliance of governments, the NFIP is a people's movement. The organization is trying to support and organize indigenous people in particular as they struggle for independence and autonomy against nuclearism. The NFIP has built a surprising solidarity across the vast island-dotted ocean, especially with the Micronesians and Polynesians. These people have been fragmented in the past, due largely to Western colonial policies, but "the times, they are a changin'." The NFIP has built transnational bridges and has created a cultural and political network among these people.

The Nuclear Free and Independent Pacific network has convened four international conferences, at Fiji (1975), Ponape, in

Micronesia (1978), Hawaii (1980), and Vanuatu (1983). The movement has supported Palau's nuclear free constitution and Vanuatu's denial of access for American warships.

Broadly, the NFIP continues to press towards the goal of a totally Nuclear Free Pacific. Its Vanuatu Conference (1983) declaration stated: "We strongly condemn the deployment of nuclear weapons systems into the Pacific, especially the Tomahawk cruise missile. We support the efforts of the Kwajalein landowners of the Marshall Islands to stop the MX and other missile testing on their lands and the restoration of the land to the rightful owners."

The Results of Nuclear Testing

How many Americans have heard of Kwajalein? How many could locate it on a map of the Pacific? Harold Jackson, a *Manchester Guardian* journalist, describes this part of the Marshall Islands as "the strangest looking South Sea island in the world, bristling with enormous radar dishes and radio antennae among the coconut palms. Its airstrip is capable of landing the world's largest aircraft and it houses a town of 3,000 expatriates which is so totally modelled on the American dream that, were it miraculously dropped overnight into the middle of Nebraska, no one there would notice a single thing out of the ordinary."[11]

The "expatriates" are American military personnel, scientists, and support workers. This is their "home on the range"—the missile-range, that is. The ocean between the southern tip of Kwajalein and nearby Lib Island is designated the "impact zone" for Intercontinental Ballistic Missiles fired from the California proving grounds. The Marshallese have been "relocated" to nearby Ebeye, where they have separate but hardly equal facilities—in terms of education, recreation, general lifestyle—as compared to the Americans on Kwajalein.

Kwajalein symbolizes the American military presence. There is no nuclear testing at Kwajalein, but within a year of Hiroshima, the United States began testing in the Marshall Islands of Micronesia which it administered as a UN Trust Territory. The

US conducted 66 atmospheric nuclear tests in the Marshall chain, at Bikini and Eniwetok between 1946 and 1958, and then 25 explosions at Johnson and Christmas Islands in the mid-Pacific, during 1958 and 1962.

We mentioned that in 1954 the United States conducted a hydrogen-bomb test at Bikini, code-named "Bravo." This was an ill-fated test! Malevolent winds blew radioactive particles eastward about 300 miles over Rongelap and Uturik Islands. Political scientist Michael Hamel-Green describes the results of "Bravo" in a publication of the Victorian Association for Peace Studies:

> Twelve years after the "Bravo" test, the cruel consequences began to appear. In 1966, 52 percent of the young people on Rongelap Island who had been under ten at the time of the test were found to have thyroid cancer or abnormalities. Twenty-two years after the test, 69 percent of the same group had developed thyroid tumors. Throughout the sixties and seventies, miscarriages, eye cataracts, birth defects, leukemia, and other health problems increased dramatically amongst the Marshall Islanders, even amongst those who had been exposed to extremely low levels of radiation. Over 2,000 islanders are now suing the American government for billions of dollars in damages.

> But the worst may still be to come. As Rosalie Bertell, an authority on the effects of low-level radiation, has warned, Marshall Islanders aged between 24 and 37 were subjected to a threefold radiation exposure: first, before conception, by the irradiation of their parents' reproductive organs; secondly, while they were embryos in utero; and thirdly, as young children, when they were many times more sensitive to radiation injury than adults. As a result, the children of victims of American testing in the Marshalls, and *their* children, will in turn become victims of the same tests, now long forgotten by most Americans and Australians. According to Bertell, these second and third generation victims will be twelve times more vulnerable to genetic damage, asthma, heart disease, arthritis, and diabetes than non-exposed populations.[12]

Are we treating the indigenous people as guinea pigs? A Lawrence Livermore Lab study on Bikini reported in 1971: "Bikini may be the only global source of data on humans where intake

via ingestion is thought to contribute the major fraction of plutonium body burden . . . It is possibly the best available source of
data for evaluating the transfer of plutonium across the gut wall
after being incorporated into biological systems."

In 1984, a team of American scientists determined that Bikini's soil has been contaminated to a depth of 16 inches or more.
Radioactive cesium-137, they said, has been lingering in the
earth and finding its way into fruits and coconuts. Some of the
islanders returned to Bikini in 1968 when President Johnson
sounded the all clear, but were evacuated again ten years later
when tests showed high levels of radioactivity in their bodies.
But now we are told that the island can be reclaimed—and for a
total cost of about $100,000,000. If nothing is done, according
to Jonathan Weisgall, who represents the Bikini litigants in federal court, it may take nature 125 years to do the job!

American guilt is shared with the British and French—there is
plenty to go around. The British ran twelve atmospheric tests in
Australia and nine at Christmas Island during the fifties. The
British tests, according to Hamel-Green, had deadly consequences for the servicemen who conducted them—many have
since died of cancer—and for many indigenous people living in
the fallout's path. "British and Australian cover-ups have so far
frustrated efforts to discover the full extent of this tragedy," he
writes.

After Algeria became independent, the French were unable to
continue nuclear testing in the Sahara so they turned to their
Polynesian colonies. They began atmospheric testing in 1966 at
Moruroa and Fangataufa, east of Fiji and Cook Islands. The
French ran forty-one atmospheric tests and switched to underground nuclear testing in 1975 only in response to a massive
international protest.

For years French tests at Murora sent clouds of radioactive
fallout drifting across the Pacific, contaminating food and water
supplies. Australia and New Zealand appealed to the World
Court, and union bans were enacted against French shipping in
the area. New Zealand's Labour Government in 1973 sent two

frigates to the French test area to focus international outrage on the scene. After several months of monitoring French explosions on Moruroa, Commander Tyrrell of HMNZS *Otago* concluded that New Zealand had achieved its aims: "It was the first time an eye-witness account of an explosion had been broadcast live by an outside party—in fact the news from the *Otago* was in advance of all other news outlets and the French nation itself first heard of the test from the *Otago's* broadcast."

Greenpeace, an international environmental action group, sent a plucky crew sailing into the French test area in 1972, and again in 1973. The idea was to anchor so close to the site of the explosion that the French wouldn't explode the bomb. But in 1972 the Greenpeace ship was rammed by a French minesweeper and towed to shore; and when a year later the intrepid Greenpeace crew returned to the site, French commandos jumped on board and beat up the crew members! The world was shocked by photographs of the unprovoked attack on civilians, evidence of the extent to which nuclear nations will go to protect their development and use of the Bomb. That shock has been magnified many times as a result of French agents' destruction of the Greenpeace flagship, *Rainbow Warrior,* in the Auckland harbor in 1985.

The French tests go on, underground now at Moruroa, with a total of over 100 explosions by the end of 1984, and Paris denies all charges about dangerous radiation. But Hamel-Green, using the French government's own figures, has found "ominous signs that cancer is on the increase in Polynesia, with evacuations for overseas cancer treatment rising dramatically from an average of 26 per year in 1975–77 to 75 per year in 1980–83." Ironically, the name Moruroa is Polynesian for "place of great secret."

All together, America, Great Britain, and France have exploded well over 200 nuclear bombs in the South Pacific. The UN International Commission on Radiological Protection reported in 1980 that the combined effects of this nuclear testing in the Southern Hemisphere will be to kill at least 15,000 people. Hamel-Green: "The Western Powers claim to be preparing for war against Russia; in fact they have already been making war on South Pacific people. The victims of nuclear testing may not carry labels saying they were killed by this or that particular test, but they are no less victims, their deaths no less agonizing, and the nuclear powers no less culpable."

Cancer is a dreadful result, but only one of many. Scientists predict that the ocean will gradually become more poisoned as the testing continues, with the radiation affecting the food chain and working itself up through the fish and shellfish of the region, to the point where it eventually contaminates the food of the Pacific islands as well as on our own tables!

The Pentagon and Palau:
Will US Strategic Interests Prevail?

Question: when does a vote never settle an issue? Answer: in the Republic of Palau (also, Belau). Voters in this tiny Pacific island group went to the polls on February 21, 1986, for the sixth time in six and a half years, to decide on a Compact of Free Association with the United States. At stake again was Palau's nuclear-free constitution which prohibits the use, testing, storage, or disposal of "harmful substances, such as nuclear, chemical, gas, or biological weapons intended for use in warfare, nuclear power plants, or waste materials therefrom." The vote this time was 72 percent for the Compact, up from 67 percent in September of 1984.

Nevertheless, President Salii badly wanting more American aid and trade, announced that the Compact has passed. To the contrary—the Palauan Supreme Court had ruled in favor the 75 percent provision two years ago. Now, in the summer of 1986, the Court ruled again ruled that the Compact violated Palau's constitution and that, lacking the prescribed 75 percent, the Compact could not be ratified. Unfortunately, the United States then forced another referendum on the Compact, set for December 15, 1986. Meanwhile the discussion and debate continues in two committees of the US Congress, and at the United Nations where the termination of the Pacific Islands Trust Territory has been approved by the Trusteeship Council but still lacks ratification by the Security Council. There the USSR may use its veto to block implementation of the US Compact of Free Association in Micronesia—what the Soviets like to call "neocolonialism."

Palau, the home for 15,000 people in the Western Pacific region known as Micronesia, is a luxuriant paradise. Its flora and fauna attract naturalists worldwide, and its sandy white beaches bring tourists. The islanders' fertile land provides abundant tara, coconut, and banana crops, and the rich fishing grounds help sustain the people. For the Palauans, the land and sea are a sacred trust they must preserve. As one chief expressed it, "We the people here do not need money. We need our land, we need our water, we need our ocean, and we need our people much more than money, much more than military bases, much more than nuclear weapons." A Palauan woman said, "We don't want any form of military to come. What's wrong with our life today? We go fishing and to our garden and get food and cook it. If you need some money you take vegetables to market. What's the matter with this?"

Japan fortified the Micronesians in the late thirties, telling the inhabitants that the bases it was building would protect them. Instead they proved to be a target for American invasions, bringing death and destruction to an innocent people with an ancient, stable lifestyle. Palau, in fact, was the scene of some of World War II's bloodiest fighting, where Japanese dug into caves in the rocks beat off continued assaults by US marines until they succumbed. One-half of Palau's population died during the war. This experience gave rise to the Palauan proverb, "When soldiers come, war comes," and influenced the islanders' decision to stay free of foreign military systems.

The United States became administrator of the Micronesians under a United Nations trusteeship in 1947. Under a mandate to bring the islanders to self-government, the US approved and partly funded a Constitutional Convention in April 1979, which drew up a constitution banning "harmful substances." Alarmed, the US State Department sent vigorous objections to the constitutional delegates, but the charter was adopted. Then US Ambassador Peter Rosenblatt traveled to Palau and in a closed-door session with the Palauan legislature, hammered out American objections.

In June of 1979, Palau's legislature voted to nullify both the proposed constitution as well as a referendum that had been scheduled for July 9, but a pro-constitution group took the issue to Palau's national court. Washington decided to back off temporarily, and the referendum was held, under UN scrutiny. On July 9, 1979, the nuclear-free constitution was ratified by a margin of 92 percent to 8 percent, despite warnings and threats made to UN observers and to voters.

Subsequently, the United States pressured the Palauan legislature to invalidate its new constitution, and American lawyers came in to "help" draft a new document. Another referendum was held in October, 1979, and the US-drafted constitution was rejected by 69 percent of the voters. In July 1980, the Palauans voted 78 percent in favor of the original nuclear-free constitution, and so the US forced additional votes, in February 1983, September 1984, and February 1986. Each time the US-supported pro-nuclear document (compact) failed to get a 75 percent majority.

The United States has pumped a lot of money into Palau to influence the voting. Palauan peace groups charge that possibly $100,000 in bribe money was distributed before the second referendum. One campaigner commented, "It was hard for us to tell our people not to accept the money, so we told them to accept the money and reject the US version of the Constitution." Other referenda attracted US dollars too: Patrick Smith, a former Portland attorney who became legal counsel to the Ibedul chief of Palau, wrote in *The Sunday Oregonian*[13] that the US poured $400,000 into voter "education" for the 1982 referendum. According to writer and peace activist Charlie Scheiner, who spent most of February 1986, in Palau, at the time of the referendum, the US spent $325,000 for voter education in the last campaign—over fifty dollars for every yes vote!

Other methods of influencing these votes were attempted. Patrick Smith fled Palau on August 16, 1983, after both his boat and his house had been firebombed! Two Palauan Supreme Court justices anxiously announced that they would not hear any testimony relating to the arrest of the guilty parties.

Previously, a confrontation had occurred in September of 1981, when one-fourth of the government workers, led by pro-US Palauan senators, went on strike, a strike which ended with the bombing of the President's home. The (pro-constitution) President was able to restore order even though strikers took over the local radio station and the US offered to send in the Marines from Guam! Robert Aldridge, who conducted a fact-finding visit to Palau following this event, charged that "the riot was obviously provoked by outside interests," which were "attempting to set the stage for a US presence."

The American government also may have tried to cloud the wording of the ballot issue before it was presented in the February 10, 1983 referendum. The Pacific Concerns Resource Center in Honolulu charged that the wording was dictated by the US State Department, and that it was "completely misleading," in the words of international law authority Roger Clark. Only after the issue was taken to court by two Palauan senators was the wording made unambiguous. University of Santa Clara Law Professor Howard Anawalt said that the US-dictated language would have suggested to voters that a vote for approval of the nuclear provision "is a vote in favor of placing restrictions and conditions on radioactive, chemical, and biological materials, when in fact it does the contrary."

There is enough substance in these allegations of US misconduct to add up to this: the American government wants Palau in its camp badly! There are several factors that contribute to this. In the light of a possible eventual loss of the major US bases at Clark and Subic Bay in the Philippines, the Pentagon wants another option. Palau, less than 500 miles away, seems attractive. The Pentagon wants to bring nuclear warships into Palau's natural deepwater harbors. Palau's coasts are desired for training maneuvers involving landing craft and assault troops.

Although the most recent version of the US-Palau pact did not specify the storage of weapons on Palau, it would open Palauan waters and ports to US nuclear-armed vessels. It would provide the US with land for two air bases, a naval base, and a jungle warfare training ground. In addition, with only sixty days notice, the US could take more land if it wished.

American officials think they will have their way with Palau. Significantly, the name given to the main road at the Trident submarine base in Puget Sound, Washington, is "Palau Road." The contest seems unequal: the world's most powerful nation versus a tiny group of atolls. But the antinuclear movement in Palau is gutsy and vigorous and related to a nonviolent philosophy of life. There was little public opposition to the US-sponsored compact before the last referendum. In this consensus society it is considered "un-Micronesian" to make waves on divisive issues, according to Charlie Scheiner. But people like Palauan attorney Roman Bedor continue the struggle against militarism (here quoted by Scheiner):

> In 1981, with the formation of our Republic, we have, for the first time in 400 years, declared that we are a sovereign people. And we are throwing that away! When we made our constitution the central issue was the protection of the lands. Nuclear-free was one element, but even without nuclear weapons, Free Association will not benefit us. We are fighting this from the same perception as the American Indian—it denies our rights as a people. The whole operation of the military must be seen as a threat to our life.

The nonviolence of the Palauans is real and profound. In August 1981, sixteen Palauans traveled to Japan to attend ceremonies at Hiroshima and Nagasaki, and they sang several songs they had written. "No matter what you did to us, we are still your friends," they sang to a rally of 10,000 people in one of the two nations that had destroyed their islands during World War II. The Japanese wept with them.

There is hope for Palau in its battle with Goliath. The United States has spent thousands on "voter education" in the islands but still hasn't secured the 75 percent majority it wants to revise or neutralize Palau's constitution. Palau's struggle against Goliath is being widely publicized by the Nuclear Free and Independent Pacific movement and other peace groups. Overt and covert attempts to influence Palauan voting are being reported, giving Palau higher profile worldwide and raising questions everywhere about American motives, and whether the United States really believes in the right of self-determination for these islands.

In a letter written for the American peace network, Charlie Scheiner writes,

> It started to rain two hours before the polls closed on February 21, 1986. As the downpour continued and the vote-counting began, one Palauan told me, "Here we believe that a heavy rain washes away problems, allowing us to start over again. Maybe this rain will wash away the Compact for good, and we can get on with our independence."

The issue remains in doubt. Will the United States finally prevail in yet another referendum. Will the people of Palau have to keep voting until they come up with the "right" result?

Washington is worried. Palau's ultimate victory over American military interests would impress the world. Worse, in Washington's view, it could be contagious: if this tiny nation prevails over the nuclear collossus, other nations will take heart. Others will take courage. Farmers and fisherfolk, traders and local officials determined to save the Pacific for their children and grandchildren will look again at the grave implications of a strategic alliance with the United States.

Indeed, the goal of a totally non-nuclear Pacific, from Alaska to Hawaii, Japan, and New Zealand, will seem attainable.

7

Addressing the Bench: Legal Issues

"The law will never make men free; it is men who have got to make the law free. They are the lovers of law and order who observe the law when the government breaks it."

—Henry David Thoreau

"Things which are manifestly iniquitous are not to be done, even though commanded by the King."

—Hugo Grotius, 1625

"(AP) Washington, DC, June 23, 1989: In an unprecedented and far-reaching decision, the US Supreme Court today declared the federal government's nuclear weapons policy unconstitutional. The Court ordered all nuclear weapons research and manufacturing to end within 90 days and directed the President to draw up conversion plans immediately.

"The decision came as a result of the legal challenge mounted by several towns in Massachusetts to a declaration by that state's attorney general that their Nuclear Free Zone bylaws were unconstitutional. Speaking for a unanimous Court, Chief Justice Rehnquist's opinion cited international law and the 'common interests of humanity' among other arguments to support its decision."

Fanciful? Certainly. But there is a potential conflict between local and federal authorities. Nuclear Free Zone proponents will get their day in court. The conflict will not really be *decided* in the courts, for it is the people who will make the ultimate decision, one way or another, on nuclear weapons—but it will be adjudicated.

Some federal officials view the existence of Nuclear Free Zones as a threat. As NFZs proliferate in response to the proliferation of weapons, officials may feel more threatened. The Zones are not an attempt by local government to make national foreign policy, as some charge, but they do question that policy, indeed, *challenge it*. Washington will use legal tactics to challenge the challenge.

Are Nuclear Free Zones legal? Do they interfere with the federal government's warmaking powers, impede interstate commerce, deny Washington the right to "provide for the common defense?" The attorney of the state of Massachusetts declared local NFZ bylaws "unconstitutional." So did the city attorney for Portland, Oregon. Are they right?

We shall explore this question, to the extent possible without a definitive federal court decision. Nuclear Free Zones are just beginning to be tested in courts and there has not been any federal law passed regarding them. But there is sufficient legal precedent to permit a judgment as to their legality.

This, however, begs another critical question: are nuclear *weapons* themselves legal? We may discover—surprise!—that the illegal actor is the federal government, and not the towns and cities passing NFZ legislation. This broader issue will be saved for the last half of the chapter. First, as to the legality of Nuclear Free Zones, the experience of Amherst, Massachusetts provides a lens through which we can view the issues.

Town Meeting Democracy Thwarted?

May 17, 1984: Amherst, in town meeting assembled, passes a Nuclear Free Zone bylaw. September 6, 1984: Massachusetts Attorney General Francis Bellotti strikes down Amherst's bylaw, holding it unconstitutional. August 13, 1984: the Amherst Selectmen adopt a "policy" to substitute for the bylaw, Nuclear Free Zone signs are posted on roads controlled by the town, and a non-nuclear contracting policy is urged on the Town Manager.

None of these actions are subject to review by the attorney general.

Amherst is an intellectual enclave nestled in a bucolic western Massachusetts valley. Three colleges lie within its borders: Amherst, Hampshire, and a branch of the University of Massachusetts (UMass). Hampshire College has an anti-apartheid, anti-nuclear weapons investment policy, and UMass has banned classified research since 1972. Strong humanitarian, antinuclear sentiment on the campuses merged with local activism to produce a May 1982 town meeting vote in favor of the Bilateral Nuclear Freeze proposal. Citizens for a Nuclear Free Amherst and the Amherst Disarmament Coalition decided to push it another step—to make Amherst a declared, functioning, nuclear-free community.

Article 65, as the measure was called, would prohibit research, testing, manufacture, storage, and transportation of nuclear weapons or their components within town limits. Also, it would preclude the town's investing in or contracting with nuclear weapons firms. Immediately, questions arose. Would Amherst buy word processing equipment from IBM, a nuclear weapons firm, for the schools and town hall? Local officials decided to table the matter pending passage of the bylaw and/or ruling by the state attorney general. City planning director James Lindstrom said that the bylaw's effect on the town's financial policy would be "minimal," but some contracts would have to be reviewed and investments in US treasury notes reconsidered.

Article 65 also provided for a "Nuclear Free Amherst Committee," consisting of five residents, which would have these functions (here paraphrased): (1) Review any work within the town which it has reason to believe is not in compliance with the Act, and inform appropriate authorities; (2) review existing town contracts, investments, and so forth to check on compliance; (3) propose a socially responsible investment policy; (4) maintain resource materials on conversion and alternate sources of funding for civilian industry and socially productive research, available to local businessmen and to the public.

The proposal drew flak. Opponents argued that it was conceived in a "political vacuum," that a nuclear-free policy failed to recognize the intransigence of the Soviets and other realities of the cold war world. In addition, they raised objections in light of the federal war powers, First Amendment rights governing research and the reporting of same, and other legal matters. But the NFZ proponents were equally passionate. Medical personnel, for example, spoke of the fearful medical consequences of nuclear war. Robert Gage, a physician heading the UMass Division of Public Health, said that the proliferation of nuclear weapons represents "an epidemic of unprecedented proportions . . . We are talking about the impending dissolution of the world!"

Such statements were made at an explosive public hearing called by the Amherst Selectmen for April 26, 1984. Other comments made at the hearing, taken from notes made by the Select Board secretary, follow:

. . . a physician said that since there will be no escape in a nuclear war, we have to focus our energy on prevention and recovering moneys being stolen from health and welfare programs to feed the war machine.

. . . a psychologist spoke of the many patients suffering from depression due to their nuclear fears. One path out of depression is community action—a feeling of solidarity in supporting one another to make the world safe.

. . . a homeowner pointed out that the military budget had tripled since 1977, and the federal budget for education had been cut a billion dollars a year since President Reagan took office. "This town lives and breathes education. Every time we make a bomb we take money out of this town!"

. . . an apartment-dweller remembered 1945 when the bomb went off, and Americans felt exhilarated "because we had so much power!" Twenty years later his youngest son was born and he thought of what he could do to lessen the chance of nuclear catastrophe. The question is both a liberal and conservative issue, he said, and "we must come to the realistic conclusion that if we ever have a nuclear war there will be no institutions to be conservative about."

. . . a woman from the Yiddish Book Exchange said that it was a special community that could stand up and demand a morally just world. "We have an opportunity to act as responsibly as a town can to make an investment that makes sense."

. . . an attorney congratulated those who planned the hearing and said that he wanted his children to survive him, and "this is a first step in that direction!"

In the smaller Massachusetts communities, any registered voter may participate in a Town Meeting, but in a town the size of Amherst representatives are elected from the various precincts, and they do the voting. In Town Meeting on May 17, 1984, the delegates voted in favor of Amendment 65 by 101 to 60. A weakening substitute motion failed, 86 to 76. Thunderous applause from the many NFZ supporters in the hall greeted the bylaw's passage. But some restrained their joy, fearing a negative ruling by the state attorney general.

Indeed, Attorney General Francis Bellotti overruled the bylaw three and a half months later, with similar measures from other towns. Mr. Bellotti held that Amendment 65 was unconstitutional. "This would result in the 'balcanization' of the nation," he said, "it would result in the federal government losing control of its foreign policy and would deprive Congress of its warmaking power."

Consider the objections raised by the attorney general and others to Amherst's Amendment 65, as well as by opponents of Nuclear Free Zones around the nation.

"Provide for the Common Defense"

Article I, Section 8 of the Constitution states that Congress shall, "provide for the common defense and general welfare of the United States," and shall be authorized to declare war and to raise an army, navy, and militia.

The "common defense" argument appealed to some Amherst citizens. "I've been opposed (to the NFZ) from the very beginning," Amherst Selectman Frederick Steinbeck was quoted in the Boston *Globe* (7/2/84). "It seems to me we are taking the defense of the United States on our shoulders . . . Why don't we take on Mars and Saturn while we're at it?" The editor of a new, free-distribution paper, *The Sentinel,* remarked that having taken on the policies of national defense, Amherst no doubt would be soon forming its own Department of State, sending ambassadors to the UN, and placing orders with the local tailor for striped pants!

In his letter to the town clerk of Tisbury, Massachusetts, assistant attorney general O'Connell contended that Nuclear Free Zone measures did infringe on the government's national defense prerogative. In a very detailed memorandum on New Clear Vision's attempt to make Portland, Oregon, nuclear-free, city attorney Christopher P. Thomas contended, "these provisions give Congress exclusive power to determine national defense policies and to select the weapons with which the armed forces are equipped." He went on to discuss the history of nuclear arms production in this country, including the Atomic Energy Act, concluding, "In light of this history, the courts would not uphold a local ordinance intended to frustrate the federal policy of nuclear weapons proliferation."

But other lawyers disagree. The Tenth Amendment grants all powers to the states which have not been specifically reserved to the federal government. In most states (and pursuant to the Home Rule Amendment in Massachusetts), local communities have the power to legislate regarding public health and safety. NFZ proponents argue that this is what they are attempting to do: such legislation is an attempt to protect the community from the health hazards of nuclear weapons production or war. Michele L. Leaf, attorney for Citizens for a Nuclear Free Amherst, wrote in a thorough, thoughtful memorandum:

> The War Powers established in the Constitution are not without limits. They have never been held to completely preempt local zoning laws. The Constitution does not give weapons manufacturers the unlimited power to produce weapons, not does it forbid a town from regulating or prohibiting the manufacture of specified war materials within its borders.

But the "preemption doctrine," based upon the Supremacy Clause of the Constitution, Article VI, cl. 2, holds in general that where federal and state laws conflict, federal law prevails.

However, two recent Supreme Court decisions tend to support the case for NFZs. In 1976, the state of California declared a moratorium on new nuclear power plants due to storage and waste disposal concerns. Two electric utility companies sued, contending that the Atomic Energy Act of 1954 preempted the moratorium. The US Supreme Court disagreed, holding that the state's right to regulate utility companies in the interests of public health and safety was substantial. In the Karen Silkwood case, her father brought suit against Kerr-McGee to recover damages for the contamination his daughter had suffered working with plutonium as a laboratory analyst in 1974. The Supreme Court reversed a lower court on the question of punitive damages, holding that such an award was not preempted by federal law.

In a third case, the Supreme Court declined to review a decision by the Second Circuit Court against the New York City Board of Health, which had in 1981 banned the shipment of high-level radioactive materials through the city. The court held that the US Department of Transportation's ruling had preempted the city regulation. But since the US Supreme Court failed to review the case, it left the other federal courts free to disagree with the Second Circuit in other cases. Remember that a District Court had ruled in New York's favor before the federal government appealed the case to the Second Circuit.

Attorney Michele Leaf indicates that where state and federal laws exist on the same subject, there is no definitive formula for testing their validity. "State laws have been found unconstitutional (a) if they clearly conflict with federal law, (b) if Congress has clearly expressed its intent to preempt state authority, or (c) if Congress has enacted such a pervasive scheme of federal regulation that its intent to preempt can be inferred."

In sum, local zoning laws are not necessarily preempted by federal regulations. Nuclear-free legislation does not assume any power to provide for the common defense, nor does it seek to benefit from the nuclear defense "umbrella." The Nuclear Free Zone resolution may specify that a community *does not want* to be defended by nuclear weapons. And we can argue that, far from providing for the common defense, the government's nuclear program, together with that of the Soviets', represents a *suicide pact*. There is no defense against nuclear weapons and there is none in the offing, "Star Wars" notwithstanding.

At any rate, Congress can override the effect of an NFZ through specific legislation. It has not done so. Until or unless it does, we assume legality.

The Commerce Clause

Article I, Section 8 of the US Constitution also gives Congress the authority to "regulate commerce . . . among the several states." Some have challenged Nuclear Free Zones on this basis, but Portland city attorney Thomas, as a result of careful study, concluded that NFZs did not affect interstate commerce. They prohibit certain activity outright and make no distinction between interstate and intrastate commerce. As the Department of Energy indicated in a letter to Nuclear Free America, ". . . the United States government is the sole manufacturer of nuclear weapons. Government contracts are established or awarded with private industry . . . but all products or research is owned by the government." If the government owns all products and research related to nuclear weapons then commerce—in the usual sense of the competitive marketplace—is clearly not involved.

The First Amendment Issue

In part, the First Amendment prevents the federal government, and the states through the Fourteenth Amendment, from curtailing free speech. Opponents of nuclear-free legislation, especially in Amherst and Cambridge, stretched this guarantee to argue that any ban on academic research is unconstitutional. They contended that under the First Amendment, scholars should be free to pursue academic research unhindered by political considerations. Not only is the reporting of research constitutionally protected, but also the research itself—because any research is a form of "inquiry" necessary to advocacy.

Amherst activists questioned whether there is such a thing as "pure" research, or objective research without political overtones. They pointed out that the Act was worded to exclude legitimate research, "unclassified research the specific purpose of which is other than the development of nuclear weapons or components thereof," as well as "the research and application of nuclear medicine," and "uses of fissionable materials for smoke detectors, light-emitting watches and clocks and other applications in non-weapons related activities."

Many persons at the controversial public meeting in Amherst sensed the difficulty of attempting to separate research from politics, knowledge from morality. One citizen who had spent two unhappy years in the Pentagon said, "Academic freedom has to be matched with responsibility for the betterment of life." Another said it was not a question of academic freedom "but of weighing the potential harm against the potential benefit . . . . From a citizen and community point of view and an environmental point of view, the potential danger far outweighs the potential benefit to the few who may benefit from a nuclear weapons-related experiment."

To argue that a ban on weapons research is unconstitutional is to argue the untenable, that a person has a First Amendment right to develop and build nuclear weapons. The stronger argument is ours, that preventing a community from taking an antinuclear stand is a denial of its First Amendment right to expression!

Nuclear Free Zones are Legal!

Just as a number of towns and cities have considered and rejected their role in civil defense plans for nuclear war, so many are now rejecting their role of complicity with the nuclear arms race. The federal government has taken no action against those cities and six states which have rejected civil defense plans. Neither has it taken any action against Nuclear Free Zone communities. Again, if federal action is absent, we assume that Nuclear Free Zones are legal.

Nuclear Free America has developed some guidelines and suggestions for drawing up an ordinance or bylaw. Wording is critical, as any lawyer knows. Generally an ordinance includes sections on "Findings" (the rationale), "Prohibitions," "Exclusions," "Enforcement," "Severability," and "Notification." Often sections on "Nuclear Free Investment and Contracts" may be added, and "Economic Conversion." The placement and maintenance of Nuclear Free Zone signs may be specified as well. Detailed notes on the wording of such an ordinance are available from Nuclear Free America or from nuclear-free communities. (Note the sample ordinances in the Appendix.)

In addition to the *defensive* arguments that Nuclear Free Zones do not interfere with constitutional powers reserved to the federal government, a strong case can be made for Zones *conforming to international law* in a way that federal policies do not.

International Law

"Look, if you give them a nuclear freeze, the next thing you know they'll want to outlaw nuclear war altogether!" So goes the caption in a provocative Joseph Farris cartoon.

Actually the legal basis already exists, as Lucile W. Green indicates, "for prohibiting weapons of mass destruction such as the nuclear, biological, and chemical devices of modern warfare. The very same governments that are now manufacturing, stockpiling, and threatening to use them have, by their own covenants, treaties and international laws, declared them illegitimate."[1] If the leaders of today's nuclear states were tried under these laws they would be convicted as "war criminals" for preparing a nuclear holocaust that will make World War II seem like child's play. A Japanese court in the Shimoda case of 1963 concluded that the United States had violated international law in the atomic bombing of Hiroshima and Nagasaki. Although the court denied compensation to the five survivors seeking damages for their injuries, this was a unique attempt by a national court to examine the legality of nuclear weapons.

The US Constitution (Article VI) states that treaties made by the United States "shall be the supreme law of the land." The Supreme Court confirmed this in *The Paquette Habana* (1900), holding that "International Law is part of our law and must be ascertained and administered by the courts of justice of appropriate jurisdiction . . ."

But, you say, there are no treaties specifically banning nuclear weapons—therefore nuclear weapons are legal. This is a popular notion and the view held by the US military. For example, from a US government-prepared field manual, Article 613 of the Law of Naval Warfare: "There is at present no rule of international law expressly prohibiting states from the use of nuclear weapons in warfare. In the absence of such express prohibition, the use of such weapons against enemy combatants and other military objectives is permitted."[2] A decision of the Permanent Court of International Justice in 1927 seems to support this notion: states are free to do "what they are not strictly forbidden from doing."

Others, however, argue this point. The opinion of the Nuremberg Tribunal suggests the law governing warfare is not only to be found in treaties, but "in customs and practices of states which gradually obtained universal recognition" and in "general principles of justice." Long ago, the "Martens Clause" of the 1907 Hague Convention made the "laws of humanity and the dictates of public conscience" applicable to unforeseen situations in which new weapons may be contemplated. Thus a treaty specifically banning such weapons is unnecessary. Today's mega-death warheads so blatantly violate international law that only a treaty *excluding* them from the law could possibly justify their use!

What are the sources of international law? Elliott L. Meyrowitz, executive director of The Lawyers Committee on Nuclear Policy, identifies them as

. . . treaties, custom, general principles of law, judicial decisions and the writing of qualified publicists. Particularly relevant are the many treaties and conventions limiting the use of weapons in war, decreeing the fundamental distinction between combatant and noncombatant, and establishing the principles of humanity as a source of international law, including the prohibition of weapons and tactics that are especially cruel and cause unnecessary suffering.[3]

Relevant treaties and conventions include but are not limited to the following:

(1) THE DECLARATION OF ST. PETERSBURG, 1868, which declares that the only legitimate object of war "is to weaken the military forces of the enemy," that weapons of mass destruction are "contrary to the laws of humanity," and that the right to inflict injury on the enemy is "not unlimited."

(2) THE HAGUE CONVENTIONS, 1899 and 1907, expressly forbid poisons, "arms, projectiles or material calculated to cause unnecessary suffering," as well as "wanton and indescriminate destruction." Article 1 of the Hague Convention V of 1907 declares, "The territory of neutral powers is inviolable." Radioactive fallout cannot be contained by the belligerent's borders but will spread worldwide, contaminating the Swedens and the Switzerlands as well as the combatants.

(3) THE 1925 GENEVA PROTOCOL to the Peace Treaty with Germany condemns "the use in war of poisonous gases, and all analagous liquids, materials or devices." Radioactive fallout is technically not such a "gas" but would spread in a similar fashion, and as the Shimoda court declared, ". . . the pain brought by the atomic bombs is severer than that from poison and poison gas, and we can say that the act of dropping such a cruel bomb is contrary to the fundamental principle of the laws of war that unnecessary pain must not be given."

(4) THE KELLOGG-BRIAND PACT, 1928, signed by the US and forty-two nations, condemns recourse to war for the solution of international disputes, renounces war as an instrument of national policy, and agrees that all conflicts should be settled by pacific means.

(5) THE GENOCIDE CONVENTION, 1948, prohibits the murder, extermination or intentional destruction in whole or in part of a national, ethnic, racial or religious group.

(6) THE GENEVA CONVENTIONS OF 1949, as well as the 1977 PROTOCOLS ON HUMANITARIAN LAW APPLICABLE IN ARMED CONFLICT, firmly establish the distinction between combatant and noncombatant which the Red Cross holds to be the key rule of warfare. (The fact that nuclear explosions make no distinction is not lost on the nuclear powers, none of which have ratified Protocol I.)

> Protocol I espouses principles that, reasonably construed, support conclusions of nuclear illegality. For example, Article 51 provides that civilians must not be subject to attack, that indiscriminate attacks against civilians are prohibited and that attacks intended to spread terror among civilians are prohibited . . . Article 54 prohibits the deliberate destruction of objects indispensible to the survival of the civilian population such as food producing areas, crops, livestock, and irrigation works. Article 55 prohibits the use of means or methods of warfare that may be expected to cause widespread and severe damage to the environment. And, Article 56 prohibits destruction of works or installations containing dangerous forces such as dams, dikes, or nuclear generating stations.[4]

Conventional weapons injure civilians or noncombatants inadvertently and occasionally, but nuclear weapons will do it consistently and massively. Political scientist John Fried:

> It is scurrilous to argue that it is still *forbidden* to kill a *single* enemy civilian with a *bayonet,* or wantonly destroy a *single* building on enemy territory by *machine-gun* fire—but that it is *legitimate* to kill *millions* of enemy noncombatants and wantonly to destroy entire enemy cities, regions, and perhaps countries (including cities, areas, or the entire surface of *neutral* States) by nuclear weapons.[5]

(7) THE UNITED NATIONS CHARTER, 1945, imposes a legal duty upon all states to refrain from force or the threat of force. In 1961 the UN General Assembly voted 55–20, with 26 abstentions, to declare that "any state using nuclear or thermonuclear weapons is to be considered as violating the Charter of the United Nations, as acting contrary to the laws of humanity, and as committing a crime against mankind and civilization."

Unhappily the US and other NATO nations opposed the resolution while the USSR and its allies supported it. Other UN resolutions followed, including a 1983 resolution passed 95–19, with 30 abstentions, "resolutely, unconditionally, and for all time" condemning nuclear war, as well as those political and military doctrines intended to provide legitimacy for the first use of nuclear weapons. This too was opposed by the Western nuclear powers.

Legal scholar Burns H. Weston points to a basic inconsistency in the Western powers' policy. They seem determined to block any and all attempts to brand nuclear weapons as *per se* illegal. But the military manuals of the US and UK, at least, "instruct that nuclear weapons are to be judged according to the same standards that apply to other weapons in armed conflict."[6] These standards, as we've seen, preclude nuclear weapons.

Consider also that the fundamental principle guiding any rules of warfare, the whole basis for them, in fact, is the notion that war is an abnormal event, an interruption in human affairs. After the peace is secured, the society needs to return to normal as soon as possible. This is the reason for rules against weapons of unmitigated terror that cause unnecessary suffering, disproportionate damage, or ecological disaster. Nuclear war fails the test completely. It will devastate civilization and it might well destroy the fabric of life. It would not be possible to "return to normal."

Nuremberg Principles of 1946

The principles arising from the Nuremberg "War Criminals" trial following World War II, deserve special attention. The trial was based on the Charter of the International Military Tribunal, recognized by the UN General Assembly as a source of international law.

The Nuremberg Principles condemn "Crimes Against Peace," the "planning, preparation, initiation or waging of a war of aggression," which certainly precludes a first-strike nuclear policy; "War Crimes," having to do with violating the laws and customs of war, such as "the wanton destruction of cities, towns or villages, or devastation not justified by military necessity"; and "Crimes Against Humanity," involving "inhumane acts" committed against any civilian population before or during a war, whether or not they violate the domestic laws of the country in which they are perpetrated. So, the Nazi extermination of Jews was criminal even though it was legal according to Hitler's regime. The same logic makes the preparation for nuclear war criminal even though perfectly legal in the US and USSR!

The Nuremberg Tribunal addressed the abdication of moral responsibility by supposedly decent, civilized people. In Nazi Germany, the death trains rumbled to the crematoria and nobody looked, nobody saw. Nobody wanted to know. Those who knew denied responsibility too. "I just carried out orders," they said.

So the unique principle declared at Nuremberg was that individuals are accountable for the misdeeds of nations. When Frederick Flick and other German industrialists and Nazi officials told the Tribunal that war crimes were affairs of states—and they had no personal guilt in the matter—they were told otherwise. Individuals are obligated to act—even against governments—to uphold the law. "International law, as such, binds every citizen just as does ordinary municipal law. Acts adjudged criminal when done by an officer of the government are criminal when done by a private individual."

According to this standard, every American has the duty, in political scientist Richard Falk's words, "to fulfill the Nuremberg obligation." Anyone who is aware that serious crimes against humanity are being contemplated has to take what action he or she can to prevent those crimes from being committed.

Today, the death trains rumble through our towns, and across the rolling hills and mountains of America. Nobody looks, nobody sees, nobody wants to know how many trains carry how many warheads targeting how many cities with how many deaths. But some persons feel an obligation to act. Consider, as an example, Barbara Katt and John LaForge, "The Sperry Software Pair."

On August 20, 1984, dressed as quality-control inspectors, Katt and LaForge entered a Sperry Corporation building at Egan, Minnesota, and damaged two prototype computers designed to provide guidance and navigation for Trident missile submarines and F4G fighter-bombers. At their trial LaForge charged that the US in its nuclear policy was guilty of breaking the Nuremberg Principles. Interviewed later, he said, "The Nuremberg Principles make it clear that the German people and Japanese people should have been disobedient . . . Nuremberg also said that simple planning and preparation of illegal warfare is a crime—even short of the war, it's a crime!" So, he argued, if the government is preparing for an illegal nuclear war, individuals have a personal obligation to try to stop it.

Unique among jurists who generally protect the nuclear industry, Judge Miles Lord heard their entire case and gave the pair suspended sentences. The judge said nothing about Nuremberg in his opinion, but asked,

> What is so sacred about a bomb, so romantic about a missile? Why do we condemn and hang individual killers while extolling the virtues of warmongers? What is the fatal fascination which attracts us to the thought of mass destruction of our brethren in another country? How can we even entertain the thought that all people on one side of an imaginary line must die and, if we be so ungodly cynical as to countenance that thought, have we given thought to the fact that in executing that decree we will also die? Who draws these lines and who has so decreed?

In light of the unprecedented threat to the planet, almost nothing anyone does to protest or stop the insanity seems unreasonable. But some peacemakers cannot in conscience support the use of trespass or the destruction of property to try to stop the arms race. Again, Nuclear Free Zones offer us a chance to challenge nuclear policy at the local level—where, even if we are not physically destroying the weapons, we can withdraw funding from firms that serve and build the bomb. Awareness of the Bomb's criminal status gives muscle to our cause.

Counterforce and Countervalue

But the bomb's defenders have a rebuttal. They say yes, counter*value* nuclear strategy may well violate international law, but counter*force* strategy does not. The difference, again, is that countervalue strategy, or Mutual Assured Destruction, the policy of deterrence that we have been following for years, says to your adversary, "If you attack us, we'll respond with nuclear strikes on your population centers. Millions will die—so don't start anything!" Counterforce strategy, instead, targets military installations and nuclear delivery systems—missile silos, submarines, bombers, and so forth. The Reagan administration's point is that a counterforce strategy is immoral, if not illegal, since it would kill millions of civilians. Counterforce strategy, using accurate "surgical" strikes against military targets, would greatly limit the casualties to noncombatants.

Logical? Perhaps. Two serious issues remain unsettled. One is that, as Weston writes, "'Clean bombs' and 'surgical' strikes, especially in retaliation to strategic warfare, exist more in the minds of military planners than they do in reality."[7] Counterforce targeting is probably not as accurate as the military claims. After all, strategic ballistic missiles have never been tested over the courses they would take in a war—a north-south trajectory over the North pole instead of the east-west firing range currently in use. Further, granting a fair degree of accuracy, there will still be millions of deaths in a war involving counterforce strategies. An Office of Technology Assessment Study in 1979 quotes other studies by the government that indicate some two to twenty million Americans would be killed within thirty days after a Soviet attack on US ICBM silos—from the early fallout, which excludes all the residual effects. The same for the USSR, in spades. The Soviets have more military facilities located close to population centers. There are said to be sixty-two military objectives that American strategic planners have targeted within Moscow!

Obviously, counterforce is no more legal than a countervalue strategy, or MAD. *Both are mad.*

Possession and/or Threat to Use Versus Use

Many well-meaning people argue, "Yes, nuclear war would be terrible. The use of nuclear weapons, in fact, may well be a crime against humanity. But we need to possess them to keep the peace. We've prevented war by deterrence for all of these years! Surely there's a difference between use and mere possession!"

The Nuremberg Principles suggest otherwise. Conspiracy to commit crimes against humanity is proscribed, and must be resisted by individuals. The Genocide Convention, Article I, makes it criminal to *conspire, incite, or attempt* to commit genocide. Some antinuclear treaties specifically prohibit *preparation,* i.e., deployment: the 1959 Antarctica Treaty, the 1963 Partial Test Ban Treaty, and the 1967 Outer Space Treaty, for example.

Take a closer look at the distinction between possession and/or threat versus actual use. Deterrence ("If you attack us we'll wipe you out!") is paradoxical. In effect, the argument makes it somehow appear proper to prepare to do—or threaten to do—that which would be unlawful if it were actually done. But moral logic suggests that if the deed itself is illegal it is illegal to plan the deed—in the case of deadly weapons, to *possess* the weapons. As a practical matter, we have laws against carrying a concealed (or unconcealed) deadly weapon because the possession of such a weapon in public constitutes a threat to the public. Even if you concede the sanity and goodwill of the bearer, the weapon may discharge accidentally. The result? With a pistol, one death; with a nuclear warhead, at least thousands.

In addition to Nuremberg, the Genocide Convention, and the aforesaid treaties, consider the following point by Daniel J. Arbess, of the Lawyer's Committee on Nuclear Policy, New York.[8] Even if the deterrence policy justifies threatening with nuclear weapons, nuclear threats have not been restricted to that particular purpose. From the days when it had a monopoly on nuclear weapons, the United States has protected its interests abroad by threatening to use nuclear weapons in a variety of cases—and not just in retaliating to a raid on the United States. Joel Kovel states it baldly: "Without having once been actually dropped over an enemy city since 1945, nuclear weapons have been made the keystone of Western global policy."[9] The Cuban missile crisis and Vietnam are the obvious examples, but, by Kovel's count, Washington has threatened nuclear strikes on twenty-two occasions. President Carter's announced intention to fight, if necessary, for Mideast oil included a thinly veiled nuclear warning. "Administration after administration has insouciantly shown itself willing to threaten life on earth in order to advance American power," Kovel writes.

Arbess calls this a policy of "extended deterrence." He adds, "In addition to expanding the range of circumstances in which the United States is engaged in preparations to use nuclear weapons, extended deterrence increases the degree of preparedness—the promise that its threats will be carried out—to an almost irrevocable level."[10] At the battlefield level, the integration of nuclear artillery within conventional forces will make it necessary to "use it or lose it" in case your position is in danger of being overrun. At the strategic level, the policy requires more and more accurate counterforce weapons. As both sides improve their technology, making their weapons more accurate—aimed at the other sides' missiles—both sides have to be ready to "launch on warning" in a crisis, that is, triggered by computers, to avoid losing their missiles. *Irrevocable* it may be, and certainly illegal preparation by any stretch of the "laws of humanity."

Bold Strides

Given the nuclear peril, almost nothing anyone does to protest or stop the madness seems unreasonable. Thoreau, referring to the necessity to protest unjust laws, advised, "Let your life be a counter-friction to stop the machine." Hundreds here, thousands overseas, have demonstrated physically against nuclear weapons. In the United States the number arrested annually for civil disobedience at defense plants and military bases runs 4,000 to 5,000 per year. Many of those brought to trial have attempted to use a defense based partially or solely on international law. Such a defense has seldom been allowed by the presiding judge.

In addition to civil disobedience, peace activists are resorting to other paralegal means to expose the illegality of nuclear weapons. A Provisional World Parliament met in Brighton, England, in 1982, which claimed to represent a constituency of four million people across national boundaries. The Parliament was convened under a *Constitution for the Federation of Earth* that had been adopted by an international assemblage in 1977. At the Provisional World Parliament of 1982, Bill Number One, adopted unanimously, outlawed nuclear weapons.

With other legislation, the Parliament enacted a World District Court Bill. "Transgressors of world laws and in particular the legislation which outlaws nuclear weapons can, by due process, be brought for trial before the world district courts which are to be set up under this bill. The organizing force is the World Constitution and Parliament Association, a nongovernmental organization with members in fifty countries."[11]

Under the mandate of the Provisional World Parliament, Leon Vickman established a "District World Court" in Los Angeles. In June, 1983, the court issued summons to twenty-eight governments which possess or which are allegedly preparing to deploy nuclear weapons. The plaintiffs in this class action suit are listed as "The People of the Earth," and their case will be heard by a distinguished three-judge panel of international law professors, according to Vickman. Additional District World Courts are being planned. In the long run, Lucile Green writes, "World courts acting for the world community could provide a means of settling international disputes without resort to war, by making it incumbent on nations to obey the laws they themselves have made."[12]

Yes . . . if the nations will agree to it. To date, the superpowers have been notably disinclined to accept the jurisdiction of the International Court of Justice at the Hague—unless the court's opinions coincide with their perceived national interest. If at some point a national court decides against its own government on the basis of international law, that will certainly be a sign of the new age!

A minor breakthrough occurred at the state level with *Illinois v. Jarka*. For the first time, a jury was instructed by a state judge, Alphonse Witt, that the use or threatened use of nuclear weapons violates international law. On April 15, 1985, the court rendered an acquittal verdict based on "necessity," the legal doctrine that an individual may break a law in order to prevent some greater harm from occurring or to defend a higher value. (For example, a person may break into someone's burning house to rescue a child.) In *Jarka*, seven demonstrators had been charged with resisting arrest in a November 1984 action outside the Waukegan Great Lakes naval base. The protest was directed against government intervention in Central America as well as continued deployment of first-strike nuclear weapons.

Other courts and judges are awakening, gradually. When the "Plowshares 8" went before the Pennsylvania Superior (appeals) Court, a majority overturned the lower court's decision against the eight antinuclear defendants. The trial judge had disallowed any defense based on international law or justification (necessity). But Superior Court Judge Edmund B. Spaeth, Jr., disagreed: "Whenever a defendant pleads justification, the court should ask, 'What value higher than the value of literal compliance with the law is the defendant asserting?' The trial court failed to ask this question." Further, Judge Spaeth said, actions taken to prevent a greater harm "must now be measured against the greatest danger that ever existed: "no peril is greater—no peril even approaches—the peril of nuclear war." The state Supreme Court overturned the Superior Court's decision by a 4 to 3 vote, but the Chief Justice has asked the court to reconsider some of the issues.

In Canada, a coalition of peace groups known as Pacific Interfaith is asking the courts to declare nuclear weapons illegal and thus create the world's first *judicial* Nuclear Free Zone. As we have seen, Canadians are worried about the over-flights of American nuclear-capable aircraft, nuclear submarines roaming Canadian waters and cruise missile testing. Recently the Canadian Cabinet agreed to allow B52 bombers, armed with nuclear weapons, to use Canadian air space in times of "heightened international tension," and to permit nuclear depth charges to be stationed at a Canadian base. By permitting this complicity with the Pentagon, Interfaith lawyers say, the Canadian government is violating international law.

A number of religious organizations and others have joined or may yet join the legal action. Building momentum, the movement may produce, ultimately, a national consensus. The "Operation Dismantle" case, in which the Canadian Supreme Court refused to stop the testing of cruise missiles in Canada, did establish the principle that all acts of Parliament are subject to the Court's review—unlike in the US and UK, even matters of defense and foreign policy.

If a Canadian court should declare nuclear weapons illegal, it would send a shock wave around the world—a shock of the magnitude of New Zealand's brave decision to refuse port access to US warships! Indeed, it would beckon us to a possible bigger breakthrough—that grand day when an American federal judge or jury declares, loudly and unequivocally, that nuclear weapons violate the interests of humanity and the agreements that nations have made to protect and preserve the planet.

8

Divestment and Conversion

"For where your treasure is, there will your heart be also."
—Matthew 6:21 (NEB)

DO YOU KNOW WHERE YOUR MONEY REALLY IS?
DOES IT BUILD NUCLEAR WEAPONS? POLLUTE THE ENVI-
RONMENT? SUPPORT REPRESSIVE REGIMES? ENCOURAGE
ON THE JOB DISCRIMINATION? OR . . .
OR WILL YOUR MONEY CONSTRUCT A HYDRO PLANT? RENO-
VATE A NEIGHBORHOOD? PROVIDE GOOD JOBS? PRODUCE
HIGH QUALITY GOODS AND SERVICES?
—Brochure for *Good Money*

The story neither begins nor ends with him, but the Takoma Park Nuclear Free Zone saga cannot be divorced from Sam Abbott. Feisty, opinionated, controversial, Abbott was the mayor of that Washington, DC, suburb of 18,000 from 1980 to 1985. Assertive and given to strong language, Abbott is described by his political opponents as "confrontational." But he has one central passion: to rid the world of nuclear weapons.

Sam Abbott lost his re-election campaign for mayor in 1985 by just seven votes out of 3,149. Some people said he was too involved with the big issues—nuclear weapons, sanctuary, US involvement in Central America—and didn't do all the nitty-gritty things that keep a community functioning. Abbott disagrees with those who said he didn't care about local government but he concedes an interest in the more critical issues of our time. "Too many of our citizens are worried about potholes," he told me. "A nuclear bomb makes the world's biggest pothole!"

Takoma Park and Nuclear Divestment

Other citizens kept a lower profile than Abbott but worked just as hard to make Takoma Park, Maryland, a Nuclear Free Zone.

One was councilman Carl Iddings, a computer programming manager who works in Washington, DC. Together with Councilmember Lou D'Ovidio, Iddings introduced the original ordinance as well as amendments a year later which, according to him, made the Act functional; and which, according to Abbott, weakened its impact.

The first act of the new city council following the 1982 election was to endorse the Nuclear Freeze proposal and to set up a task force to study the question of Takoma Park's becoming nuclear-free. The Nuclear Freeze Task Force modified a draft ordinance supplied by Nuclear Free America and submitted it to council members and the mayor, who became a staunch supporter of the ordinance with its provisions for selective city contracting and non-nuclear investment. Following the lead of thirty-three other communities, on December 12, 1983, Takoma Park became "the thirty-fourth mouse that roared," in the words of a local columnist. The vote by the city council to make Takoma Park nuclear-free was unanimous.

Takoma Park is an unusual town. It happens to sit astride two counties. It has a large nonwhite population (about 40 percent) and tends to draw people who have a social commitment. As one resident said, "people who like to live among the real world rather than a middle-class ghetto-like existence." "It's like a little UN," a resident who is a psychotherapist said. "There are a lot of musicians, a lot of hippies, a lot of Seventh Day Adventists." The city has long been the site of the Seventh Day Adventist world headquarters, and acquired a reputation for conservatism: the sale of liquor had been banned since the town's founding in 1883 until a public referendum ended prohibition in 1983.

Recently, Takoma Park's politics have taken a more liberal turn. At the public hearing called by the Council on December

12, 1983, anger and frustration was evident. Manfred Smith, a local social studies teacher, said later:

> People have had it up to here! You felt it that night: religious groups and political groups and individuals expressing their anger toward administration policies. Billions are going to bombs while human services are being ignored. It was a weathervane of the mood of the people.[1]

The adoption of the ordinance brought Takoma Park international notice. David Wollcombe of the London-based Peace Child Foundation complimented Takoma Park for being "way ahead of the government down the street," and said he hoped that eventually the United States government "would need three brigades of soldiers to protect missiles against the ravages of people," as in Britain where soldiers have had to protect the Greenham Common missiles against the women's peace presence. Councilman Iddings and Bob Teague of the Takoma Park Nuclear Free Zone Task Force were interviewed by a Soviet television crew.

In August 1985, Mayor Abbott spread the word about Takoma Park to the delegates assembled in Japan for the First World Conference of Mayors for Peace Through Inter-City Solidarity. Officials representing sixty-three cities abroad and forty Japanese cities joined for ceremonies marking the 40th Anniversary of the dropping of the first two atomic bombs.

The fact that the manufacture and possession of nuclear warheads and weapons components is prohibited within the two square mile limits of Takoma Park is not unique. But Takoma Park was the first, and is still one of only four US communities to add a strong economic component to its NFZ legislation. The ordinance pinches the military-industrial complex two ways. It addresses (a) the investment of municipal funds and (b) city purchasing and contracts. As amended January 28, 1985, Section 8A-5 calls for a "socially responsible investment policy and implementation plan," which was to be proposed to city government by a Nuclear-Free Takoma Park Committee, a nonpartisan body to be appointed by the mayor. Section 8A-6 prevents city officials from knowingly granting "any award, contract, or purchase order, directly or indirectly, to any nuclear weapons purchaser," or "to purchase products produced by a nuclear weapons producer." Also, the city "shall phase out the use of any products of a nuclear weapons producer which it presently owns or possesses." (For the complete ordinance, see Appendix.)

Assistant Administrator Beverly Habada, a Seventh Day Adventist, has been researching the divestment issue. She wants to see it work but explained some of the difficulties. The city makes use of a statewide Local Government Investment Pool but the pool lacks the ability to screen investments to remove nuclear weapons firms. Another limitation is the fact that, by law, city funds must be invested in federally insured institutions—banks are insured but they reinvest funds in diverse stocks and bonds, many of which are related to nuclear weapons companies. Federal bonds, of course, are "dirty" investments too.

"We are novices," Habada said, "we don't quite know how to do this. But we're learning." In terms of purchasing and equipment, she asked, "what do you do with your IBM typewriters? Phase them out?" The answer seems to be yes, according to the ordinance. "What about our current use of AT&T telephone systems?" AT&T is a nuclear weapons-related firm. Sam Abbott argues, "There is always an alternative" to buying from a nuclear manufacturer. Takoma Park, for example, buys only Chrysler cars for its police since both General Motors and Ford have immense nuclear defense contracts.

The issue of nuclear-free contracting erupted when the Police Department needed new radios. The Police Department prepared a bid package calling for "state of the art" radio equipment using the 800 MHz frequency band. The only two bidders were Motorola and General Electric, both nuclear weapons companies (because the proposal had been written to their technical specifications!).

The ordinance forced city officials to look hard at the police radio system and examine their options. Mayor Abbott and City

Administrator James Wilson, with technical help from various sources, researched the issue. Research on the existing equipment revealed that the preventive maintenance contract had been violated by the city's maintenance of the radios, or the lack of it. In addition, the Police Department had allowed its FCC license to elapse. Mayor Abbott also found that there were available frequencies outside of the 800 MHz band: notably in the "T" band, frequencies already being used by the police in adjoining counties. Eight non-nuclear manufacturers of "T-band" radio equipment were discovered, again bids were submitted, and a non-nuclear supplier was offered the contract. Currently a top-quality radio system is being installed by a non-nuclear firm at a savings of 40 percent below the cost of a Motorola or GE system. By acting on principle the city saved money too—always a happy outcome.

Police Chief Tony Fisher still had to be convinced. Fisher wanted Motorola or GE radios—they are the leading suppliers and they have a reputation in the field. Concerned about public safety, Fisher took a "show-me" attitude towards the system being installed. He still wants a more flexible purchasing policy where public safety is involved. "I'm for nuclear disarmament," he told me. "Let's send a message, but let's not harm the messenger in sending the message!"

The police radio flap evolved into a lively public debate over amending the Nuclear Free Zone ordinance of December 12, 1983. Some of the city council, led by Carl Iddings, wanted to provide city administrators with more flexibility in awarding city contracts: what if there were no viable alternatives to nuclear-weapons firms? The council appointed an ad hoc six-member Nuclear Free Zone Committee to study the ordinance and consider amendments. The committee did so, unanimously recommending five amendments designed to strengthen the Act. However, the committee split evenly over the controversial issue of whether to adopt a formal policy for granting exemptions (waivers) to the purchasing requirement.

At two public hearings on the issue, in December 1984 and January 1985, a few citizens spoke for the waiver amendment but the vast majority spoke against it. Yet the Council approved the waiver proviso by a five-to-two vote after three hours of testimony on January 28. Mayor Sam Abbott, disgusted with the "gutting" of Takoma Park's NFZ ordinance, threw down the gavel and walked out of the meeting.

But the amendment doesn't gut the ordinance. As amended, the city may not purchase from nuclear weapons firms if a product or service can reasonably be obtained from another source. Only in special circumstances related to public safety, such as when non-nuclear vendors are unavailable or the costs of purchasing from them are prohibitive, can exceptions be made. The amendment's supporters think it strengthens the Act by giving the city more flexibility and making the non-nuclear policy "workable."

Takoma Park's abrasive ex-mayor disagrees, but he has to live with it—at least until he runs for mayor again. He should be proud. Despite the amendment (or because of it, in Iddings' view), Takoma Park has a workable antinuclear weapons policy, a model for other communities. The city has set an example of refusing support to the federal government "for policies that can only be called suicidal," in Abbott's words. "We've got the sense to know that providing for the common defense does not mean providing for the common obliteration." Abbott is determined to abolish nuclear weapons. His brother was among the first group of American military personnel to enter Nagasaki after the bomb. Sam Abbott lost his job as a result of promoting Bertrand Russell's antinuclear petition campaign following World War II. In some quarters it was unpatriotic to oppose the American nuclear program.

Seventy-eight year old Abbott is a talented artist as well as a courageous politician. One of the gifts he presented to Japanese officials in August, 1985, was a print of one his own oil paintings. It showed the horrible effects of a nuclear blast, an artistically terrible apocalypse. Frightened faces are shown above, people fleeing the explosion; below, a bomb shelter with a skeleton identified by its dog tag as Edward Teller, father of the H-bomb. The skeleton hugs its hoard of dehydrated water, books on how to survive thermonuclear war, and a shotgun to keep the neighbors away. Abbott is not subtle. He is direct and uncompromising. Like his words, Sam Abbott's painting is a grim and serious warning to a worried world.

The Economics of Arms

Citizens are becoming more sensitive to and alarmed by the economic consequences of the arms race. Worldwide the nations spend $800 billion a year for military programs. Since World War II the superpowers have spent $3 to $4 trillion to build nuclear arsenals which, if used, will mean the end of civilization. Priorities? The budget of the US Air Force alone, according to Ruth Sivard, is greater "than the total educational budget for 1.2 billion children in Africa, Latin America, and Asia excluding Japan. The Soviet Union in one year spends more on military defense than the governments of all developing countries spend for education and health care for 3.6 billion people."[2]

Globally, national budgets reflect an increasing preference for military power in comparison with constructive social programs or with peaceful strategies for resolving conflict. Sivard quotes Adolfo Perez Esquivel of Argentina (1984) who put it clearly: "Usually we speak of violence only when it has reached an extreme. But it is also violence when children are dying of malnutrition, when there is not freedom of unions, when there is not enough housing, not enough health care."[3]

Within our society, the astounding, accelerating military focus forces more and more scientists and engineers into military research and development, to the detriment of nondefense industries. One-third to one-half of our technical talent works directly on military-related projects. This diversion of American talent from the civilian sector affects our ability to compete in the international marketplace with such industrial powers as Japan and West Germany.

But there is a greater tragedy. Bright young minds who could be devoting their energies and gifts to finding cures for cancer and AIDS, or inventing new methods of birth control, or harnessing hurricanes, or alleviating hunger with high-nutrition foods, are being lured into ballistic missile design and researching exotic plans for space-based defense.

Nationally, the Reagan bucks-for-bombs and cut-social-programs philosophy has severely hurt minorities and the poor. The economic squeeze is felt most intensely in our nation's cities, where critical human services have been severely cut as the Reagan administration poured billions more into the Pentagon. In one year alone, Baltimore lost $99,000,000 in federal aid. The national Jobs with Peace campaign has stirred many communities to revolt against federal budgetary priorities. In the November 1982 elections, 50 cities and towns approved such resolutions with an average 65 percent yes vote. For example, in November 1982, Baltimoreans passed a charter amendment, Question 1, popularly known as the Peace Budget, by a majority of 60 percent at the polls. The amendment declares:

> More federal funds should be made available to the Mayor and City Council of Baltimore for local jobs and programs—in quality education, transportation, energy-efficient housing, improved health care, and other essential services. This should be accomplished by reducing the amount of tax dollars spent on nuclear and conventional weapons systems and programs of foreign military intervention. The Department of Finance shall cause to be published annually in at least five prominent Baltimore newspapers (i) the above appeal to the Federal Government to cut military spending and (ii) a detailed statement of taxes paid per person and in total by the citizens of Baltimore City to Federal Government that are allocated to military spending.

As Takoma Park has done, Baltimore and other cities could write purchasing and investment policies to squeeze the military-industrial complex and force a rethinking of priorities in Washington. By withdrawing their economic support from companies that profit from the arms race, towns and cities give the federal government notice that they "are fed up to here" with the production of bombs and missiles, and they want to see their government take initiatives to reduce arms and create a just and peaceful world.

Certainly any NFZ legislation becomes more concrete with the addition of policies for purchasing and investing only with companies unrelated to nuclear weapons. A Nuclear Free Zone *is* symbolic. Perhaps for some people in Washington, or behind the desks in IBM, GE, and Lockheed offices, the most potent symbol is the dollar sign. Remove the dollars from the nuclear weapons business and you "give it the business." You hit it in its soft underbelly—profits.

Boycott!

But, you may say, if a town refuses to purchase from or invest in companies dealing in nuclear weapons—this is a boycott! Yes, it is. Are boycotts ethical? Good question.

Certainly there are precedents for refusing to buy from or invest in or use services offered by certain people, firms, or governments. Historian Gene Sharp has catalogued economic boycotts, with examples even prior to the invention of the term in 1880, when peasants of Mayo County, Ireland, were protesting the policies of a certain Captain Boycott.[4] In America, prior to the War of Independence, colonists boycotted a number of British commodities in resisting the infamous Stamp Act and the Townshend Acts. Refusing to buy or consume any East-India tea led to the Boston Tea Party, enraging the British and stirring the colonies to revolt. Boycotting was an important nonviolent contribution to America's independence; similarly, and to a greater extent, Gandhi's strategy of asking Indians to boycott British cloth and salt, and spin cloth and produce the salt themselves led to Indian independence.

Boycotts are not necessarily moral; that is, the grievance impelling a boycott may or may not be related to a real injustice. Prices may be too high, or a union may feel that it's being unfairly targeted for wage cuts, and in such cases it may be hard to ascribe the conflict to real injustice—the question of whether prices are too high or wages too low is very subjective. If a boycott is called because working conditions are dangerous or because a company's products are physically or psychologically harmful or threaten harm in some way, then it clearly becomes a moral issue. Led by the Rosa Parks example, blacks in 1955 boycotted the bus lines in Birmingham, Alabama, to end racial discrimination in seating. Sharp cites other examples from the civil rights movement:

> In 1938, as part of a jobs-for-Negroes movement led by the Rev. Adam Clayton Powell, A. Philip Randolph, and the Rev. William Lloyd Imes, Negroes in Harlem, New York City, conducted a "blackout boycott" every Tuesday night by turning off electricity and lighting candles to induce Consolidated Edison Co. to hire Negroes in jobs above the unskilled level. In Nashville, Tennessee, shortly before Easter 1960, Negroes supporting a student sit-in to integrate lunch counters decided not to buy new Easter clothes as a means of influencing Nashville merchants. On May 10 the lunch counters of the six downtown stores were integrated. During the summer of 1960 about 250,000 people in the Philadelphia area carried out a "selective patronage program" against the Tasty Baking Co. of Philadelphia, in order to obtain equal job opportunities for Negroes.[5]

More recently, the grape boycott sponsored by United Farm Workers and Cesar Chavez was effective in producing more favorable working conditions and salaries for California's farm laborers. And the massive international boycott of products made by Nestle, including Stauffer foods and many other commodities, paid off when Nestle announced a more humane policy for marketing baby formula in the third world. There are many ongoing boycotts, as well as a newsletter that periodically details the latest "Unshopping List."[6]

INFACT, the organization that pushed the Nestle boycott, has announced plans for a nationwide boycott of General Electric products. GE is a likely target for antinuclear consumers since it manufactures many consumer items, unlike such companies as Lockheed, which produce little else than military hardware. General Electric, the nation's fourth largest military contractor, manufactures engines for the F-18 fighter and the B1 bomber, nuclear reactors for submarines and aircraft carriers, and the Mark 12-A warhead for the Minuteman and MX missiles—also certain military satellites that would be used in nuclear warfighting. But GE (whose slogan ironically is "We bring good things to life") also produces everything from refrigerators to light bulbs for the general public, under the GE and Hotpoint labels. A community that's serious about boycotting nuclear weapons firms needs to secure a list of the major nuclear weapons firms. (See appendix for help.) Doing your homework comes first, then implementation.

South African Divestment and the Churches

Divestment aimed at South African apartheid models the kind of economic pressure that we need to crank up against the nuclear weapons industry. Between 1977 and 1985, fifty-four American colleges and universities divested a total of $251 million in holdings of South African-related assets. As of January 1, 1986, thirty-three American colleges and universities were following full-divestment policies, and fifty-one partial divestment. Unions, states, and municipalities have been considering divestment. By 1983 Massachusetts, Connecticut, and Michigan, and such cities as Philadelphia, Wilmington, and Berkeley had passed legislation calling for the sale of stocks and bonds from any company doing business in South Africa. In 1984, the New York City Employees Retirement System became the largest pension fund to line up against apartheid, requiring the city to sell over $600 million invested in South African-related companies.

These efforts are starting to pay off. The Commerce Department reported a 10 percent drop in private investment in South Africa in three years. According to the Investor Responsibility Research Center in Washington, nine American companies left South Africa in 1983, six in 1984, and at least sixteen in 1985. Paul Wilson, director of the Human Rights program of the Christian Church (Disciples of Christ), visited South Africa in late 1984 and reported that South African whites were preoccupied with US divestment. It worried them. Most South African blacks welcomed it. They felt that the South African government dreaded economic sanctions from outside and the withdrawal of foreign businesses. "They also saw the divestment efforts as encouraging signs that there is support outside South Africa for their struggle for liberation and freedom."[7]

In addition to divestment, other forms of pressure are being applied by churches in the anti-apartheid campaign here. The Interfaith Center for Corporate Responsibility announced that on May 20, 1985, fifty-four Protestant denominations had agreed on a campaign to pressure twelve US corporations doing business in South Africa, "key investors in apartheid." Petitioning, letter-writing, and shareholder resolutions will be among the tactics used to encourage these firms to withdraw completely from that police state unless "significant progress is made" towards eliminating apartheid by the end of 1986.

If we can target apartheid, *we can target nuclear weapons.* Already, several religious bodies have divested funds from the "Armageddon firms." Such actions were taken by the United Presbyterian Church Board of World Ministries, the Sisters of Mercy, and the United Presbyterian Church in the USA. The latter, at its General Assembly on June 26, 1982, voted to remove the church's investments from twenty-one weapons-related firms. The Board for World Ministries of the United Church of Christ has adopted guidelines calling for divestment from any company depending on military contracts for over 20 percent of its sales; the Board of National Ministries of the American Baptist Churches has a policy specifying 15 percent. In early 1983, thirteen Roman Catholic congregations in the Chicago area divested $1.8 million in stocks and bonds from nuclear weapons-related corporations.

The investment guidelines of the Sisters of Mercy are stringent. Their "Assets Management Program" excludes corporations which "(1) Receive over $200 million in defense contracts in a given fiscal year, (2) Derive 5 percent or more of their total sales from nuclear weapons production; and (3) Engage in nuclear weaponry through nuclear weapons production of delivery vehicles." The board of pensions of the United Methodist Church also has a 5 percent policy, and several theological seminaries have taken divestment action.

Responsible Investing

In a Nuclear Free Zone, the funds withdrawn from the arms race should be invested in constructive and beneficial programs: agencies, companies, and projects benefiting human beings. It is not enough to boycott the nuclear industry. We have to define what a *good company* is. Generally, antinuclear investors look for companies involved in constructive work such as low-income housing or solar energy, and whose employment policies are enlightened and equitable.

There may be local projects worthy of support: loan-making agencies funding community co-ops or worker-owned enterprises, and firms involved in high-priority needs such as renewable energy sources, urban agriculture, adult education, and job retraining. The profits on alternative investments such as these may not match the dividends accruing from General Electric or Rockwell International but

> . . . the returns are actually greater. The money invested in local projects stays in the community and becomes part of a "natural" cycle of generating more revenue and more jobs, lower costs for coping with social pathologies, and a renewed sense of community. Further, if a sizeable number of investors were willing to avoid nuclear weapons manufacturers, then these firms would have to reconsider their involvement in the arms trade.[8]

The Interfaith Center for Corporate Responsibility has published a *Directory of Alternative Investments*[9] which describes fifty-five investment opportunities in four categories: cooperatives, credit unions/banks, housing projects, and enterprise development projects. The list will be updated periodically.

For cities, churches, schools, and individuals with money to invest—who want to make ethical investments—there are many resources. Investment counselors with an ethical sense exist. Ethical investment newsletters exist also: *Market Conscience, Good Money, Insight*. Mutual funds like Dreyfus Third Century Fund and Pax World Fund screen investments on various ethical criteria, excluding some firms and including others that make a positive contribution. Pax World tries to invest in life-supporting business such as firms engaged in pollution control and renewable energy systems.

Pax World Fund began in 1971 when a group of United Methodist ministers decided to set up a socially responsible investment fund. They went to Wall Street for assistance, but the market experts said "it couldn't be done." So the Methodists formed Pax and proved the experts wrong. Amy Domini, author of a recent book on ethical investing, says that:

> Pax was the first firm to adopt a broad range of issues for its screens. It pioneered much of the territory ethical investors explore today. It demonstrated that defense companies are not a necessary part of a successful investment portfolio.
>
> Luther E. Tyson, president of Pax World Fund, told me that whenever a violation of Pax's social criteria obligates it to sell its shares in a corporation, he contacts the management and tells it of Pax's decision and the reasons behind it.[10]

good policy for a Nuclear Free Zone community to follow!

Is socially responsible investment profitable? Apparently so, as the slogan attests: "doing well while doing good." When a major New York bank analyzed the *Fortune* 500 between 1977 and 1982, comparing the performance of companies invested in South Africa with those who were not, the latter well outperformed the former. Also, in 1983 the Pax World Fund racked up an impressive 24.17 percent return to outperform the Standard and Poor's 500 Index; and the Calvert Social Investment Fund's Money Market portfolio outperformed any other money market fund in 1984. The pattern is that socially-responsible funds do at least as well as the market as a whole, proof that the righteous don't have to finish last!

Socially-responsible investing is making Wall Street take notice. Major financial institutions such as Franklin Management and Shearson-American Express have opened departments that specialize in it. "As near as anyone can calculate," Joe Kane reported in November 1983, "the net total of socially screened investments has doubled since 1981, will probably double again by 1985, and will continue to double in even shorter periods of time." Why this new interest in ethical investing? Is it the result of the hippie generation growing up and getting money, as someone suggests? Or just a revival of social responsibility in America? Who knows? Whatever the reason, it is happening—and because of it, there are investment channels for Nuclear Free Zone people wanting to impact the arms race economically.

Of course, there may be a good reason for keeping some money in an unsavory company. Shareholders have some clout in the company's affairs, and if they own enough stock, they can introduce shareholder resolutions at company meetings which are designed to affect that firm's policies. A number of religious denominations retain just enough stock in a company like General Electric to act as gadflies, annually introducing resolutions calling for the company to withdraw from defense contracting or other evils. In 1983, according to Amy Domini, over two hundred social responsibility resolutions were proposed for proxy statements, compared to just two in 1973. For example, my friend William Whistler, a former GE engineer, introduced a resolution calling for General Electric "to support efforts to ban weapons in space; to direct research and development funds to peaceful uses of space; to cease involvement in the use of space for nuclear warfare-related systems; and to stop nuclear weapons manufacture."[12]

Almost never do these resolutions gather a significant number of votes, but the process has an educational value. Officials in Nuclear Free Zone communities, however, may not have time to attend corporate meetings and introduce resolutions. Total divestment from the "Armageddon firms" may be the best policy.

Massive divestment has the potential to squeeze the military-industrial complex until it hurts; indeed, to force the federal government to reorder its priorities and, with or without Soviet cooperation, suffocate the arms race. A divestment strategy, as Max Obuszewski of Nuclear Free America says, "forces the issue of conversion onto the public agenda, from which a discussion of a wide range of alternatives should develop. These alternatives—alternate use planning and alternate investment and taxation policies—hold promise for converting the slogan 'Fund Human Needs' into reality."

Conversion Plans

Conversion—a religious term evoking images of revival, hymns like "Just As I Am," Billy Graham, and being "born again." Yes, but it also evokes a matter of *economics*. Here we suggest that a restructuring of values, a radical reordering of priorities, in short, a conversion of the spirit—shall lead to or bring about a conversion of defense industries to constructive, life-enhancing purposes. Swords into plowshares, spears into pruning-hooks? Yes, and bombs into bread, tanks into tractors, missile plants into eggplants.

So we pursue conversion, that this heavily militarized world may, by degrees, be transformed into a life-enhancing global economy where human needs and not military needs take first place. Indeed, nuclear-free zoning requires us to consider conversion. If a community passes legislation to *stay* nuclear-free, nuclear weapons firms are banned. But when they are *banished,* that is, when a community orders firms within its borders to stop making nuclear components by a certain date, conversion comes into play. The idea is not to destroy a business, leaving people without jobs; rather, to find ways to convert it to nonmilitary function. This will keep workers employed, and employees are happier producing services that are *needed* and beneficial to society.

Economic conversion has been accomplished in other areas without much fuss. The American automobile industry successfully converted its factories to wartime production during World War II, and after the war, the industry reconverted to peacetime production. In other times and places, an outmoded or failing business has managed to switch to producing something else. Indeed, the Pentagon's Office of Economic Adjustment has helped a number of communities faced with military base closings to develop projects to provide jobs for displaced workers. Advance planning is the key to making successful transitions.

China provides a remarkable example. Matthew Goodman and Randall Forsberg visited China in August 1985 and discovered that, since 1980, virtually every weapons factory has switched to civilian production. This was the result of a decision to give greater priority to economic development and to postpone large-scale military production until China has access to more modern technology. The conversion is not permanent, however:

> Civilian products—sewing machines, bicycles, cars, trucks, and precision instruments—are made in factories where the same personnel will, at times, revert to military production. This unique "dual capacity" offers four benefits: production facilities are kept in full use, rather than standing idle when military demand is low; dual production helps transfer advanced technology from the military to the civilian sector; the civilian goods produced benefit the national economy; and there is no pressure on the government to produce unneeded weapons merely to sustain production capacity for future use.[13]

In China, the impetus for economic conversion comes from the government, which may dictate terms to its industry. In a democracy, the impetus may come from management or from the workers but it will probably not take place without the consent and cooperation of both. If the company is large and diversified rather than locally-based, it will be less interested in retooling and hearing workers' ideas about alternate products.

Workers at the Lucas Aerospace Company in Britain furnish an inspiring model. Faced with diminishing military contracts in the 1970s, Lucas laid off some 5,000 of its 18,000 workers. The unions, motivated by fear of more layoffs and the conviction that the company didn't have to depend on military contracts, began to study conversion seriously. They sent a questionaire to the workers. From over 1,000 suggestions a list of 150 products was compiled, and several prototypes built. These included a road-rail car, a heat pump, and a kidney dialysis machine. The company rejected their ideas, but the solidarity the workers experienced, and their creative output, gave them confidence and strengthened their ability to resist further layoffs.

When it declared London nuclear-free, the Greater London Council allocated $2.5 million to underwrite conversion projects at London-area defense companies employing some 90,000 workers. "An alternate use committee has suggested conversion to desalination plants as one of several projects, at the Barrow in Furness shipbuilding yard in northwest England, where 12,000 workers assemble Trident submarines. Says Daniel S. Pearson, a union leader: 'We became concerned that all of our eggs are in one basket.' "[14]

In the United States, people are talking about conversion at both federal and local levels. The federal executive is doing very little, but conversion bills have been introduced in Congress. The Defense Economic Adjustment Act, first introduced by Senators McGovern and Mathias and by Representative Ted Weiss of New York has been reintroduced by Weiss and had collected fifty-two cosponsors as of August 1985.

The stated purpose of the Weiss bill, introduced in the House in the 97th Congress (1982) as H.R. 6618, was

. . . to provide the means through which the United States can promote orderly economic adjustment which will (1) minimize the dislocation of workers, communities, and industries, (2) assure that such dislocations do not compound recessionary trends, and

(3) encourage conversion of technologies and managerial and worker skills developed in defense production to projects which serve the civilian sector.

Actually, the Dodd-McKinney amendments, attached to the Public Works and Economic Development Act, predated and prefigured the Weiss Bill. Dodd-McKinney passed the House in 1979 but failed to survive a House-Senate conference committee.

Representative Ted Weiss' Economic Adjustment Act, which has been endorsed by the AFL-CIO Industrial Union Department, requires a one-year prenotification by the government of plans to cut back or terminate a defense contract or military base. A Defense Economic Adjustment Council would be established to oversee the program, and an Office of Economic Adjustment to provide necessary staff support for the Council. The Council would publish a Conversion Guidelines Handbook for use by industries or bases in process of conversion. At every defense facility employing at least one hundred persons an "alternate use committee" of at least eight members "shall undertake economic conversion planning and preparation for the employment of the personnel and utilization of the facilities in the event of a reduction or elimination of any defense facility or the curtailment, conclusion, or disapproval of any defense contract."

The military itself has done some study on conversion. At a stormy meeting on July 11, 1985, called by the South Shore Conversion Committee to discuss economic conversion at the General Dynamics shipyard in Quincy, Massachusetts, Navy research was cited. The Navy report listed various alternative products for shipyards and their potential markets: bridges and road beds, $300 billion; piping and power plants, $10 billion; warehouses, $10 billion; sewer pipe and tunnels, $50 billion; oil rigs and refineries, $50 billion; trash incinerators, $100 billion. In terms of ocean thermal energy conversion, the production of three plant ships per year would provide 27,000 jobs to a shipyard. Elizabeth Sherman of the South Shore Conversion Committee called for the creation of a "collective vision of the shipyard as a healthy, productive center," and urged the development of coalitions to secure that kind of a future.

Acting Locally

The most significant conversion research is being pursued by private organizations working at a local or regional level. The Bay State Conversion Center in Massachusetts and the Center for Economic Conversion in California are developing plans based on these assumptions: that there is a vast silent majority aware of the threat of a nuclear holocaust and who want to turn the arms race around; that workers engaged in the defense industry feel trapped, uneasy with the result of their labors but unable to risk job security by leaving their work; and that by developing mechanisms that free workers to move from dependence on military contracting it will be possible for the nation to examine its priorities and consider foreign policy decisions on their merits without job security entering the equation.

Too often that doesn't happen. "Job blackmail" is used to save weapons systems or prevent military cutbacks. When President Carter threatened cancellation of the B-1 bomber in 1977, Rockwell International and the Pentagon cited possible layoffs of 6,000 workers in Los Angeles County. Consequently, United Auto Workers lobbied with Rockwell to have the program restored—a classic case of defense dependency producing job blackmail. Unnecessary weapons, inflation, budget deficits are the result.

Securing the support of labor is a key element here. Conversion activists are working together with labor unions to develop conversion models and to encourage industry to consider conversion. The International Association of Machinists and Aerospace Workers (IAM) has embraced conversion as a goal and is trying to educate its own people, and the United Auto Workers leadership is favorable. The Center for Economic Conversion in California has worked with the IAM, as has the St. Louis Economic Conversion Project. In Seattle the Puget Sound Conversion Project has cooperated with the International Woodworkers Union.

Overseas, the labor movement is a major force within the peace movement, according to Gene Carroll in a publication of the Center for Economic Conversion:

> For example, the British Trades Union Congress (equivalent to the AFL-CIO) has adopted a platform calling for unilateral nuclear disarmament and for the establishment of a National Industrial Conversion Committee . . . IG Metall, the West German metalworkers union (the largest single union in the 'free world' with more than 2.2 million members) is urging cutbacks in military exports and production and encouraging the development of economic conversion and alternative use committees at the plant level.[15]

Many other powerful trade unions in Western Europe and the Pacific are working to end the arms race and are proposing economic conversion programs to ease the transition:

> Workers and their unions are beginning to see that the cold war reality has real economic consequences for them: more capital intensive military production employs less and less people, draining resources and weakening the bargaining and political power of unions—all in the name of national security—while all around there is increasing evidence that the world is becoming *less secure* because of increasing militarization.[16]

We need to build bridges and forge alliances. NFZ activists need more dialogue with the labor movement and more support from the national unions. Working people need to understand that peace activists are not going to desert them when weapons contracts are defeated. We have to preserve their jobs or help them find alternatives. In the long run conversion will benefit everyone—studies show that the same number of dollars invested in nonmilitary industry produces more jobs than when invested in defense work.

Working-people have shown significant ingenuity when faced with plant closings. In Charleston, South Carolina, the United

Electrical Workers local has developed an "alternate use" committee to prevent the impending shutdown of General Electric's steam turbine plant. The local brought in William Niven, an economic conversion expert from England, for consultation. He used a shop floor survey to search for alternate products, seeking ideas from the rank-and-file. Ultimately the union rejected several proposals for military products in favor of environmental protection and alternative energy devices, such as antipollution "scrubbers" for coal-burning power plants. To date, GE management has not accepted the idea.

Worker-sponsored conversion proposals also are in process at three government-owned uranium enrichment plants in Appalachia. These plants, located in Piketon, Ohio, Paducah, Kentucky, and Oak Ridge, Tennessee, are slated to close within the next decade. The conversion of these massive government complexes would be different from any other conversion project, as Jeoffrey Sea reports from Piketon:

> We advocate "site conversion" as distinct from "plant conversion." The main process buildings on the sites are, without doubt, unsuited to any alternative use due to their vast size, their level of contamination, and highly specialized nature of the process equipment. However, the sites also house multi-purpose, relatively uncontaminated buildings such as warehouses, machine shops, laboratories, as well as switchyards, railyards, water treatment facilities, and developed access to power, water, and road/rail transport. In other words, the developed infrastructure at the sites makes them ideal for the development of new large industries.[17]

Sea reports that possible alternative industries include toxic waste treatment, alcohol fuels production, timber processing, and greenhousing and food processing. But there are still two hurdles: (a) getting company owners to accept the idea of conversion—management has seldom reacted favorably to workers' suggestions—and (b) providing financial support for workers temporarily displaced.

We need to encourage workers to leave their jobs in nuclear weapons industries. A job that puts all humankind in peril is not a constructive job. The song lyrics apply: "My work is more than my job/ my life is more than my work." But we cannot discount the economic results for individuals and their families: the temporary loss of income is a serious problem for many.

If the workers are not adequately supported by government, local communities can help. In the Catholic Diocese of Amarillo, Texas, in which the Pantex nuclear weapons plant is located, a Solidarity Peace Fund was established in 1983 to assist Pantex employees who for reasons of conscience want to transfer to other work and need financial help in the meantime. Archbishop Leroy T. Matthieson writes, "We have provided such help for one worker and are currently (2/10/86) offering help to another. The fund currently stands at $21,000." Local activists can provide a financial safety net for concerned workers. Such funds need to multiply until or unless state and federal governments provide similar assistance.

The Center for Economic Conversion, formerly the Mid-Peninsula Project, is located in the heart of California's Santa Clara valley, which is packed with defense industry. The Center's objectives are to "increase the expertise of workers and other concerned citizens regarding the political, economic, and technical dimensions of conversion planning and to foster broad public awareness of and political support for economic conversion. CEC publishes a newspaper, *Plowshare Press,* a slide show, and several other resources including a Conversion Organizer's Packet.

The packet includes a model ordinance that has been proposed to the Palo Alto, California, city council. The bill would, if adopted, set up a "Peace and Security Commission" which, among other duties, would study the feasibility of making Palo Alto a Nuclear Free Zone. In addition, the document includes a "Conversion" section mandating the city council to assist local industry in moving to nonmilitary activity. The bill would provide for both positive and negative incentives to industry. The document mandates studies of "the feasibility of possible zoning, utility and other incentives the city could provide to companies willing to submit to a binding commitment not to enter into defense-related work," and "the feasibility of a special tax on defense-related industries to support the city's conversion program." So, with the carrot and the stick, the new age dawns!

States Take Notice

Proposals for conversion legislation have been considered by activists in several states, including Massachusetts, California, Washington, Connecticut, Minnesota, and Oregon.

Activists in Oregon have an ambitious initiative going in 1986. Their Economic Conversion Bill would have allowed a 30 percent tax credit to companies that convert from the production of nuclear weapons to consumer products. That is, firms involved in conversion would have received tax benefits worth up to 30 percent of the investment they make in retooling plants and retraining workers within a three year period. A Governor's Task Force would have been empowered to assist the companies, and the new law would have phased out all nuclear weapons components in Oregon by 1990.

The initiative failed at the polls, losing by a 60–40 margin on November 4, 1986. Very unfortunate. Another attempt will likely be made in the future since Oregon seems an ideal state for this kind of social experiment. There would not be a huge industrial relocation since their are few firms in Oregon working on nuclear weapons. Also, there is a pro-environment sentiment, and the state has a number of communities and counties that are nuclear-free already.

If it happens in Oregon or another state, those citizens will be "born again" to a new hope, a vision of a world without arms; like Takoma Park a model for other communities, states, and countries around the earth.

Conversion, we say. Yes, indeed. This weary world needs a new-fashioned revival, first *a metamorphosis of spirit,* of consciousness and *conscience;* and then, economic conversion follows, an important step on the road out of the nuclear abyss.

9

From Paralysis to Empowerment

"Hope is the capacity to live with danger without being over-whelmed by it; hope is the will to struggle against obstacles even when they appear insuperable."
—American Catholic Bishops' Pastoral Letter on War and Peace

"As human beings, our greatness lies not so much in being able to remake the world—that is the 'myth' of the 'atomic age'—as in being able to remake ourselves."

—Gandhi

Imagine a huge boulder teetering on the edge of a cliff above your house. Would you go on living in its shadow or would you do something about it? Or, imagine yourself and your family sitting on a flimsy raft cruising down river. You hear the noise of an approaching rapids, unmistakable, growing louder. Are you going to try to paddle for shore?

The answer is yes to both questions, of course. But in the face of an unparalleled and terrible threat to our global home, to this flimsy raft, to amend the spaceship earth metaphor—as a species we are doing very little to avert disaster. In light of the peril—the threat not only of our own individual deaths but of the "second death," as Schell puts it, the extinction of life on earth—the response made so far by homo sapiens is remarkably weak, incredibly inadequate.

Never have so few objected so little to so great a disaster. Jonathan Schell remarks on the imminence of this biocide or *omnicide* that threatens us:

"Embracing, as it does, the life and death of every human being on earth and every future human being, it embraces and transcends all other issues." And because extinction threatens not only our lives but "every larger cause," everything and everyone that we might want to give our lives for, it threatens even "the *meaning* of our lives.[1]"

With amazing foresight, Lewis Mumford in 1954 remarked on the "extraordinary fact about the postwar period that mass extermination has awakened so little moral protest. It is as if the Secretary of Agriculture had authorized the sale of human meat during the meat shortage, and everyone had accepted cannibalism in daily practise as a clever dodge for reducing the cost of living."[2] More recently, psychologist Robert Jay Lifton has said, "Indeed one of the great scandals of our time is the paucity of human and material resources mobilized to cope with the absolute question of our time."[3] That is changing slowly, he adds, as more and more people from various professional groups begin to work for peace, but still . . . in light of the peril, our response to date seems so puny!

Hear a prophetic voice from the nineteenth century, that of Alfred Nobel, the inventor of dynamite who left a part of his fortune to be awarded in peace prizes. He remarked to his friend Bertha von Suttner, a writer and peace activist, "Perhaps my (munitions) factories will put an end to war sooner than your (peace) congresses. The day when two army corps can annihilate each other in one second, all civilized nations, it is to be hoped, will recoil from war and discharge their troops."[4]

That day is now. Today two army corps using nuclear artillery can annihilate one another in a second. Two submarines with nuclear missiles can annihilate each other's countries within a few seconds. And two nations, eyeing each other uneasily along the silo-sights of their ICBMs, can annihilate all of humankind within a few minutes.

But are we shocked enough to act? Have the world's civilized nations "recoiled from war in horror?" Not yet. Why not? "Don't be silly," we're told, "we have to learn to live with the Bomb!" But learning to live with the Bomb is like going to sleep with cobras loose under the bed or living in a house full of tarantulas. Do you say, "we have to learn to live with tarantulas," or do you try to get rid of them?

What will it take to arouse people? We stand stunned before an ocean of apathy. We, the activists, that is—the campaigners for a freeze, for a test ban, for Nuclear Free Zones.

But lest we become self-righteous, let us individually remember the courses we've trod: the pain, the awakening, the mixed feelings about speaking out, the difficulty of breaking with friends or family on this vital issue. I have "come a long way, baby!" You too?

Paralysis and Catharsis

Apathy, in fact, may be the wrong word for the prevailing public mood. Joanna Rogers Macy, in her excellent primer on despair-work, identifies *apathy* as a Greek word that literally means *nonsuffering*. "Given its etymology, apathy is the inability or the refusal to experience pain."[5]

Many people are, subconsciously for the most part, refusing to feel, refusing pain. They don't want the pain of grieving for a terminally ill world. Robert Jay Lifton mentions several kinds of repressed feelings, *psychic numbing*. For one, he tells of "the numbing of massive death immersion" observed in the stories told by Hiroshima and Nagasaki survivors: disfigured people wandering in slow motion after the blast, unable to function normally, their minds disconnected. They were aware of people around them dying in horrible ways but they simply *ceased to feel*.

There is another, different psychic numbing, that experienced by the atomic scientists who, over time, managed to suppress their fears about the possible carnage as they worked on the Bomb and, like the rest of us, learned to coexist. And we *have* learned to coexist with it (can that be called *living?*) to a certain extent. But the price of that lesson is high: depression, mental disorders, even the increased teenage suicide rate may be, in part, a result.

So we all lead double lives. We live the ordinary life of our daily existence, shopping, working, going to church, watching television, but always aware, at some level of consciousness, of the fact that we're looking into the barrel of a nuclear gun. It is unpleasant to think of such things, so we try not to. A paralysis results, a *nuclear numbing* takes over, in Lifton's phrase. "Further," he writes,

> We *domesticate* these weapons in our language and attitudes. Rather than feel their malignant actuality, we render them benign. In calling them "nukes," for instance, we render them small and "cute," something on the order of the household pet . . . What are we to make of terms like "nuclear exchange," "escalation," "nuclear yield," "counterforce," "megatons," or of "window of vulnerability" or (ostensibly much better) "window of opportunity." Quite simply, *these words provide a way of talking about nuclear*

weapons without really talking about them. In them we find nothing about billions of human beings incinerated or literally melted, nothing about millions of corpses.[6]

So our military and political leaders, lest they awaken the numbed masses, the *apathetic,* use "nukespeak" to address this grim subject. Nukespeak is a desensitized language that will slide by us without arousing our outrage.

Do not assume, however, that the entire silent majority feels no pain. Some, at least on the conscious level do not. They simply refuse to hurt, they refuse pain. But many of our friends and neighbors *are* in pain. They are grieving for an endangered world. Like us, they suffer with every new chemical spill, every Bophal, every Greenpeace misadventure, every round of weapons development; certainly, with every new revelation of a "nuclear winter." They suffer, but they don't talk about it. It hurts more when you talk. It is easier to suppress your fear, seek diversions, pretend the disaster won't happen. Retreat into fantasy or busyness—live for the moment. For such, the prevailing mood is not apathy (in its literal meaning) but *inability.* People are silent, unable to speak, or immobilized, unable to act. Their tongues are numbed, and their wills; not their feelings.

But Nuclear Free Zones testify to the widespread, growing conviction that we *can* survive—indeed, create a brave new weaponless planet for ourselves and posterity—if we are willing and able to *speak out* and *act out* our feelings. Acting out our fear, anger and love constructively, we can turn the arms race around. Start a peace race. Abolish nuclear weapons!

Joanna Macy describes the benefits that come from unblocking our feelings, that is, from self-disclosure, sharing our common grief for the world. It is a healing process, and it activates. In *Despair and Personal Power in the Nuclear Age,* she provides ways and means—creative exercises for reflection, togetherness, healing, and empowerment. By sharing our pain for the world,

. . . we can open to power, and this power is not just our own, it belongs to others as well. It relates to the very evolution of our species. It is part of a general awakening or shift toward a new level of social consciousness.[7]

So perhaps the first step is to get people to share their feelings about the state of the world—the fate of the earth. Many a peace group has begun that way, with a small circle of concerned individuals. People often get involved in the Freeze, Jobs With Peace, or NFZ campaigns as a result of someone asking them, "What do you think about all these nuclear weapons in the world?" We have to invite people to express their feelings and even share their grief. That invitation may lead to self-discovery, and to action.

"But," you say, "turning the arms race around is a huge undertaking—and all the success stories in your book won't alter that fact." Yes, but—and thank God for the "buts" of life—there are ways. In this last chapter I want to consider three aspects of empowerment, ways and means of motivating ourselves, awakening others, and staying the course. In sum, we shall be talking about self-motivation, interpersonal persuasion, and spiritual stamina. The latter comes largely from imaging and hope.

Force-Field Analysis

If the problem seems too big for you, break it down and systematically attack its separate parts. That's the value of force-field analysis,[8] a problem-solving model developed by Kurt Lewin. Let's use it to examine the problem we face in promoting nuclear disarmament. First, consider the *present state* and the *goal state*. We all know about the present state: it is grim and frightening. As for the goal state, we want a world without nuclear weapons. (Or, without weapons of any kind, but let's not push it that far at the moment.) In the following chart are a number of factors that tend to promote change in the desired direction, and others which seem to obstruct it. These are the Impelling and Restraining Forces. (I have listed the factors that struck me as most important—you may think of others.) The same force-field model could be used to plot the factors facing activists in a local NFZ campaign: the goal state would be a nuclear-free ordinance and/or community. But here we'll apply the model to the larger problem.

In chapter two, I discounted so-called expert opinion. But the "experts" are right about something: the nuclear weapons establishment is deeply entrenched. It cannot be removed overnight, for the Restraining Forces are formidable. But wait—don't overlook the other side, the Impelling Forces! Often as we examine a problem we become very aware of the obstacles but fail to see the available resources, the immense strength and variety of Impelling Forces.

Now, the idea is, *first,* to weaken or eliminate the Restraining Forces, or as many of them as we can; *second,* to strengthen the Impelling forces, if possible. You may have to prioritize the Restraining Forces and attack them in order of their importance. There may be a few factors in the field which you cannot affect; for example, the lure that pure science has for some young people. But most of the Restraining Forces can be attacked and removed, or weakened.

Consider the ones charted. Generally, the way to deal with self-serving ideologies is through indoctrinating people into a more responsible world view. The methods of dealing with official intransigence include education to correct faulty assumptions; severing the connections between Congress, the military-industrial complex, and academia; and removing certain stubborn officials by means of the ballot box. The economic basis of nuclearism can be combatted through curtailing defense-industry profits (boycotts and divestment!), providing conversion plans, and helping workers with compensation and skill-training as they make the transition to nonmilitary work. If the home and church are doing their job, spiritual training can overcome a good deal of the amorality that makes it possible for keen minds to design weapons of death.

But the Restraining Forces *in me* are more disturbing (let me

FORCE-FIELD ANALYSIS:

Present State: the existence of 50,000 nuclear warheads, others added daily; and with all known complicating factors.

RESTRAINING FORCES

THE POLITICAL/SOCIAL SETTING . . .

+ Self-serving ideologies, prejudice and stereotyping; and the political games that nations play to extend their global spheres of influence . . .

+ Official stubbornness, resistence to change, and the nuclear deterrence mindset; faulty assumptions, and the inability to reason creatively.

+ Greed and cost-plus defense contracts; and the economic tentacles of a system involving many jobs.

+ The lure of pure science and the challenge of problem-solving for technicians; the indifference to moral principles on the part of many engaged in research, testing, and deployment of weapons.

BUT THE RESTRAINING FORCES WITHIN ME
are more disturbing . . .

1) *denial:* "Nuclear war? It's a nightmare, it can't (shouldn't, won't) happen!"
2) *powerlessness:* "There's nothing I can do to stop the arms race so why try?"
3) *cowardice:* "I'm afraid of what my spouse (boss, friends, neighbors, children, parents) will say if I speak or ack out my fears and conviction."

ONE WAY TO WORK ON THE PROBLEM IS TO REDUCE OR REMOVE THE RESTRAINING FORCES. First, I need to work on the ones inside me.

+ *denial:* Accept the possibility, "It can happen!"
+ *powerlessness:* Assume responsibility: "Together with others, I can prevent it from happening!"
+ *cowardice:* Take courage and act: "The first thing I'm going to do about it is _____ "
(and fill in the blank with the first thing you're going to do!

THE PROBLEM OF NUCLEAR WEAPONS

Goal State: a world without nuclear weapons—and with careful international monitoring to preclude weapons being covertly manufactured or deployed.

IMPELLING FORCES

EDUCATION, RESULTING IN . . .

+ public awareness of the results of nuclear explosions; the threat they pose to the ecosystem, putting everything at risk . . .

+ perception of the likelihood of nuclear war; knowing the circumstances that could provoke it; becoming aware of the possibilities of accidental war . . .

+ being aware of our Judeo-Christian heritage, as well as the humanistic values most Americans share, emphasizing the sacredness of life, justice, compassion, and the importance of sharing this globe's abundance with the Third World . . .

+ the inspiration of community leaders, both the known (Paul Newman, Mark Hatfield, Helen Caldicott) and the unknown (NFZ organizers and others) who are taking stands for disarmament, peace, social justice . . .

RESULTING IN . . . THESE EMOTIONS:

FEAR for the fate of the planet, and regarding the possible extinction of life.

ANGER at the insanity of the arms race and those who have brought us to this pass—and the fact that immense resources are being wasted in the effort to catch up (get ahead of) the other side.

LOVE for the world and all its beauty . . . and for art and architecture and technology (rightly applied) and all the good things in civilization that have been put at risk . . . all that is worth cherishing and worth preserving.

WORK ON THE IMPELLING FORCES TOO! STRENGTHEN AND CHANNEL THEM INTO POSSIBLE, POSITIVE ACTION!

be very personal), and they are multiplied in others. These are the numbing factors: denial, a perception of oneself as powerless, and cowardice. When Gandhi was warned about the "demonic" British he replied, "I am worried more about the demons in me." I have to admit that my real enemies are not the Communists, or the hawks in the Pentagon, or the defense contractors, or the engineer I know who designs missiles—but the denial, sense of powerlessness, and cowardice *in me*. Dealing with my internal enemies enables me to deal with the external "adversaries." I need to work on myself even as I work with others to change the political and social soil that nurtures and nourishes the Bomb.

Awareness and education, in time, erode our denial: the holocaust *can* and may happen. This awareness combined with a healthy rage tends to break down our cowardice. But the feeling of powerlessness is perhaps the most difficult to eradicate.

Indeed, the power often *seems* to be in the hands of the militarists and businessmen and politicians who further the arms race, who won't listen to reason, who plow on towards an unhealthy end. When I think of the fact that the President, or any number of submarine commanders, can launch missiles and unleash a nuclear war without my say-so, indeed, without any vote in Congress as dictated by the Constitution, I feel powerless, and I am angry.

We have to remember that *we* have put our elected officials in office, and *we* can unelect them. We are paying for the bombs and missiles with our tax dollars, and *we* can refuse to pay. *We* are providing the land, workers, and support for the research and manufacture of the deadly weapons that may destroy us someday, and *we* can refuse to provide these things. We are not powerless! Indeed, with Nuclear Free Zones we take back power that is rightfully ours.

Next, consider the Impelling Forces and let them work for you, especially the emotions at the bottom of the chart. Again, the top of the chart represents factors affecting society at large; the bottom, factors in me and you.

Using Your Feelings

We tend to think of two emotions, fear and anger, as negative or debilitating. Often they are, but they don't need to be. For many persons promoting Nuclear Free Zones, the journey *starts* with fear. The very legitimate fear of what may happen to ourselves, our children, posterity, and the globe drive us to action. Franz Alt quotes the German novelist Gunther Anders who said that we need to find the courage to fear, and to make others afraid. "Frighten your neighbor as yourself," Alt writes.

> Naturally, this kind of fear has to be something very special. (1) A fearless fear, since it excludes fear of those who might jeer at us for being afraid. (2) An animating fear, since it ought to get us out of our corners and into the streets. (3) A loving fear, which should worry about the *world,* and not just about what might happen to *us.*[9](italics mine)

What about anger? Religious activists may be uncomfortable with anger, but we have to be honest about our feelings. As a Christian, I am not ashamed of anger. Jesus was angry more than once, and if we are not enraged by injustice and insanity there is something wrong with us. The political situation *is* outrageous, and we should be outraged! Conducting business as usual in a world brimming with weapons is obscene, and we should be scandalized!

So, driven by anger, I write letters, circulate petitions, join direct action events at defense plants. Without that motivating anger, a good deal of social change would never happen. Take Mothers Against Drunk Driving, aptly named MADD. It was an angry grieving mother who began the political process that has resulted in significant anti-drunk driver legislation in virtually every state. Historically, it was anger that declared American Independence, got rid of slavery, took us out of Vietnam, produced sweeping civil rights laws. Let the establishment know you're angry. Control your anger, but use it, channel it to bring about change!

"But the greatest of these is love." (1 Cor. 13:13b) Alt says that we need a "loving fear," a fear that worries about the world. Surely, when we think of all that would be lost in a nuclear war—depicted so dramatically in the thousands of banners paraded about Washington for the Ribbon Project in August, 1985—we find so much to love! My own list would include bluebirds and meadowlarks, tasseled cornstalks and bushy green broccoli, porpoises and giant pandas, bicycling and cool spring water, black raspberry ice cream and blueberry pancakes, ball games and band concerts, Wilder's plays and Bradbury's stories, sunsets and smiling faces, the joy of creative work, and a good backhand shot down the line.

So the journey that starts with fear ends with love. Many Christians believe that "God so loved the world" that he sought to save it through Jesus Christ; Jews, that he will save it through the long-awaited Messiah. In a more physical sense, it is because of *our* love affair with the world that *we* want to save it. That we *demand* that it be saved; no, that we *take responsibility* for saving it. Thinking and loving globally, we act lovingly, locally to save our planet from destruction.

Persuasion and Social Movements

Briefly, consider some of the insights from studies in persuasion that may help us plan our tactics. Many of these are evident in the Nuclear Free Zone campaigns we've discussed.

(1) *Balance theory* holds that people try to keep their beliefs consistent. They want to keep their beliefs, rhetoric, and behavior harmonious. If there is any disharmony between or among our values and beliefs, we try to eliminate it. Similarly, if there is a contradiction between what we think, say, or do, we're uncomfortable. We try to restore balance, and there are various ways of doing that.

Persuaders attempt to make the principle work for them. They will demonstrate to an individual that he or she holds a belief or value that is inconsistent with certain facts; for example, the idea that missiles make us secure won't wash in light of the fact that every missile becomes a target for a missile on the other side, or in light of the fact that the more machinery of death we have, the more likely it is that an accidental firing may occur.

If a person sees the inconsistency, he or she may react in various ways. One is to deny the new information, or reject it by discrediting the source; another is to accept the persuader's point. If the point is pivotal for this individual, conversion to the antinuclear cause has occurred.

But now the new convert has another balance problem, for he or she holds an antinuclear *position* but has not taken antinuclear *action*. Applying the balancing strategy again, the activist will point this out, gently, and/or simply suggest some ways of acting that are consistent with the individual's convictions.

Another approach is to argue that your position *supports* or *extends* the persuadee's values and desires. Here, the case might be stated as follows. "You want to be safe. You want a world free from the threat of a holocaust. You want to see your tax dollars used for the elderly, for education, for low-income housing, mass transit, feeding the world's poor, and so forth, instead of poured by the billions into weapons—then join with us abolitionists and work for a Nuclear Free World!" This strategy works to the extent that your audience says yes to each of the implied questions, or to the extent that you can relate your theme to the actual values of your audience.

Notice how Martin Luther King, Jr., reached his listeners' values by grounding his theme (racial integration) in both Americanism and the Judeo-Christian heritage:

> I still have a dream. It is a dream deeply rooted in the American dream. It is a dream that one day this nation will rise up and live out the true meaning of its creed: "We hold these truths to be self-evident; that all men are created equal' . . . I have a dream that one day every valley shall be exalted, every hill and mountain shall be made low, the rough places will be made plane and crooked places will be made straight, and the glory of the Lord shall be revealed, and all flesh shall see it together.[10]

We can appeal to people's values in stressing the urgency of ending the arms race and the utility of Nuclear Free Zones.

(2) The balancing goes on, multiplied many times in a community where NFZ campaigners are active as persuasion takes place person-to-person or through the media. Often, a two-step flow process occurs. Studies show that new ideas are adopted in many communities only when they are first accepted by *opinion leaders*.

These opinion leaders are not the so-called experts, the Washington technocrats and military strategists. They are respected local citizens, professional people, union officials, newspaper editors, the mayor and council, clergy. So the ideas flow from the activist group to opinion leaders to the public at large; or from the media to opinion leaders to the public. It is critical that nuclear-free activists bring some opinion leaders on board early in their campaign. Clearly, activists in Ashland, Amherst, and the other communities that we've examined were aware of this.

(3) Getting people to make a *public commitment* is important. When a person takes a public stand he or she internalizes a commitment, and it becomes more difficult for that person to stray. "Crossing the line" into peace work may be taken quite literally, as when, driven by conscience, a person crosses a boundary line onto a defense plant or a military base, and is placed under arrest. That person is very likely to repeat his or her action.

With Nuclear Free Zone campaigns, rather, a more subtle but significant step is taken when a person agrees to have his or her name added to a published list of sponsors in the newspaper, or carry a Nuclear Free Zone banner in a local parade down Main Street. Once seen by others, that individual's commitment is firmed and strengthened. So, widespread participation is good, and the more it becomes public the stronger the cause becomes.

(4) One of the basic principles of selling is to *ask for more than you expect to get.* The insurance salesman, the United Way solicitor, and others, will often start you off at twice the amount he or she expects you to take (or give), then settle for less. The union representative will demand a stronger wage package than the union expects management to accept, and *vice versa.* With

the bargaining process, if you ask for too little, you will get less than you want.

By this logic, Nuclear Free Zone campaigners should not ask a city council for a resolution, if that is what they expect to get, for they may wind up with nothing. Ask for an ordinance. And if you expect to get an ordinance, package a powerful one! Include whatever you think is morally right, and whatever you think is at all politically possible. If there is strenuous opposition, you may have to settle for less. Compromise, if necessary, later. In Takoma Park activists had to accept a compromise to their investment and purchasing clauses, but Takoma Park still has one of the nation's strongest NFZ ordinances.

Everett M. Rogers, who has studied the process by which ideas are distributed and adopted in society,[11] speaks of the "reinvention" of an innovation. Modifications are made as a result of the corrective feedback during the innovation's trial period. Rogers' studies concerned technological innovation and so his findings need to be applied cautiously elsewhere, but we can make some tentative predictions about the spread of public policy ideas.

Rogers says that when the adoption percentage reaches 10 to 15 percent the curve takes off. To get to that point you have to educate and explain it to the public; and once an innovation is known by 20 to 30 percent of its target population, the rate of adoption proceeds much more rapidly. Currently, the average American isn't aware of Nuclear Free Zones. As awareness spreads, adoption takes place slowly. But if Rogers' theory applies to Nuclear Free Zones, it appears that when the idea is known to 20 to 30 percent of the population, the rate of adopting communities will soar.

Most of the above discussion of persuasion follows a reason-oriented philosophy. We are assuming that our listeners think logically and that we can use a *rational* approach on them. The media persuaders often operate very differently: they assume that humans are essentially *emotional* beings. Tony Schwartz offers a *resonance model* of persuasion.[12] The resonance or "evoked recall" theory assumes that it's better to get a message out of an audience than to put one into it. It relies on the experiences and memories, value-images, that people have stored within themselves. The persuasive message is designed to evoke these images. For example, picture a television spot in which a kindly grandfather sits on an ivy-covered front porch playing chess with his granddaughter. She asks, "Will I grow up to be good enough to win my college chess championship like you did, Gramps?" He looks solemn, smiles wistfully, and says, "I hope so, dear. But I wonder . . ." Voice over: "Help reduce the threat of nuclear war. Support your local Nuclear Free Zone ordinance!"

Heart-tugging advertisements, like emotionally-geared speeches, may present an ethical problem. Each group of peace activists needs to examine the ethical issues in persuasion in light of their own values and objectives.

Also, consider how movement campaigns evolve. Charles U. Larsen suggests that the Yale model, originally designed to interpret emerging nations' identity-development, can be applied to idea campaigns as well.[13] The model suggests five developmental stages: identification, legitimacy, participation, penetration, and distribution.

A movement like Nuclear Free Zones has to develop an *identification*. It has to be recognized widely. Flags, logos, slogans, and T-shirts help, in addition to the basic theme of the movement, or as a means of dramatizing that theme. (Of course, it helps to get oneself on national television!) *Legitimacy* refers to establishing a power base. NFZ campaigns may do this by getting the local editors on their side, or putting the council in their camp, or a sufficient number of opinion leaders. In this stage, the participants are known supporters. In the so-called *participation* stage, the organizers try to involve previously uncommitted persons. The movement then swells and grows. In an NFZ community, the petition drive or newspaper signatures would be a way of doing this. Fourth, the *penetration* stage is reached when the movement can show that it has some "clout." NFZ campaigners usually demonstrate this clout by producing a significant number of voters. However, an opinion poll could also demonstrate the extent of penetration. Finally, with *distribution,* the campaign succeeds and its goal is implemented.

Nuclear Free Zone campaigners need to be aware of the need to *monitor the implementation* of NFZ legislation. If the ordinance provides for a monitoring committee, make sure it is appointed. If there is no such provision, appoint an unofficial "watchdog committee" from the campaign organization to stay in touch with officials and make sure that implementation occurs. Be courteous, and assume that local officials want to comply with the ordinance. (If they resist, then go back to the city council and squawk!)

We need to be honest with local officials. There may be some discomfort as the policy is implemented, and some administrators may have trouble adjusting. People may suffer a little temporarily, but there's a new order coming, and these are its birth pains.

For the Long Haul

We need stamina—moral, spiritual, and physical stamina. William Perry, formerly the public affairs director at Lawrence Livermore Laboratory, left his job in 1982 for ethical and spiritual reasons. He had decided that nuclear weapons are an immoral business and he couldn't be a party to it any longer. His concern is that the peace movement "will dissipate."

> One of the things that the establishment has going for it, *always had going for it,* is patience. It has money, it has time, and it thinks that it can outlast any movement. I've seen them try it with the civil rights movement. I've seen them try it with the women's movement.[14]

How do we keep the movement strong and vigorous for the long haul? How do we keep ourselves pumped up? It's not easy. Burnout occurs. People join the movement, others drop out—hopefully, the losses are temporary.

Jo Claire Hartsig, who served as peace programs staffer at Kirkridge Retreat Center in Pennsylvania, provides a way of looking at a person's response to the nuclear peril. Dr. Kubler-Ross looked at how people respond to their imminent death; she found the stages are denial, anger, bargaining, depression, and acceptance. But Hartsig has creatively reversed the stages to demonstrate how we may indeed choose life as opposed to meekly accepting death.[15] Most NFZ advocates, indeed, most peace activists, have taken the journey Hartsig suggests:

(1) We *accept* the presence of nuclear weapons and nuclear weapons-makers among us. Congress passes another defense budget bill and we yawn. We hear the rhetoric about the "missile gap," or the "window of vulnerability," and shrug. And we comply with our government's demand that we support the military machine with our tax money—every hour, 38 million dollars of our money is spent for Pentagon programs with our permission. (2) When our consciousness is raised, when we're made aware of the magnitude of the problem, our natural response is *depression.* We feel down, and blue. We wonder at the wisdom of bringing children into such an insane world. Hopefully, this stage is short-lived. (3) Some people skip the third stage, *bargaining,* but not all. The bomb shelter craze was an attempt by some people to bargain their way out of death, to avoid the holocaust. Civil defense schemes are a kind of collective bargaining too. (4) *Anger* is the fourth stage: we've discussed anger and found that it can be constructive if it is properly channeled; if indeed, it leads to the next stage, (5) *resistance* (denial). We are not talking about the denial of death as a reality—as in the Kubler-Ross patients—but the denial of power to those planning our collective death. We confront the warmakers. We refuse to comply with their demands. We protest, divest, convert, and drag our feet on civil defense plans. We resist with all our might the continuance of the nuclear status quo! Nuclear Free Zones are part of a creative, ongoing resistance movement.

But what keeps the resisters resisting? What keeps *us* going? Aside from the Impelling Forces we've charted, *community helps.* That is, being a part of an active, supportive group builds self-esteem as well as conviction. We have to be loved in order to live out our love for the world, to say nothing of how a caring community helps you keep your sanity in a crazy world. A friend living at Jonah House in Baltimore with other peacemakers, told me, "We get up in the morning and tell each other we're sane—and that really helps!"

Another thing that helps is visioning.

Visioning and Hope

Positive visioning brings empowerment, dispels despair, and builds stamina for the long haul. Psychologist Victor Frankl, in his influential account of experiences in a Nazi concentration camp,[16] explained that those who survived, those who held themselves together despite brutality and deprivation, had one characteristic other victims lacked: the vision of a future.

Imaging builds a future by enabling us to see what the goal would look like when we get there, what the "peaceable kingdom" might be like. If we want a world without weapons we have to dream it, imagine it, image it, or as Kovel puts it, "prefigure" it. Visioning is critical. We need utopian thinking today.

It is possible to dream good dreams, or bad ones; to conjure negative visions or more positive ones. Our slogans generally reflect negative images of the future: "Nuclear War is Nuclear Suicide" and "War is Unhealthy for Children and Other Living Things." At a peace demonstration in front of a weapons plant, one poster was addressed to the workers: "Will Your Children Survive Your Work?"

Currently, negative visions abound. People in despair workshops share impressions that came to them about friends burned horribly in nuclear war, or familiar buildings and landmarks vaporized. Joanna Macy reports an experience a college professor related to her:

> . . . when I crossed the campus on my way to class I saw the buildings crumble. The library and the science building, they just began to go in a cloud of dust. I stopped dead and closed my eyes—and for a moment I was afraid to open them again.[17]

The nuclear-winter scientists have helped us imagine what the world would look like after a full-scale nuclear war. They have done us a service. But that is a negative vision, a nightmare, not a dream. We need to stack up some positive images alongside it. What is the shape of the peaceable kingdom? What form would a utopian dream take? What would a world without weapons look like? Indeed, "What If They Gave a War and Nobody Came?"

The two sets of visions, negative and positive, are avenues to outcomes. Each of them, the apocalyptic vision and the more hopeful one, may be self-fulfilling prophecies if we dwell on them. Clearly, we need to imagine the constructive outcome more frequently and more completely than we have.

Elise Boulding, a Dartmouth sociologist who has been leading workshops on "Imaging a World Without Weapons," says that you cannot really work for something you cannot visualize. In one of her workshop exercises people are asked to pick a date, say thirty years from now, when they have gathered to celebrate the fact that there is no longer any danger of nuclear war. Questions are raised. What does it feel like? What has happened to our institutions? Our government? Schools? Churches? Relationships? Our view of the Soviet Union? The global community?

Often people are asked to reflect in silence, then work as a group to fill in the intervening history. What events have taken place to get us to this point? What were the headlines? Groups often produce unusually creative time-lines showing just how their goal of a nuclear-free world was reached. This might be an excellent process for a group of Nuclear Free Zone organizers. Visioning is empowering.

Nobody knows exactly what a peaceful world would be like, but we can dream. We can imagine! We have a few clues in songs like "Ain't Gonna Study War No More," "Vine and Fig Tree," and especially, "Last Night I had the Strangest Dream." The Bible offers images too. For Jews and Christians it's hard to improve on Micah 1:1–4:

> In days to come
> the mountain where the temple stands
> will be the highest one of all,

towering above all the hills.
Many nations will come streaming to it,
   and their people will say,
"Let us go up the hill of the Lord,
   to the temple of Israel's God.
For he will teach us what he wants us to do;
   we will walk in the paths he has chosen.
For the Lord's teaching comes from Jerusalem;
   from Zion he speaks to his people."
He will settle disputes among the nations,
   among the great powers near and far.
They will hammer their swords into plows
   and their spears into pruning knives.
Nations will never again go to war,
   never prepare for battle again.
Everyone will live in peace
   among his own vineyards and fig trees,
   and no one will make him afraid. (TEV)

We can bring this vision up to date, or translate it into our experience. Try paraphrasing. Instead of beating swords into plows (or plowshares) think about hammering nose cones into bird baths or converting nuclear submarines into floating hospital ships. We can redeem the land around missile silos by tilling the soil again for corn, wheat, or barley. And we can live in our homes and condominiums unafraid to venture into the hallway or into the streets, for there is a new spirit in the land, and no one will frighten us anymore. These are just a few images that the Micah passage suggests to me. Add your own.

Wellsprings of hope arise from scripture, from the writings of wise men and women and from their brave deeds, and from within ourselves. Visioning empowers by making the future concrete, and that also fosters hope (not optimism). Optimism comes hard these days, but there is a difference between optimism and hope, as Randall Kehler, former national coordinator of the Nuclear Weapons Freeze Campaign, said:

    I am often asked whether I am optimistic about stopping and reversing the nuclear arms race. The answer is no, I am not optimistic. But I *am* hopeful. That is to say, I am not convinced that we *will stop the nuclear arms race and prevent the ultimate catas-trophe. But I am absolutely convinced that it is possible* for us to stop it. For me, this is a matter of faith. And because I have faith that the possibility exists, I believe that we must keep trying. In short, I know that for myself I must cultivate not only faith but fortitude.[18]

Fortitude, yes. A full-bodied hope gives us stamina for the long haul. "Love never ends," the Bible says (1 Cor. 13:8), and hope is longsuffering and longlived too. Consider Emily Dickinson:

> Hope is the thing with feathers
>   That perches in the soul—
> And sings the tune without the words
>   And never stops—at all—

Peacemaking is a work that never stops. The crusade for nuclear abolitionists will end when nuclear weapons are gone. But of course there is more to peacemaking than getting rid of nuclear weapons. There is so much more to the problem of violence, some say, that eliminating nuclear weapons won't make a dent on the problem.

This becomes an argument against action, a justification for standing-pat. To those who argue that there is other violence in the world, and other weapons besides the nuclear ones that are just as fatal, and should we not rid the world of war, we say: "Yes, to all of the above! But abolishing nuclear weapons is a first step. You take aim at the dragon's head, and if you hit your target, the whole beast may fall."

Please recall the two primary effects of the multiplication of Nuclear Free Zones mentioned in chapter two. The first is the liberation of territory, the denial of land and resources to the bomb-makers. As Nuclear Free Zones multiply they will surely begin to suffocate the arms race. The second is that such an unprecedented people's crusade will produce a new world view, a marvelous new *zeitgeist*. Even getting close to a nuclear weaponless world will foster an unparalleled spirit of brotherhood and sisterhood among the world's peoples. Getting to zero would release much of the billions presently devoted to megadeath for humanitarian, life-saving projects around the world. Certainly that would put us in a position to heal the world's wounds, deal with problems such as overpopulation, acid rain, poverty, and hunger, and create an environment which fosters health, justice, and joy.

Aside from the money and resources, an incredibly healing spirit will surely be released, like a lark from its cage, into this old battered world. We are not prepared for the spiritual shock effect of that new spirit—it will energize, enlighten, and ennoble human beings as never before. It may surprise us, this "new-clear" explosion of the spirit—but let it come!

This new spirit will be an empowering one, but it will not give us power *over* as, historically, individuals and nations have tried to gain power over others, to impose their will on them and to use them for their own advantage. Historically, power became identified with dominance, or domination. The power we need to learn for the new age is power *with,* or *within.* Working *with* our fellow humans beings we become agents of change, instruments of healing and joy, and we learn at last to live *within* our fragile environment.

Power, then, which is the ability to effect change, works not from the top down, but from the bottom up. It is not power-over, but power-with; and this is what systems scientists call *synergy.*[19]

So when the day of real *shalom* comes, hopefully on the heels of Abolition—or we bring it to pass, God willing—we shall have power *with,* and *within.* There is a power *within* that connects us to the web of life and reminds us that we need to live and work *within nature.* For too long we have used our environment, trying to dominate it as we dominate people, and have left it eroded, poisoned, or decaying.

Now there is the *shalom* of peace *with* and *within.* We dream new dreams. We have a new vision. We are connected to all that is on the planet; we feel responsible for it. What happens to the Aleuts and the Samoans is just as important to us as what happens to our American neighbors, and what happens to the alligators and aardvarks and ash trees is also important. After all, we have no other home—this planet is the only one available to us—and we have to *preserve* and *conserve* it.

The New Abolitionists—with many other peacemakers—are trying to birth an earth where reason and responsibility prevail, where individuals consider themselves *world citizens* and want to preserve life in all its richness. How do we get there? In this chapter we've examined the persuasive process: motivating ourselves, convincing others, and building spiritual stamina through the kind of visioning that breeds hope.

The Unarmed Truth

Proverbs and poetry are comforting. "When it is dark enough," someone said, "you can see the stars." "In a dark time," Theodore Roethke wrote, "the eye begins to see."[20]

We live in a dark time, but not without hope. In a 1963 Nobel Lecture, Linus Pauling spoke of nuclear weapons as a "vestige of barbarism, a curse to the human race," then went on to say, "we are privileged to be alive during this extraordinary age, this unique epoch in the history of the world, the epoch of demarcation between the past millenia of war and suffering and the future, the great future of peace, justice, morality, and human well-being."

These are the assumptions underlying Nuclear Free Zones, that humanity is redeemable, that the future is alterable, that if we work hard for a world free from dread we shall have it. The 19th century social critic William Graham Sumner observed, "A wise rule would be to make up your mind soberly, and then to get ready for what you want; for what we prepare for is what we shall get."

There is an elemental logic here. If we prepare for war we shall most likely get war, and if we prepare for nuclear war, we shall probably—despite our whispered prayers—get that. To go on living with nuclear weapons is a dismal prospect. They threaten to steal our past and our future; indeed, they have already stolen our present, for as we live and breathe we are haunted by them.

Shall we not then prepare for peace?

Let us begin by removing the curse from our own communities, then join others. Linking Nuclear Free Zones around the world, the people of Earth can create a solidarity with enough clout to challenge the death-machine, to reverse the tide. "Join hands until there are millions of hands," poet Olga Cabral writes. "Cry out together, from millions of throats!"[21]

Each local Nuclear Free Zone foreshadows a time when the world itself will be nuclear-free. *Thinking globally and acting locally,* we invite and invent a new age. Each new Zone brings us one step closer to that ideal emancipated earth.

A Fictional Epilogue

They wandered through the Peace Park, joking, scoffing, arguing, confirming one another. Mother, daughter, father and
son . . . they meditated on the monuments and stared at the stat-
uary. The birds sang and the breeze blew, and they sipped honeysuckle and breathed clover and wild roses and held buttercups to
each other's chins and noses. Across the street from the park,
kids with faces that mirrored all ethnic heritages played stickball
shouting and arguing like banshees, having a jolly good time
until mom and dad yelled that dinner was ready, the chores
needed doing, and did they know what time it was?

The idea for the Peace Park came from a letter to the editor:
"Dear Sir: There seem to be a lot of bronzed generals in this
world. We're about to enter the New Age, and I don't want my
kids looking up to the warriors. Where can I take my son or
daughter to see the statue of a peacemaker?"

Wiser than most, this editor launched a campaign. They
carved the park out of the ugliest of all slum sections of the city.
Now, graced with fragrant shrubs, reflecting pools and foun-
tains, and bordered on the street by a section of attractive low-
cost homes, the Peace Park was an inviting place to spend a
Sunday afternoon.

Here were bronzed and marble champions of peace and
justice . . . reconcilers, healers and helpers, caretakers and cus-
todians of earth . . . statues of men and women who reverenced
life. There were Albert Schweitzer, Gandhi, Dorothy Day, Rosa
Parks and Martin Luther King, Jr., James Meredith and Bishop
Tutu, Dag Hammerskjold and David Lange. There was a statue
of the Greenpeace photographer, Fernando Pereira, who died
when the *Rainbow Warrior* was sabotaged in the Auckland, NZ,
harbor on its way to prevent French nuclear testing, and one of

Olof Palme, beloved Swedish Prime Minister and disarmament advocate, slain by an assassin outside a Stockholm theater.

There were marble memorials to the members of Witness for Peace and Peace Brigades, and others who offered themselves as living barriers to violence on contested borders, wherever human rage and revenge threatened to outrun reason. And there was a special exhibit honoring the women of Greenham Common, UK, who endured hostile police and fickle weather to witness against the missiles stored at the American air force base.

The family paused at the Statue of the Unforgotten Abolitionist. They sat gazing at the immense figure, neither black nor white, male nor female: a stylized, commanding presence with a compassionate face. This artwork honored all the abolitionists who endured insults, threats and the loss of friends and jobs, staving off Armageddon until a peace race could start up, gain momentum, and end humanity's bondage to the Bomb.

The inscription under the statue read: *The Meek Shall Inherit the Earth—Provided There's Anything Left When the Warriors are Through.* They had done the impossible, these abolitionists. They had dragged the hawks kicking and screaming into the New Age.

"Mommy," the boy asked, "was there really a bomb big enough to blow up the world."

"At least Pennsylvania, or a country the size of Spain. But there were lots of those bombs, honey."

"Daddy," the girl asked, "my teacher said something today about Libya. Do they have a big bomb?"

"There's been some kind of test explosion," he said gravely. "The UN dispatched a surveillance team. If the Libyans have built a bomb in defiance of international law, the world won't stand for it!"

"Not any more."

"No way. We've had one crisis since Abolition, when it appeared that South Africa was secretly making warheads. Evidence accumulated. South Africa refused surveillance. But as a result of a global boycott they had to comply. You have to export your marketable goods for a country to survive."

"Mommy," the boy begged, "tell us about the dominoes again!"

His father chuckled, muttering, "dominoes again," and tickled his son. "You smart, too-good-for-your-britches kid!" They all laughed and grimaced.

"The dominoes fell, dear," the mother said. "One by one by one back in the 1980s and 1990s. New Zealand was the first, I think, to make the world take notice. By then the Latin countries were part of a Nuclear Free Zone. Soon the island nations were nuclear-free, then Scandinavia, Holland, Britain, Belgium, and Spain and then the Mediterranean. African nations followed, and several Warsaw Pact countries, despite ominous signals from Moscow. In Asia, India and Pakistan signed a non-aggression pact and joined the peace parade.

"By this time the nuclear powers' navies were finding it hard to dock their ships. Refused port access around the world, they were being confined to small areas of water.

"But what about here?" the boy asked. "The US of A?"

"In these United States," the father said, "Nuclear Free Zone communities doubled almost every year for six years. Whole states declared themselves, beginning with Oregon and Massachusetts, where some firms making nuclear weapons parts were converted by state fiat. Astonished and frightened, of course, the military-industrial complex struck back. Federal prosecutors took mayors and council members to court and charged them with treason. Courts declared some zones unconstitutional, but more judges and juries began to apply international law."

"What about Massachusetts? The state line?"

"When federal marshalls tried to escort a truck convoy carrying weapons components into the state they were forced to turn back at the Connecticut border by state police."

"And Oregon! Tell us about Oregon!"

"Confrontation! Oregon threatened to secede if its nuclear-free law wasn't recognized. In the celebrated case, *The United States v. Oregon* in 1992, the Supreme Court ruled the state law constitutional and declared the federal government in violation of international law. They held that Washington was involved in criminal activity by preparing to wage nuclear war!

"The White House rocked with the blow, the Pentagon likewise. Dozens of nuclear weapons firms began to draw up conversion plans. Hundreds of local communities voted to divest. Civil disobedience against the Armageddon companies increased and hundreds, thousands were jailed. Thousands more took their places. A massive general strike was called for October 4, 1993. Around the world millions stayed home—didn't work. Business stood still. Wall Street shivered. The Pentagon shuddered, and hastily rammed more anti-Communist invective into its propaganda mill.

"In the Soviet Union, where peace activities had been controlled by the authorities, independent peace groups took heart. Despite threats and beatings, they bravely took the streets in Moscow and in many other towns and cities. The Kremlin had to listen! The Party Secretary announced that the USSR would dismantle 100 warheads a week, down to 500, and called on the US to follow suit. The White House did so, surprising the world.

"So . . . a peace race. At the summit, both sides agreed to cut down to zero. Amazing! Politicians who had said it couldn't be done were eating their words. The once-proud military-industrial hawks fluttered like frightened pigeons from one shaky perch to another, trying to escape the tidal wave of abolitionism. Vainly they protested this mad rush toward peace, warning of a takeover by the other side, but now their dire doomsaying failed to impress."

"I don't think I understand all that," the boy frowned. "Especially the hawks fluttering like pigeons."

"Just a figure of speech," the father continued. "Within two years of the famous General Strike it was over. The Bomb was banned, the missiles gone. Treaties had been signed, sealed and delivered. The UN would keep the peace. On the day that the last two H-bombs were dismantled under world scrutiny—with satellite television beaming the wondrous sight to every nation on earth—everybody celebrated! From Moscow to Washington, from Paris to Sidney, Calcutta, Buenos Aires and Madrid, shouts of joy! Dancing, singing, jubilation!"

"Hooray!" the boy yelled, scaring two pigeons from their perch on Gandhi's stone shoulder. "That's why we have VNW Day!"

"Victory Over Nuclear Weapons!" cried the girl.

"And we celebrate every year on September 6th," the boy said.

"Exactly a month after the anniversary of Hiroshima!" the girl announced.

They pounced on her. "You smart, too-good-for-your-britches kid!" they chuckled, and tickled each other, and made faces.

And the birds sang and the breeze blew, and they sipped honeysuckle and breathed clover and wild roses, and held buttercups to each others' chins and noses. Across the street from the park, kids with faces that mirrored all ethnic heritages played stickball shouting and arguing like banshees, and having a jolly good time until mom and dad yelled that dinner was ready and the chores needed doing, and did they know what time it was?

It wasn't a perfect world. Africans and Asians still died at alarming rates from starvation and disease. But the gap diminished. Resources once poured into the mighty maw of Mars were being diverted to projects that elevated and improved life.

It wasn't a perfect world, since Abolition . . . but a much safer one.

Endnotes

1. Taking Responsibility

1. Andrew Malcolm, "Chicago Declares Itself Nuclear Weapon-Free Zone," *New York Times,* March 13, 1986.
2. Senator Matthias (R-MD), *Congressional Record,* May 6, 1982.
3. Gene Sharp, *The Politics of Nonviolent Action,* 3 vols. (Boston: Porter Sargent, 1973).
4. John Naisbitt, *Megatrends* (NY: Warner Books, 1982).
5. Naisbitt, p. 167.
6. Michael Nelson, "Power to the People," *Saturday Review,* Nov. 24, 1979, p. 17.
7. W. Clyde Tilley, "Believing the Bible in an Age of Nuclear Madness," *Baptist Peacemaker* (April, 1985).
8. *Waltonian* interview (student newspaper, Eastern College, St. Davids, PA).
9. Douglas John Hall, *Christian Mission: The Stewardship of Life in the Kingdom of Death* (NY: Friendship Press, 1985).
10. US Rep. Lehman, *Congressional Record,* Vol. 131, Mar. 25, 1985.
11. Hall, p. 72.
12. Tom Sine, "Bringing Down the Final Curtain," *Sojourners* (June-July, 1984): 13.
13. Sine, p. 14.
14. Tilley, p. 8.
15. John R. W. Stott, "Involvement: Is It Our Concern?" *Faculty Dialogue,* Fall 1985, p. 24.
16. George Kennan, "A Christian's View of the Arms Race," *Theology Today,* 1982, pp. 162–170.
17. Leonard Sweet, "'Give Me Liberty Or Give Me Death!' and the Nuclear Arms Race," *The American Baptist* (March, 1984) p. 5.
18. Franz Alt, *Peace is Possible: The Politics of the Sermon on the Mount* (New York: Schocken Books, 1985), p. 88.
19. Richard Barnet, *The Giants* (New York: Simon & Schuster, 1977).
20. Olga Cabral, "Join Hands," in *What Will It Take to Prevent Nuclear War?* Pat Farren, ed. (Cambridge, MA: Schenkman, 1983), p. 74.

2. A New World Vision

1. Benjamin Spock, *The Common Sense Book of Baby and Child Care*, 1946.
2. Paul Boyer, *By the Bomb's Early Light: American Thought and Culture at the Dawn of the Atomic Age* (NY: Pantheon, 1985), p. 23–24.
3. Quoted in Boyer, p. 211.
4. Gregg Herken, *Counsels of War* (NY: Alfred A. Knopf, 1985).
5. Joel Kovel, *Against the State of Nuclear Terror* (Boston: South End Press, 1983), p. 173.
6. Sidney Lens, *The Day Before Doomsday*, 1977.
7. *Voter Opinions on Nuclear Arms Policy* (NY: The Public Agenda Foundation, 1984), p. 9.
8. *Nobel: The Man and His Prizes*, ed by the Nobel Foundation (New York: Elsevier, 1972), p. 36.
9. Helen Caldicott, *Missile Envy* (NY: William Morrow, 1984), p. 316.
10. Boyer, p. 344.
11. Barry M. Casper, "Appeal to Physicists," *The Bulletin of the Atomic Scientists* (Oct. 1984): 13.
12. National Conference of Bishops, *The Challenge of Peace: God's Promise and Our Response* (Washington, DC, 1983).
13. David McReynolds, newsletter of the War Resisters League.
14. Jonathan Schell, *The Abolition* (NY: Alfred A. Knopf, 1984), p. 112.
15. Schell, *The Abolition*, p. 113.
16. Harvard Study Group, *Living With Nuclear Weapons*, 1983.
17. Schell, *The Fate of the Earth* (NY: Alfred A. Knopf, 1982), p. 226.
18. Marilyn Ferguson, *The Aquarian Conspiracy: Personal and Social Transformation in the 1980s* (Los Angeles: J. P. Tarcher, Inc., 1980), p. 411.
19. Joanna Rogers Macy, *Despair and Personal Power in the Nuclear Age* (Philadelphia: New Society Publishers, 1983), p. 27.
20. Macy, p. 28.
21. Herbert F. York, "Bilateral Negotiations and the Arms Race," *Scientific American* (Oct., 1983).
22. Barnett, p. 100.
23. Marek Thee, "The State of the Globe: Rethinking Problems of the Nuclear Arms Race," *Bulletin of Peace Proposals*, 15. (1984) #4.
24. Thomas J. Downey, "START . . . SALT . . . The Freeze," *Bulletin of the Atomic Scientists* 38 (Dec., 1982): 58.
25. Gerald C. Smith, "The Arms Control and Disarmament Agency: An Unfinished HIstory," *Bulletin of the Atomic Scientists* 40 (April, 1984).
26. Anders Thunborg, "National Security and Nuclear Weapons," *Bulletin of Peace Proposals*, 15, (1984) #4.
27. Schell, *The Abolition*, p. 119.
28. *Ibid*, p. 139.
29. Lewis C. Bohn, "ZNA: Let's Take Nuclear Disarmament Seriously," *UCAM Network News* (March, 1986): 3.

30. Dietrich Fischer, *Preventing War in the Nuclear Age* (Towata, NJ: Roman and Allenheld, 1984), p. 33.
31. Thee, p. 374.

3. Americans Opt Out

1. Arthur Levine, *When Dreams and Heroes Died: A Portrait of Today's College Students* (San Francisco: Jossey-Bass, 1980).
2. Howard J. Ehrlich, "The University-Military Research Connection," *Thought & Action: The NEA Higher Education Journal,* (Fall 1984): 118.
3. Bill Bell, "Making a Statement For Peace," *Daily News,* June 1, 1984, M-3.

4. The Abolitionist Connection

1. Freeman Dyson, *Weapons and Hope* (NY: Harper & Row, 1984), p. 201.
2. Nicholas Humphrey, *Consciousness Regained* (Oxford: Oxford Univ. Press, 1983).
3. Jacob Bronowski, *Science and Human Values* (New York: Julian Messner, Inc., 1956), p. 89.
4. Dale Aukerman, *Darkening Valley: A Biblical Perspective on Nuclear War* (New York: Seabury, 1981).
5. Howard Webber, "In Preparing for Nuclear War, We Have Sinned," *The Episcopalian* (January 1985).
6. David McReynolds, undated publication, War Resisters League.
7. Fran Fortino, "My Turn: Make Amherst Nuclear-Free," *Amherst Bulletin,* May 16, 1984, p. 13.
8. David Brion Davis, *Slavery and Human Progress* (New York: Oxford Univ. Press, 1984) p. 13.
9. Sidney Lens, *The Day Before Doomsday* (New York: Doubleday, 1977).
10. London *Observor,* June 27, 1948.
11. Brien McMahon, speech before US Senate, Sept. 18, 1951.
12. Robert William Fogel and Stanley L. Engerman, *Time on the Cross: The Economics of American Negro Slavery* (Boston: Little, Brown, 1974).
13. Anon, quoted in *The Abolitionists: Immediatism and the Question of Means,* Hugh Hawkins, ed. (Boston: D. C. Heath, 1964).
14. Lens, p. 55.
15. Gordon Adams, *The Iron Triangle* (Council on Economic Priorities, 1981).
16. David Donald, "Abolitionist Leadership: A Displaced Social Elite," in *The Abolitionists: Reformers or Fanatics?* Richard O. Curry, ed. (New York: Holt, Rinehart, and Winston, 1965). p. 43.
17. Frank Thistlewaite, "The Movement Derived Largely From England," in *The Abolitionists,* ed. Curry, p. 64.
18. Gilbert H. Barnes and Dwight L. Dumond, eds., *Letters of Theodore*

Dwight Weld, Angelina Grimke Weld, and Sarah Grimke, 1822–1844, 2 vols. (Gloucester, MA: 1965), I, p. 98.

19. Wendell P. and Francis J. Garrison, *William Lloyd Garrison, the Story of His Life as Told by His Children,* 1805–1879 (New York: 1885–1889), I, p. 228.

20. Gerald Sorin, *Abolitionism: A New Perspective* (New York: Praeger, 1972), p. 39.

21. Dwight L. Dumond, "The Abolition Indictment of Slavery," in *The Abolitionists,* ed., Hawkins, p. 22.

22. Cartleton Mabee, *Black Freedom* (Toronto: Collier-Macmillan, 1970), pp. 239–240.

23. *Liberator,* William Lloyd Garrison, ed., Oct. 4, 1850.

24. Howard Zinn, "The Tactics of Agitation," *The Age of Civil War and Reconstruction,* Charles Crowe, ed. (Homewood, IL: The Dorsey Press, 1966), pp. 215–216.

25. Mary G. McEdwards, "Agitative Rhetoric: Its Nature and Effect," *Western Speech,* (Winter 1968): 38.

26. Jane H. and William H. Pease, *Bound With Them in Chains* (Westport, Conn: Greenwood, 1972), p. 217.

27. Dyson, p. 201–202.

28. Thomas Harwood, "British Evangelism: A Divisive Influence on Protestant Churches, *The Abolitionists,* Curry, p. 76.

29. Dyson, p. 313.

30. Zinn, p. 222.

31. James Russell Lowell, *The Anti-Slavery Papers of James Russell Lowell,* 2 vols. (Boston: 1902), II, pp. 82–83.

5. Declaring Interdependence

1. Jonathan Steele, *Soviet Power* (New York: Simon and Schuster, 1983), p. 79.

2. Steele, *END* magazine (European Nuclear Disarmament), issue 7.

3. Gene Sharp, *Social Power and Political Freedom* (Boston: Porter-Sargent, 1980).

4. Gene Sharp, *Making Europe Unconquerable* (Cambridge: Ballinger, 1985).

5. Robert Jay Lifton and Richard Falk, *Indefensible Weapons: The Political and Psychological Case Against Nuclearism* (NY: Basic Books, 1982), p. 165.

6. Daniel Ford, Henry Kendall, Steven Nadis, *Beyond the Freeze* (Boston: Beacon, 1982), pp. 108, 6.

7. Ford, *et. al.,* p. 109.

8. Albert Donnay, *The New Abolitionist,* June 1983.

9. David Albright, "Eyes Only for Each Other," *Greenpeace Examiner,* (Oct.–Nov. 1984).

10. Leonard Specter, *The New Nuclear Nations* (New York: Vintage, 1985). Second annual nuclear proliferation report, commissioned by Carnegie Endowment for International Peace.

6. Is a Nuclear Free Pacific Possible?
1. William Arkin, "Tomahawk: Ominous New Deployment," *Bulletin of the Atomic Scientists*, 40: 4.
2. "New Zealander Assails US Ship Ban Reaction," *The Sun* (Baltimore), Feb. 27, 1985, p. 4a.
3. Gillian Thomas, "In New Zealand, Our Side's Winning. Here's Owen Wilkes," *Peace* magazine, (Feb. 1986): 16–17.
4. Thomas, p. 51.
5. Thomas, p. 17.
6. *Hearing Before the Subcommittee on Asian and Pacific Affairs of the Committee on Foreign Affairs, House of Representatives,* Ninety-ninth Congress, March 18, 1985 (Washington: US Govt. Printing Office), p. 155.
7. Hearing, p. 3.
8. *Nuclear-Free,* Journal of the New Zealand Nuclear Free Zone Committee, Christchurch, NZ (March/April 1985).
9. *Hearing,* p. 25.
10. Toshiyuki Toyoda, in *Bulletin of the Atomic Scientists* (August 1985) p. 62.
11. Harold Jackson, "Victims of the Nuclear Colonists," *Manchester Guardian Weekly,* July 15, 1984.
12. Michael Hamel-Green, "A Future for the South Pacific—Nuclear-Free," *Peace Dossier 8,* Dec. 1983. p. 1.
13. Patrick Smith, "U.S. Usurping Emerging Nation's Right to Self-Determination," *The Sunday Oregonian,* Oct. 9, 1983, D3.

7. Addressing the Bench: Legal Issues
1. Lucile W. Green, "Making Nuclear War Illegal," *Open Exchange* (Oct.–Dec. 1983): 33.
2. Quoted in Richard A. Falk, "The Shimoda Case: A Legal Appraisal of the Atomic Attacks Upon Hiroshima and Nagasaki," *American Journal of International Law* 59: 784.
3. Elliott L. Meyrowitz, "Are Nuclear Weapons Legal?" *Bulletin of the Atomic Scientists* (Oct. 1983): 50.
4. Meyrowitz, p. 51.
5. John H. E. Fried, "First Use of Nuclear Weapons: Existing Prohibitions in International Law, *Bulletin of Peace Proposals* 12, p. 28.
6. Burns H. Weston, "Nuclear Weapons Versus International Law: A Contextual Reassessment," *McGill Law Journal* 28: 571.
7. Weston, p. 586.

8. Daniel J. Arbess, "International Law Revisited: Meeting the Legal Challenge of Nuclear Weapons," *Bulletin of Peace Proposals* 16, #2.
9. Kovel, p. 35.
10. Arbess, p. 110.
11. William Durland, *The Illegality of War* (Colorado Springs, CO: The National Center for Law and Pacifism, 1983), p. 48.
12. Green, p. 33.

8. Divestment and Conversion

1. *The Sun* (Baltimore), January 8, 1984, p. A-8.
2. Ruth Sivard, *World Military and Social Expenditures 1985* (Washington, DC: World Priorities, 1985), p. 5.
3. Sivard, p. 7.
4. Sharp, *The Politics of Nonviolent Action,* p. 220.
5. Sharp, pp. 223–224.
6. *The Grapevine,* edited by Osha Davidson, P.O. Box 1319, Ames IA 50010.
7. Paul Wilson, "Six Weeks in Southern Africa," *The Corporate Examiner* 14 (1985) #3.
8. *The New Abolitionist* (July/August, 1984): 3.
9. ICCR, 475 Riverside Drive, Rm. 566, New York, NY 10115-0050.
10. Amy L. Domini, *Ethical Investing* (Menlo Park, CA: Addison-Wesley, 1984), p. 135.
11. Joe Kane, "Ethical Investment: Making Money in Good Conscience," *New Age Journal* (Nov., 1983): 84.
12. Domini, p. 199.
13. Matthew Goodman and Randall Forsberg, "China: The Mountains Move," *Defense and Disarmament News* (Oct.–Nov. 1985): 8.
14. "A Bold Tactic to Hold on to Jobs," *Business Week,* Oct. 29, 1984, p. 70.
15. Gene Carroll, "Why Labor?" *Plowshare Press* (Sept.–Oct., 1983): 4.
16. Carroll, p. 5.
17. Geoffrey Sea, "Converting an Industry," *Plowshare Press* (Jan.–Feb., 1984): 5.

9. From Paralysis to Empowerment

1. Schell, *The Abolition,* p. 4.
2. Lewis Mumford, *In the Name of Sanity* (New York: Harcourt, Brace, 1954), p. 67.
3. Robert Jay Lifton, "Toward a Nuclear-Age Ethos," *Bulletin of the Atomic Scientists* (August 1985).
4. *Nobel: The Man and His Prizes,* ed. by the Nobel Foundation, 3rd. ed. (NY: Elsevier, 1972), p. 12.
5. Macy, p. 4–5.
6. Lifton/Falk, p. 106–107.
7. Macy, p. 34.

8. For a fine discussion/application of the force-field model, see Rodney W. Napier and Matti K. Gershenfeld, *Groups: Theory and Experience* (Boston: Houghton Mifflin, 1983), pp. 225-231.

9. Alt, p. 91.

10. Martin Luther King, Jr., "I Have a Dream," *American Rhetoric from Roosevelt to Reagan,* Halford R. Ryan, ed. (Prospect Heights, IL: Waveland, 1983) pp. 171-172.

11. Everett M. Rogers, *Diffusion of Innovations,* 3rd ed. (New York: The Free Press/Macmillan, 1983).

12. Tony Schwartz, *The Responsive Chord* (Garden City, NY: Anchor Press/Doubleday, 1973).

13. Charles U. Larsen, *Persuasion: Reception and Responsibility* (Belmont, CA: Wadsworth, 1986), p. 205ff.

14. William Perry, "Why I Quit My Job," *Fellowship* (March, 1984).

15. Jo Claire Hartsig, "In the Shadow of the Bomb," *Catholic Worker* (Oct.-Nov., 1983).

16. Victor Frankl, *Man's Search for Meaning: An Introduction to Logotherapy* (New York: Washington Square, 1963).

17. Macy, p. 42.

18. Randall Kehler, "The Freeze: Three Years After," *Fellowship* (July-Aug., 1984).

19. Macy, p. 30.

20. Theodore Roethke, "In a Dark Time," *The Collected Poems of Theodore Roethke* (NY: Doubleday; London: Faber & Faber, 1966), p. 239.

21. Cabral, p. 74.

Appendices

A. Organizations Promoting Nuclear Free Zones, USA
B. Socially Responsible Investing
C. Miscellaneous Resources
D. List of Nuclear Free Zone Communities, USA
E. Nuclear Free Zone Ordinance, Takoma Park, Maryland
F. Nuclear Free Zone Ordinance, Hoboken, New Jersey
G. Declarations by Religious Organizations
    1. Church of the Brethren, General Board
    2. Our Lady of the Angels Convent
    3. Wheadon United Methodist Church

Appendix A.

Organizations Promoting Nuclear Free Zones, USA

NUCLEAR FREE AMERICA
325 East 25th St.
Baltimore, MD 21218
    International clearinghouse for Nuclear Free Zones. Publishes newsletter, *The New Abolitionist,* many other resources. Organizing packet

available, as well as literature on legality, divestment, other issues. Has profiles, consumer products, and other information on the top fifty nuclear weapons contractors.

NUCLEAR FREE ZONE REGISTRY
P.O. Box 172
Riverside, CA 92502
Maintains a file of private homes, businesses, and schools that are declared NFZs. Particular focus on schools, educational work.

NUKE WATCH
c/o The Progressive Foundation
315 West Gorham St.
Madison, WI 53703
Specializing in highway surveillance for nuclear weapons convoys, Nuke Watch also produces Nuclear Free Zone organizing material.

MOBILIZATION FOR SURVIVAL
853 Broadway
Room 2109
New York, NY 10003
Broad peace concerns; major focus recently on the Nuclear Free Harbor campaign in the New York area. Also promotes NFZs.

RELIGIOUS TASK FORCE
85 S. Oxford St.
Brooklyn, NY 11217
Formerly under the wing of MOB, now independent. Circulates data and promotes NFZs in the religious community. Has information on "twinning" with New Zealand churches.

NOTE: In your locality Clergy and Laity Concerned of the Nuclear Weapons Freeze Campaign, or some other peace group, may be promoting NFZ legislation. Although the Freeze campaign is not the same as Nuclear Free Zones—you may want to investigate . . .
PEACE SITES
435 N. Union Ave.
Cranford, NJ 07016

Appendix B.

Socially Responsible Investing

NEWSLETTERS

Good Money
  Center for Economic Revitalization
  28 Main St.
  Montpelier, VT 05602

Insight
  Franklin Research and Development
  222 Lewis Wharf
  Boston, MA 02110

The Corporate Examiner
  Interfaith Center for Corporate Responsibility
  475 Riverside Drive, Rm. 566
  New York, NY 10115

News for Investors
  Investor Responsibility Research Center
  1319 "F" St., N.W., Suite 900
  Washington, DC 20004

CEP Newsletter
  Council on Economic Priorities
  30 Irving Place
  New York, NY 10003

SOCIALLY RESPONSIBLE INVESTMENT FUNDS

Calvert Social Investment Fund. Invests in firms keyed to change meeting human needs, not in firms related to nuclear energy, South

Africa or weapons. Minimum investment $1,000. Calvert Group, 1700 Pennsylvania Ave., Washington, DC 20006.

Dreyfus Third Century Fund, Inc. Invests in firms which enhance the quality of life, protection of the environment, etc. Dreyfus Third Century Fund, 600 Madison Ave., New York, NY 10022.

New Alternatives Fund, Inc. Concentrates on solar and other alternative energy investments. Minimum $2,650. New Alternatives Fund, 295 Northern Blvd., Suite 300, Great Neck, NY 11021.

New Concepts Fund. Invests in firms that make a positive contribution to the quality of life. New Concepts Fund, 100 Park Ave., New York, NY 10017.

Pax World Fund. Founded by United Methodist Ministers in 1971, it avoids firms engaged in military activities or in gambling, liquor, or tobacco. Minimum $250. Pax World Fund, 224 State St., Portsmouth, NH 03801.

Solar T-Bill. Earns the prevailing federal treasury bill rate, but 80 percent of your investment is used to help finance the installation of solar technology in homes. Minimum $2,500. Attn: Susan Howell, Continental Savings and Loan, 2099 Market St., San Francisco, CA 94114.

Working Assets Money Fund. A labor-oriented money market fund taking a variety of social issues into account and excludes nuclear power and weapons. Minimum $1,000. Working Assets, 230 California St., San Francisco, CA 94111.

IN ADDITION, there are several reputable investment advisors who will use ethical screens according to their clients' desires. (Write Nuclear Free America for list.)

THE CENTER FOR ECONOMIC REVITALIZATION is a worker-owned business providing information, investment analysis services, and networking organizations and individuals in the field of social investing. Write Susan Meeker-Lowry, Center for Economic Revitalization, Box 363, Calais State Road, Worcester, VT 05682.

THE INTERFAITH CENTER FOR CORPORATE RESPONSIBIL-
ITY is an organization for religious institutional investors concerned
about the social impact of corporations. Researches corporate activity for church investors and supplies information on community-
owned businesses and other alternative investment opportunities.

THE INVESTOR RESPONSIBILITY RESEARCH CENTER con-
ducts research and publishes impartial reports on contemporary social and public policy issues and their impact on major corporations
and institutional investors. IRRC, 1319 "F" St. N.W., Suite 900,
Washington, DC 20004.

Appendix C.

Miscellaneous Resources

For legal advice, write Nuclear Free America or . . .
  Lawyers' Committee on Nuclear Policy, Inc.
  225 Lafayette St.
  New York, NY 10012

For the Ashland Organizer's Manual
secure "How to Make Your Community a Nuclear Free Zone"
  ($5) . . .
  Prints of Peace House
  P.O. Box 524
  Ashland, OR 97520

For advice on economic conversion,
secure the Organizer's Packet ($10) from . . .
  Center for Economic Conversion
  222C View St.
  Mountain View, CA 94041

For information on Jobs With Peace . . .
National Jobs with Peace Campaign
76 Summer St.
Boston, MA 02110

Appendix D

List of Nuclear Free Zone Communities, USA
1,380,7135 Americans in 109 Nuclear Free Zones, April, 1986

	Location	Population	Date (Y/M/D)	Type*
1.	Hawaii County, HI	92,053	81/2/4	county council ordinance
2.	Garrett Park, MD	1,200	82/5/3	referendum ordinance
3.	Sykesville, MD	1,800	82/6/14	city council resolution
4.	Ashland, OR	15,000	82/11/2	petition initiative ordinance
5.	Roosevelt, NJ	850	82/11/2	referendum resolution
	Roosevelt, NJ		83/1/12	town council ordinance
6.	Waldron, WA	100	82/11/13	town meeting resolution
7.	Isla Vista, CA	16,700	83/2/??	community council resolution
8.	Ellenville, NY	4,405	83/3/7	village board resolution
9.	Leschi, WA	5,300	83/3/23	community council resolution
10.	Barksdale, WI	788	83/4/??	town meeting resolution
11.	Bayfield, WI	625	83/4/??	town meeting resolution
12.	Bayview, WI	324	83/4/??	town meeting resolution
13.	Bell, WI	248	83/4/??	town meeting resolution
14.	Delta, WI	200	83/4/??	town meeting resolution
15.	Keystone, WI	352	83/4/??	town board resolution
16.	Lincoln, WI	284	83/4/??	town meeting resolution
17.	Marengo, WI	267	83/4/??	town meeting resolution
18.	Mason, WI	291	83/4/??	town meeting resolution
19.	Morse, WI	469	83/4/??	town meeting resolution
20.	Russell, WI	822	83/4/??	town meeting resolution
21.	Washburn, WI	390	83/4/??	town meeting resolution
22.	Tisbury, MA	3,110	83/4/5	town meeting by-law
23.	Leverett, MA	1,500	83/4/30	town meeting resolution
24.	New Salem, MA	359	83/5/??	town meeting resolution
25.	Heath, MA	500	83/5/2	town meeting resolution
26.	Gay Head, MA	220	83/5/11	town meeting by-law
27.	West Tisbury, MA	250	83/5/17	town meeting by-law
28.	Brookline, MA	55,062	83/5/31	town meeting resolution
29.	Wilde Lake, MD	10,000	83/8/15	village board resolution
30.	Wallingford, WA	50,000	83/10/19	community council resolution
31.	Somerville, WA	77,372	83/11/8	referendum resolution
32.	Madison, WI	171,590	83/11/15	city council ordinance

33.	San Juan County, WA	7,838	83/11/29	county commission resolution
	San Juan County, WA		84/2/7	referendum advisory question
	San Juan County, WA		84/4/3	county commission ordinance
34.	Placerville, CA	6,739	83/12/5	city council resolution
35.	Azusa, CA	25,271	83/12/5	city council ordinance
36.	Chico, CA	26,601	83/12/6	city council resolution
	Chico, CA		84/8/7	city council ordinance
37.	Takoma Park, MD	16,231	83/12/12	city council ordinance + +
38.	Claremont, CA	30,950	84/1/10	city council resolution
39.	Sun Prairie, WI	12,931	84/2/7	city council ordinance
40.	Moretown, VT	1,221	84/3/6	town meeting resolution
41.	Pike County, PA	18,271	84/3/15	county council resolution
42.	Newton, MA	83,622	84/3/19	board of aldermen resolution
43.	Sausalito, CA	7,338	84/3/20	city council resolution
44.	Provincetown, MA	3,536	84/3/21	town meeting by-law
	Provincetown, MA		84/3/20	town meeting by-law
45.	Martinez, CA	22,582	84/3/21	city council resolution
46.	Nantucket, MA	5,087	84/4/2	referendum resolution
47.	Meadowbrook Twp., WI	202	84/4/3	town meeting resolution
48.	Williamsburg, MA	2,237	84/4/5	referendum resolution
49.	Maui County, HI	70,847	84/4/6	county council ordinances (2)
50.	Ashfield, MA	1,458	84/4/7	town meeting resolution
51.	St. Helena, CA	4,898	84/4/10	petition initiative ordinance
52.	Magnolia, MI	2,000	84/5/??	board of directors resolution
53.	Shutesbury, MA	1,049	84/5/5	town meeting resolution
54.	Worthington, MA	932	84/5/7	town meeting resolution
55.	Dennis, MA	12,360	84/5/7	referendum resolution
56.	Wendell, MA	694	84/5/7	town meeting resolution
57.	Takilma, OR	600	84/5/10	community referendum
58.	Belchertown, MA	8,339	84/5/14	town meeting resolution
59.	Amherst, MA	17,926	84/5/17	town meeting by-law + +
60.	Chatham, MA	4,554	84/5/17	referendum resolution
61.	Fairfax, CA	7,661	84/7/9	city council resolution
62.	Flathead Reservation, MT	19,629	84/7/13	tribal council law
63.	Ladysmith, WI	3,826	84/7/23	town board resolution
64.	Marshall Twp., WI	540	84/7/??	township board resolution
65.	Rusk County, WI	14,238	84/8/21	county board resolution
66.	Hoboken, NJ	42,460	84/9/20	city council ordinance + +
67.	Union County, NJ	504,094	84/10/25	county board resolution
	Union County, NJ		84/10/30	county board ordinance
68.	Northampton, MA	29,286	84/11/6	petition init. advisory question
69.	Skagit County, WA	64,138	84/11/6	petition init. advisory question
	Skagit County, WA		85/5/16	county commission ordinance
70.	Whatcom County, WA	106,701	84/11/6	petition initiative ordinance
71.	Baker County, OR	16,134	84/11/6	petition initiative ordinance
72.	Bandon, OR	23,011	84/11/6	petition initiative ordinance
73.	Clatsop County, OR	32,489	84/11/6	petition initiative ordinance
74.	Coos County, OR	64,047	84/11/6	petition initiative ordinance
75.	Grant County, OR	8,210	84/11/6	petition initiative ordinance
76.	Harney County, OR	8,314	84/11/6	petition initiative ordinance
77.	Lincoln County, OR	35,264	84/11/6	petition initiative ordinance
78.	Tillamook County, OR	21,164	84/11/6	petition initiative ordinance
79.	Union County, OR	23,921	84/11/6	petition initiative ordinance
80.	Wallowa County, OR	7,273	84/11/6	petition init. advisory question
81.	Napa, CA	50,879	84/11/6	city council ordinance
	Napa, CA		85/1/2	

82.	New York City, NY	7,895,563	84/11/8	city council resolution
83.	Davis, CA	36,640	84/11/14	city council resolution
84.	Grandmont, MI	6,000	84/12/2	community board resolution
85.	Miller, IN	4,400	85/3/11	citizens' corporation resolution
86.	Skyview Acres, NY	200	85/3/17	annual meeting resolution
87.	Telluride, CO	1,047	85/3/21	town council resolution
88.	Greenfield, MA	18,116	85/4/2	public advisory question
	Greenfield, MA		85/6/19	town council resolution
	Greenfield, MA		86/4/1	petition initiative ordinance
89.	North Newton, KS	1,222	85/4/2	petition initiative ordinance
90.	Barnstable, MA	30,876	85/4/9	public advisory question
91.	Union Township, PA	6,200	85/4/16	supervisors' resolution
92.	Monterey, MA	900	85/5/4	town meeting resolution
93.	Jamestown, CO	240	85/5/6	town council resolution
94.	W. Stockbridge, MA	1,280	85/5/6	town meeting resolution
95.	Sandwich, MA	8,727	85/5/9	public advisory question
96.	Stockbridge, MA	2,200	85/5/20	town meeting resolution
97.	Taos County, NM	19,456	85/7/10	county commissioners' ordinance
98.	Franklinville, NC	660	85/8/5	town board ordinance
99.	Louisville, KY	298,491	85/8/13	aldermanic board resolution
100.	Mill Valley, CA	12,967	85/9/3	city council resolution
101.	Jersey City, IA	223,532	85/9/12	city council ordinance + +
102.	Iowa City, IA	50,508	85/9/24	city council ordinance
103.	Evanston, IL	73,700	85/10/28	city council resolution
104.	Oberlin, OH	8,660	85/11/5	petition initiative ordinance
105.	Boulder, CO	76,685	85/11/5	petition init. advisory question +
106.	Las Vegas, NM	14,322	85/11/13	city council resolution
107.	Wooster, OH	19,289	85/12/2	city council ordinance
108.	Lansing, IL	29,039	85/12/3	village board resolution
109.	Chicago, IL	3,005,072	86/3/12	city council ordinance

* All types of NFZ legislation except resolutions are legally-binding.

+ + Indicates NFZ legislation that prohibits public investments and/or contracts with nuclear-weapons industries.

In addition, the following had become Nuclear Free Zones as of November 5, 1986: Frankford Twp., NJ; Vernon Twp., NJ; Lafayette Twp., NJ; Hardwick Twp., NJ; Franklin Twp., NJ; Berkeley, CA; Marin County, CA; Eugene, OR; Hood River County, OR; Lane County, OR.

Appendix E

Nuclear Free Zone Ordinance
Takoma Park, Maryland

CHAPTER 8A. NUCLEAR-FREE ZONE.

§8A-1. Title
§8A-2. Purpose.
§8A-3. Findings
§8A-4. Nuclear facilities prohibited.
§8A-5. Investment of city funds.
§8A-6. Eligibility for city contracts.
§8A-7. Exclusions.
§8A-8. Violations and penalties: other remedies.
§8A-9. Definitions.
§8A-10. Notification.
 8A-11. (Reserved)
 8A-12. Nuclear-Free Takoma Park Committee.

Sec. 8A-1. Title

This chapter shall be known as the "Takoma Park Nuclear-Free Zone Act."
(Ord. No. 2703, § 1, 12/12/83.)

Sec. 8A-2. Purpose.

The purpose of this Act is to establish the City of Takoma Park, Maryland, as a nuclear-free zone in that work on nuclear weapons is prohibited within the city limits and that citizens and representatives are urged to redirect resources previously used for nuclear weapons toward endeavors which promote and enhance life, such as human services, including child care, housing, schools, health care, emergency services, public transportation, public assistance and jobs.
(Ord. No. 2703, § 2, 12/12/83.)

Sec. 8A-3. Findings.

It is the finding of the Mayor and Council of the City of Takoma Park, Maryland, that:

(a) The nuclear arms race has been accelerating for more than one-third ($^1/_3$) of a century, draining the world's resources and presenting humanity with the evermounting threat of nuclear holocaust.

(b) There is no adequate method to protect Takoma Park residents in the event of nuclear war.

(c) Nuclear war threatens to destroy most higher life forms on this planet.

(d) The use of resources for nuclear weapons prevents these resources from being used for other human needs, including jobs, housing, education, health care, public transportation and services for youth, the elderly and the disabled.

(e) The United States, as a leading producer of nuclear weapons, should take the lead in the process of global rejection of the arms race and the elimination of the threat of impending holocaust.

(f) An emphatic expression of the feelings on the part of private citizens and local governments can help initiate such steps by the United States and the other nuclear weapons powers.

(g) Takoma Park is on record in support of a bilateral nuclear weapons freeze and has expressed its opposition to civil-defense-crisis-relocation planning for nuclear war.

(h) The failure of governments of nuclear nations adequately to reduce or eliminate the risk of ultimately destructive nuclear attack requires that the people themselves, and their local representatives, take action.

(i) In view of the Nuremberg Principles, which hold individuals accountable for crimes against humanity, and the illegality of nuclear weapons under international law, in adopting this chapter, this community seeks to end its complicity with preparations for fighting a nuclear war.
(Ord. No. 2703, § 3, 12/12/83.)

Sec. 8A-4. Nuclear facilities prohibited.

(a) The production of nuclear weapons shall not be allowed in the City of Takoma Park. No facility, equipment, components, supplies or substance used for the production of nuclear weapons shall be allowed in the City of Takoma Park.

(b) No person, corporation, university, laboratory, institution or other entity in the City of Takoma Park knowingly and intentionally engaged in the production of nuclear weapons shall commence any such work within the city after adoption of this chapter.
(Ord. No. 2703, § 4, 12/12/83; Ord. No. 1985-4, § 1, 1/28/85.)

Sec. 8A-5. Investment of city funds.

The City Administrator in conjunction with the Nuclear-Free Takoma Park Committee shall propose, within six (6) months of the Committee's creation, a socially responsible investment policy and implementation plan, specifically addressing any investments the city may have or may plan to have in industries and institutions which are knowingly and intentionally engaged in the production of nuclear weapons. The proposed policy and plan shall be presented to the Mayor and Council, who shall conduct a public hearing on the policy and plan before considering it for adoption.
(Ord. No. 2703, § 5, 12/12/83; Ord. No. 1985-4, § 1, 1/28/85.)

Sec. 8A-6. Eligibility for city contracts.

(a) The City of Takoma Park and its officials, employees or agents shall not knowingly and intentionally grant any award, contract or purchase order, directly or indirectly, to any nuclear weapons purchaser.

(b) The City of Takoma Park and its officials, employees or agents shall not knowingly and intentionally grant any award, contract or purchase order, directly or indirectly, to purchase products produced by a nuclear weapons producer.

(c) The recipient of a city contract, award or purchase order shall certify to the City Clerk by a notarized statement, that it is not knowingly or intentionally a nuclear weapons producer.

(d) The City of Takoma Park shall phase out the use of any products of a nuclear weapons producer which it presently owns or possesses. For the purpose of maintaining an otherwise prohibited product during its normal life use, Sections 8-A6(a) and (b) above shall be advisory rather than prohibitive.

(e) The City Council, upon the advice of the Nuclear-Free Takoma Park Committee, shall within six (6) months of its appointment and annually thereafter establish and publish a list of nuclear weapons producers to guide the city, its officials, employees and agents, in the implementation of Sections 8A-6(a), (b) and (c) above. Said list shall not preclude application or enforcement of these provisions to or against any other nuclear weapons producer.

(f) Waivers.

(1) The provisions of Section 8A-6(a) and (b) above may be waived by the City Council only if the City Administrator in conjunction with the Nuclear-Free Takoma Park Committee advises after diligent search that a necessary good or service cannot reasonably be obtained from any source other than a nuclear weapons producer and only after public hearing.

(2) The reasonableness of an alternative source shall be determined upon the consideration of the following factors:

(A) The intent and purpose of this Act.

(B) Documented evidence establishing that the necessary good or service is vital to the health or safety of the residents or employees of the city, with the understanding that the absence of said evidence shall diminish the necessity for waiver.

(C) The recommendations of the City Administrator and the Nuclear-Free Takoma Park Committee.

(D) The availability of goods or services from a non-nuclear-weapons producer reasonably meeting the specification or requirements of the necessary good or service.

(E) Quantifiable substantial additional costs that would result from the use of a good or service of a non-nuclear-weapons producer, provided that this factor shall not become the sole consideration.
(Ord. No. 2703, § 6, 12/12/83; Ord. 1985-4, § 1, 1/28/85.)

Sec. 8A-7. Exclusions.

Nothing in this chapter shall be construed to prohibit or regulate the research and application of nuclear medicine or the use of fissionable materials for smoke detectors, light-emitting watches and clocks and other applications where the purpose is unrelated to the production of nuclear weapons. Nothing in this chapter shall be interpreted to infringe upon the rights guaranteed by the first amendment to the United States Constitution nor upon the power of Congress to provide for the common defense.
(Ord. No. 2703, § 7, 12/12/83; Ord. No. 1985-4, § 1, 1/28/85.)

Sec. 8A-8.   Violations and penalties; other remedies.

(a) Any violation of this chapter shall be a municipal infraction, the abatement of which shall be ordered by the issuance of a municipal infraction citation. The fine for each initial violation shall be one hundred dollars ($100.) and for each repeat or continuing violation shall be the maximum allowable by law. Each day for which the violation exists after issuance of a municipal infraction violation shall constitute a separate offense.

(b) Without limitation or election against any other available remedy, the city or any of its citizens or any other aggrieved party may apply to a court of competent jurisdiction for an injunction enjoining any violation of this chapter. The court shall award attorney's fees and costs to any party who succeeds in obtaining an injunction hereunder.
(Ord. No. 2703, § 8, 12/12/83.)

Sec. 8A-9.   Definitions.

As used in this chapter, the following terms shall have the meanings indicated:

(a) *Component of a nuclear weapon* is any device, radioactive substance or nonradioactive substance designed knowingly and intentionally to contribute to the operation, launch, guidance, delivery or detonation of a nuclear weapon.

(b) *Nuclear weapon* is any device the sole purpose of which is the destruction of human life and property by an explosion resulting from the energy released by a fission or fusion reaction involving atomic nuclei.

(c) *Nuclear weapons producer* is any person, firm, corporation, institution, facility, parent or subsidiary thereof or agency of the federal government engaged in the production of nuclear weapons or their components.

(d) *Production of Nuclear Weapons* includes the knowing or intentional research, design, development, testing, manufacture, evaluation, maintenance, storage, transportation or disposal of nuclear weapons or their components.
(Ord. No. 2703, § 7, 12/12/83; Ord. No. 1985-4, § 1, 1/28/85.)

Sec. 8A-10.   Notification.

(a) Upon adoption of this chapter and annually thereafter, the Mayor and Council shall present a true copy of this chapter to the President of the United States, to the Premier of the Union of Soviet Socialist Republics, to the ambassadors of all nations at that time possessing nuclear weapons, to the Secretary-General of the United Nations and to the Director of the International Atomic Agency.

(b) In addition, true copies of this chapter shall be sent to the Governor of the State of Maryland, to the United States Senators from Maryland, to the United States Representatives representing Takoma Park, to our State Delegates and Senators, to the County Executives of Montgomery and Prince George's Counties and to the Council members of the respective counties.

(c) The Mayor and Council of Takoma Park, Maryland, shall choose a town or city of approximately seventeen thousand (17,000) inhabitants within twenty (20) miles of Moscow or some other city or town in the Union of Soviet Socialist Republics, as the Mayor and Council may deem appropriate, and shall send a true copy of this Takoma Park chapter and a letter urging the chosen town to take similar action. (Ord. No. 2703, § 11, 12/12/83.)

Sec. 8A-11.   (Reserved)

Sec. 8A-12.   Nuclear-Free Takoma Park Committee.

(a) Within sixty (60) days of the effective date of this chapter, the Mayor shall appoint, with the approval of the City Council, a nonpartisan Nuclear-Free Takoma Park Committee to oversee implementation of and adherence to this Act. The Committee shall consist of seven (7) Takoma Park residents, with staffing to be provided by the City Administrator. Committee members shall have collective experience in the areas of science, research, finance, law, peace and ethics.

(b) Residents appointed to the Committee shall serve two-year terms, except that three (3) of the initial appointees as designated by the Mayor and Council shall serve one-year terms. The Committee shall appoint its own chair and establish its own bylaws, both subject to approval by the Mayor and Council.

(c) The Committee shall have the following duties and responsibilities:

(1) The Committee may review any work within the city which it has reason to believe is not in compliance with Section 8A-4 of this Act. The Committee shall inform appropriate legal authorities of suspected violation of this Act.

(2) The Committee shall review existing city contracts, awards, purchase orders and investments and may review proposed contracts, awards, purchase orders and investments to assure compliance with Sections 8A-5 and 8A-6 of this Act. If the Committee finds any contracts, purchase orders or investments in violation of this Act, it shall, in conjunction with the City Administrator, make recommendations to the Mayor and Council regarding the existence of reasonable alternatives.

(3) The Committee, in conjunction with the City Administrator, shall propose a socially responsible investment policy and implementation plan as specified in Section 8A-5 above and, upon the adoption of the policy and plan, shall annually thereafter review said investment policy to ensure its conformity to this Act.

(4) The Committee shall, through the collection of materials, newsletter articles, cable television programming, public forums and other means, provide public education and information on issues related to the intent and purpose of this Act. In performing this task, the Committee shall cooperate with city staff, the Nuclear Freeze Task Force and other interested community groups and individuals.

(5) The Committee shall maintain a collection of current materials concerning the production of nuclear weapons and the components thereof. From this information and from consultations with individuals and organizations involved in the nuclear weapons debate, the Committee shall annually prepare and report to the City Council a list of nuclear weapons producers to guide the city, its officials, staff and agents in the implementation of Sections 8A-5 and 8A-6 of this Act.

(6) Before a waiver of the provisions of Sections 8A-6(a), (b) or (c) above pursuant to Subsection 8A-6(f) might be sought, the Committee in conjunction with the Administrator shall conduct a diligent search to determine the availability of reasonable alternative sources for a necessary produce or service.

(Ord. No. 1985-1, § 1, 1/28/85.)

Appendix F

Nuclear Free Zone Ordinance
Hoboken, New Jersey

(1) FINDINGS: The People of the City of Hoboken hereby find that:
  (a) Nuclear weapons production, in the United States and in other countries, is draining the world's resources and presenting humanity with an ever-increasing threat of nuclear war.
  (b) Any participation in the nuclear war industry, locally, federally, or otherwise, directly condones the possible annihilation of our civilization. We see this as a crime against the sacredness of our humanity.
  (c) The emphatic expression of our community, along with communities throughout the world, can help initiate steps by the United States, the Soviet Union, and other nuclear weapons powers to end the arms race and the proliferation of all nuclear weapons systems.

(2) POLICY: Hoboken shall be established as a Nuclear Free Zone.
  A Nuclear Free Zone shall be defined by these requirements:
  (a) No nuclear weapons, delivery systems for such weapons, or components expressly intended to contribute to the operation, guidance or delivery of a nuclear weapon shall be produced or stored within the city or its port.
  (b) No waste from the production of nuclear weapons, their components, or commercial nuclear power shall be stored within the city or its port.
  (c) No research furthering nuclear weapons development shall be conducted within the city, subject to rights guaranteed under the First Amendment to the U.S. Constitution.
  (d) The Mayor and Council of the City of Hoboken shall request the United States Department of Transportation and the New

Jersey Department of Transportation to provide the city with advance notification of any radioactive waste shipment through the city limits. Upon such notification, the Mayor and Council shall act to prevent transportation of radioactive waste through the city by seeking an exemption from preemption by Department of Transportation regulations or using other legal means at their disposal.

(e) The Mayor and Council of the City of Hoboken shall not do business or award any municipal contract to any person, firm, or organization engaged in the production of nuclear weapons or components.

(3) **This ordinance expresses the policy of the City of Hoboken. It is not intended to make violations subject to forfeiture and nothing in this ordinance shall be construed to prohibit or regulate any activity not specifically described in Subsection (2).**

(4) **SEVERABILITY: If any portion of this Ordinance is hereafter declared invalid, all remaining portions shall remain in full force and effect, and to this extent, the provisions of this Ordinance are severable.**

NOTE: The above ordinance was also issued in Spanish.

Appendix G

Declarations of Religious Organizations

1. Church of the Brethren, General Board

STATEMENT DECLARING GENERAL BOARD PROPERTY TO BE "NUCLEAR FREE ZONES"

Believing that peace is God's intention for all creation, including all people of the earth, and that the presence of nuclear weapons do not contribute to peace;

Confessing that all war is sin and all participation in war is sin, and feeling a confessional need to eliminate elements of warmaking that exist in our lives;

Affirming our stewardship of creation and the particular responsibility for any property over which we have been given management; and

Desiring to give a witness to the world of Jesus Christ as the Prince of Peace, to warn the world of the perils of the nuclear arms race, to take this concrete step as peacemakers,

The Church of the Brethren General Board, meeting at Elgin, Illinois, March 3–7, 1984, declares all of the property held by this corporate body to be "nuclear free zones." Specifically,

1. Our property shall not be used to design, test, produce, store or deploy nuclear weapons.
2. We state to our government that we do not wish such property defended by the use or threat of nuclear weapons.
3. We ask all nuclear powers of the world to avoid targeting these properties with nuclear weapons.

Having declared those properties for which we have stewardship to be "Nuclear Free Zones," we now encourage all parts of our church to consider similar action: acting corporately as districts, congregations, seminary and colleges, retirement homes and hospitals, camps; acting personally as members regarding residences, businesses, and other properties.

The General Board will maintain at the General Offices (1451 Dundee Ave., Elgin, IL 60120) a record of all such corporate and personal resolutions, and will periodically publish a listing of "Nuclear Free Zones" resolutions. The Board will also provide a standard form for the "Nuclear Free Zones" resolution and an identifying sign for those who desire to use it.

2. Our Lady of Angels Convent

DECLARATION

WHEREAS THE NUCLEAR ARMS RACE IS DRAINING THE WORLD'S RESOURCES AND PRESENTING HUMANITY WITH THE EVER MOUNTING THREAT OF NUCLEAR HOLOCAUST; AND

WHEREAS THE USE OR THREATENED USE OF NUCLEAR WEAPONS IS A CRIME AGAINST LIFE ON THE PLANET; AND

WHEREAS TACIT APPROVAL OF NUCLEAR WEAPONS AND THE NUCLEAR ARMS RACE IS INCONSISTENT WITH THE APOSTOLIC ACTIVITY OF ALL IN THE FRANCISCAN ORDER; NAMELY, TO ANNOUNCE PEACE WITH OUR LIPS WHILE BEING CAREFUL TO HAVE IT EVEN MORE WITHIN OUR HEARTS; AND

WHEREAS THE LAND IS THE LORD'S AND AS STEWARDS WE ARE RESPONSIBLE FOR ENSURING THAT THE PROPERTY OWNED AND CONTROLLED BY OUR CONGREGATION SHALL BE USED FOR SOCIALLY CONSTRUCTIVE PURPOSES; AND

WHEREAS AN EMPHATIC EXPRESSION OF FEELINGS ON THE PART OF PRIVATE CITIZENS CAN MOVE THE UNITED STATES GOVERNMENT TO EN-

DORSE A FREEZE, FOLLOWED BY REDUCTIONS, IN THE LEVELS OF NU-
CLEAR ARMS,

THEREFORE, BE IT KNOWN THAT WE THE UNDERSIGNED, RESIDENTS
AND EMPLOYEES, DECLARE OUR LADY OF ANGELS CONVENT,
ASTON, PA, TO BE A NUCLEAR FREE ZONE. AS SUCH OUR
LADY OF ANGELS CONVENT IS OFF LIMITS TO THE DESIGN, TEST-
ING, PRODUCTION AND DEVELOPMENT OF NUCLEAR WEAPONS; NO
OTHER ACTIVITIES SUPPORTING THE DEVELOPMENT OF NUCLEAR WEAP-
ONS ARE CONDONED; WE RENOUNCE THE RIGHT TO BE DEFENDED BY
THE USE OR THREATENED USE OF NUCLEAR WEAPONS.

3. *Wheadon United Methodist Church*

DECLARATION

IN SOLIDARITY WITH the poor of the world who suffer because of
the massive excesses of the rich,

IN SOLIDARITY WITH those of our foreparents who, within the vision of their times, lived and worked for justice and freedom in the
world,

IN SOLIDARITY WITH people around the world whose lifestyle and
social harmony have been disrupted and destroyed by the intruding
forces of other nations,

IN SOLIDARITY WITH all of those persons who are discriminated
against because of the hierarchical structures of our world,

WE, THE HUMAN BEINGS IN THIS PLACE, DECLARE THE
FOLLOWING:

WE choose LIFE for ourselves and the world;

WE wish that our bodies be not "defended" by dropping nuclear bombs on other people—soldiers, civilians, children, women or men;

WE wish that neither we nor anything that is ours be made "safe" by threatening to use such weapons;

WE do not want any part of any nuclear weapon system to be helped by us or by our money or by the political system to which we belong;

WE wish to use ourselves and our possessions to dismantle nuclear weapons and nuclear weapons systems, replacing them with human sharing, work, friendship and understanding;

WE WANT THIS TO HAPPEN NOW.

WE will not leave this to other people to do for us. In partnership with others we will find ways of doing something about it ourselves.

WE wish that it not come to pass that our own land or bodies, or the bones of our foreparents, or the bodies of our great grandparents or grandparents, or the bodies of our parents, our children, our grandchildren, or of any offspring into the future, be vaporized, torn apart or mutated by any of these bombs going off over us.

WE NAME OURSELVES AND ALL THAT IS OURS AND THIS PLACE WHERE WE STAND AS A NUCLEAR WEAPON FREE ZONE FOREVER.

**Wheadon United Methodist Church,
2214 Ridge Av., Evanston, IL 60201**

ACT OF CONSECRATION: "In the name of God the Creator, Jesus Christ the Redeemer and the Sustaining Holy Spirit, nuclear hell shall not be built, stored, or launched from at least this place."